Second Edition

ARREST-PROOF YOURSELF

An Ex-Cop Reveals

- How Easy It Is for *Anyone* to Get Arrested
- How to Just Say No to Car Searches
- How to Legally Defend Yourself with Firearms
- How to Keep Lawmen Out of Your Phone and Computer

Dale C. Carson and Wes Denham

CHICAGO
REVIEW
PRESS

The Library of Congress has catalogued the first edition as follows:

Carson, Dale C.
  Arrest-proof yourself : an ex-cop reveals how easy it is for anyone to get arrested, how even a single arrest could ruin your life, and what to do if the police get in your face / Dale C. Carson and Wes Denham.
     p.   cm.
  ISBN-13: 978-1-55652-637-4
  ISBN-10: 1-55652-637-7
  1. Arrest. 2. Detention of persons. I. Denham, Wes. II. Title.
  HV8080.A6C38   2006
  363.2'32—dc22

                                                      2006017597

All photographs courtesy of Dale Carson or
Wes Denham unless otherwise noted.

Cover design: Visible Logic, Inc.
Front cover image: Howard Berman/The Image Bank/Getty Images
Interior design: Sarah Olson

© 2007, 2014 by Dale C. Carson and Sam Wesley Denham III
All rights reserved
Published by Chicago Review Press, Incorporated
814 North Franklin Street
Chicago, Illinois 60610
ISBN: 978-1-61374-804-6
Printed in the United States of America
10 9 8 7 6

To the thousands of young men in jail for petty offenses.
It's not right.
It's not just.
America can do better.

CONTENTS

≫ PART III ≪
ARREST PROOFING IN YOUR CAR

≫ PART IV ≪
GUNS, KNIVES, AND SELF-DEFENSE

⟫ PART V ⟪
AMERICA, LAND OF THE SURVEILLED

⟫ PART VI ⟪
AIDS TO LEARNING

THE GOLDEN RULES

>> **#1: IF COPS DON'T SEE YOU, THEY CAN'T ARREST YOU.**

>> **#2: KEEP YOUR DOPE AT HOME.**

>> **#3: GIVE COPS YOUR NAME AND BASIC INFO, THEN SHUT THE HECK UP!**

>> **#4: WHEN POLICE ASK TO SEARCH YOUR VEHICLE, JUST SAY NO—POLITELY!**

INTRODUCTION | TALKING SHOP WITH AN OLD COP

You've heard about how-to books? This is a how-not-to book—how not to get arrested and tossed into jail for petty and avoidable offenses of the sort that fill every jail in the United States. The title, *Arrest-Proof Yourself*, is hype, since no one, not even the president, is arrest *proof*. What this book does is make you arrest *resistant*.

This book is for people who are not career criminals. It's not about how to beat the system, but about how to avoid letting the system roll over you and ruin your life in ways that may not become apparent until years after an arrest. For career criminals, arrest is inevitable. For people with lapses in judgment, bad manners, a taste for marijuana, and no knowledge of how the criminal justice system operates, arrest is not inevitable, it's optional. That's right—optional.

Far too many black Americans, Hispanics, and poor whites think that arrest and prison are just going to happen—that resistance, as they say, is futile. They think the system is rigged against them. Get over this attitude. By understanding cops and the criminal justice system, you can make choices and adapt your behavior—especially in the presence of police—to minimize your chances of getting arrested. Even if you're not the most upstanding citizen, you can take charge and stay out of the system long enough to give yourself a second chance.

Clear your brain of thoughts about victimhood, racism, social ills, poverty, etc. Those things are not going away. This book is not about saving society; it's about saving *you* when you're standing in front of a police officer who is wearing a blue uniform and a gun. It's about your choices— how you can act, speak, and behave in order not to get arrested. The police officer can choose to arrest you or not arrest you. You can choose to act in ways that will encourage the police to let you go or, better yet, to not stop and question you at all.

This book uses the word *you* to mean "the person most likely to get arrested." If you're a parent, *you* generally means your kids.

"Who, me?" you say.

Yes, you! Changes in law enforcement technique and doctrine that have occurred over the last few years mean that police are making more arrests than ever. You are more likely to get busted today than in the past.

"But I'm a good guy," you protest. If you're a parent, you may say, "I have nice kids. Why should I worry about them getting arrested?"

No matter how upstanding you are, you are likely to have encounters with police that can result in arrest. Here's why:

>> Improved technology and training enable police to arrest people for petty crimes that in the past were ignored due to lack of manpower and resources.

>> A law enforcement doctrine called proactive policing has spread across the land. It calls for zero tolerance of petty offenses, including such things as jaywalking, loitering, and drinking a beer on the street. Proactive policing has reduced crime—no question—but to do so it requires huge numbers of arrests of petty offenders who in years past would never have seen the inside of a jail.

>> The volume of arrests has caused a boom in jail and court construction and the creation of a criminal justice system that employs hundreds of thousands and requires ever more arrests to justify its existence.

>> The near universal installation of computers in police cruisers, and their ability to access law enforcement databases instantly, allows police to make more arrests for what I call administrative crimes. These are failure to maintain tags, licenses, and car insurance; outstanding arrest warrants; driving with suspended licenses; failure to appear at

court hearings; and violation of probation and parole. None of these crimes involves theft, violence, or injury. They are not offenses against people but against the state. In the past, paper records made arrests for these crimes difficult, especially when the offender moved to another state. With the advent of computers, the jails are stuffed with people guilty of not paying fees, not doing paperwork, not showing up in court, and in general thumbing their noses at the system.

》》 People are shocked to discover that they can be arrested for things they didn't even know were illegal. For example, millions of parents chauffeuring the kids in the van or SUV don't realize that the stimulants and antidepressants prescribed for hyperactive children are scheduled narcotics. Kids carry these pills around in their pockets and book bags. The pills scatter inside the vehicle and can get Mom busted if she cannot produce a written prescription during a routine traffic stop.

》》 Let's talk about dope. Marijuana has been partially decriminalized in 18 states. Each state is different. Some allow medical use only and some medical and recreational use. Some simply reduce penalties to traffic-ticket levels. These laws change constantly and can vary county by county within a state. So before you load your ride with herb, bongs, hubble-bubbles, and rolling papers, make sure you know the law in your state, county, and city. Bone up on this while you're straight! And remember, even in places where pot has been decriminalized, you can still be arrested for illegal or unlicensed distribution if you carry large quantities. In addition, marijuana is illegal under federal law, so you can get busted by the feds even when the local constabulary give you a pass. In 32 states, the drug remains illegal, including all the states south of the Mason-Dixon Line. So if you drive through Dixie, dump your dope. If you're caught, you'll get stuffed into jails already filled to bursting with clueless potheads.

Most important, even in states where the stuff is legal to some degree, you can get busted for driving *under the influence* of marijuana. If you shoot someone while wasted, you may not be able to assert self-defense in court. This means you'll get hammered for manslaughter or murder. As you'll see repeatedly in this book, it's always wise to keep your dope at home.

》 People have worse manners than in the past. Whether this is due to less effective parenting, a decline in church attendance, increased use of drugs, disorder at public schools, or the pervasive influence of TV shows where everyone is "in your face" is a topic best left to the talk shows. All I know for a fact is that people don't know how to behave. They act out in front of cops and get busted for being obnoxious.

NEWS FLASH FOR AMERICAN WOMEN

Ladies, you, yes you, are paying for a major portion of the American criminal justice system. The system is not funded exclusively by that perennially overburdened group, the taxpayers. A big chunk of system funding comes from defendants' families. By and large this means women are paying thousands of dollars to get the men they love legal representation, reduced sentences, and freedom. Women pay the lawyers, women pay the bail bonds, women pay the drug court costs, and women pay the probation fees. When men get arrested, women get poor.

Every day, at the courts, in attorneys' offices, and in probation departments, one sees a stream of women clutching money orders funded by mortgaging their homes and liquidating their savings. Often it's more than one woman. It's mom, sister, aunt, and cousin who have cleaned themselves out to get their man out of jail. Money that would have funded a new home or car, an education, or a retirement is swallowed up in an instant by the financial black hole that is the criminal justice system.

The system devours the investment capital of poor Americans and is one of the major reasons the poor stay poor. Elected officials love to describe how much money they pour into poor neighborhoods and community services. They never, ever, discuss how much is drained out by the criminal justice system. Ladies, the best way to keep your savings in the bank and your folding money in your purse is to keep your men away from cops and out of jail. So read on and prosper.

BYE-BYE, AMERICAN DREAM

One of the terms my coauthor and I created is the *electronic plantation*. This is the lifetime restriction on jobs and opportunities that derives from the instant accessibility of arrest information. Increasing use of background checks and widespread access to the National Crime Information Center (NCIC), the federal government's database of every arrest made in the United States and its territories, means that the record of your arrest follows you around for life.

Even if your arrest record is expunged or sealed or adjudication is withheld or the charges were dismissed or you were acquitted at trial, the arrest record is permanent. Worse, it's easily accessible. Because employers tend to regard an arrest as tantamount to a conviction, a single arrest can deny you job opportunities forever.

The word *plantation* was chosen because it's a fighting word for black Americans. I want the danger of this new plantation to get attention and be understood. The masses of young black and Hispanic men in jails are too much to bear. The electronic plantation restricts them to a lifetime of low-wage work once they're free. Their only hope is to avoid the system long enough to grow up, get educated, and get on with their lives. To do so they must not be penalized forever for arrests that took place during their youth.

The electronic plantation has destroyed one of the greatest features of American life: the opportunity to get a second chance. In the age of paper records, once you paid your debt to society, you were done. You could hang out your thumb, jump the train, or hop the 'hound, and go west, east, north, or south to escape your past. You could start over and forget old legal troubles. The records were thousands of miles away. Records of offenses by juveniles and offenses where adjudication was withheld or where charges were dismissed were truly inaccessible. Not so today. An arrest should not be a life sentence, but it is.

THE SLIPPERY SLOPE: REASONABLE SUSPICION— PROBABLE CAUSE—JAIL

Arrest proofing is all about not attracting police scrutiny and about allaying suspicions when you are confronted by police. Throughout this book, my coauthor and I try to avoid hairsplitting legalisms and stick to standard English. Here, however, are some useful definitions of terms you hear all the time but may never have had explained.

JAIL VS. PRISON. *Jail* is used in this book with its common understanding as a pretrial detention facility. It's where you go after being arrested. *Prison* is where you serve your sentence after trial or a plea. Both facilities have cells with bars, but they are quite distinct in the criminal justice system.

REASONABLE SUSPICION. This means that police suspect that you are about to commit a crime. Reasonable suspicion is the standard that allows police to stop you on the street or pull over your car.

PROBABLE CAUSE. This means that it is more likely than not that a crime has already been committed. Police require probable cause to make an arrest.

MISDEMEANOR. Also known as "Mr. Meaner" in the trailer park and the 'hood. This refers to an offense for which the penalty is generally one year in prison or less.

FELONY. This refers to crimes punishable by one year or more in prison. Felonies often carry lifetime penalties such as the loss of the rights to vote and to own a weapon. In my state a felony conviction creates a lifetime ban on holding any job that requires a state license, such as health care, law, insurance, real estate, finance, television and radio broadcasting, and barbering and hairstyling.

The path from reasonable suspicion to felony conviction is a slippery slope down which you slide to jail and a ruined life with amazing speed. This book is all about staying off that slope.

ABOUT COPS

This book tells you how to avoid cops and minimize their opportunities to arrest you and your children, but it's not a criticism of modern police. The problem today is not—repeat *not*—that police are untrained, incompetent, racist, or corrupt. It's precisely the opposite. Because police are *better* educated, *better* trained, and more *tightly* disciplined, you're more likely to get arrested than ever before. Police generally make lawful arrests and are accurate and truthful in their reporting and court testimony. Fewer mistakes mean fewer chances for an attorney to set you free.

The improvement in modern policing is profound. When I was a kid, the police in my city were an organized criminal conspiracy. They ran gambling, prostitution, booze, and loan-sharking, and collected their vig (short for *vigorish*, the usurious interest charged by loan sharks) like a bunch of redneck Sopranos. Lawyers, politicians, and city hall fixers called the shots. Anything, even a murder rap, could be handled for "value received." Inconvenient people were "shot while fleeing arrest." In 1955 Florida governor Leroy Collins suspended the sheriff and appointed my father, an FBI agent, to head the police department and clean up that rat's nest, and that's what he did.

For the past half century, police departments all over America have been modernized, trained, and educated. Crooked cops have been arrested and rogue cops fired. The result is the superbly trained police of the new century. Cops today are generally honest and practically ubiquitous, and they'll arrest you for tossing a gum wrapper!

Nonetheless, police routinely use tactics, such as inciters, that provoke suspects to run, resist, and fight. Using these tactics is called putting a suspect in the trick box. They allow cops to transform a traffic ticket or misdemeanor into a felony arrest guaranteeing incarceration for suspects and impoverishment for the families who pay the legal fees, bail bonds, court costs, and probation charges. Although generally legal, these tactics are highly unethical. I ought to know. I have seen them for years. This book gives detailed instructions on how to avoid getting suckered by cop tricks. It analyzes the famous heads-cops-win-tails-you-lose questions that cops ask before vehicle searches. The chapter "Dirty Cop Tricks" explains many of these tricks, ranging from legal inciters to grossly illegal tactics such as planting drugs and "throw-down" guns on innocent suspects. In "Emergency Procedures," you will even receive instruction on what to do in the worst of all circumstances—when you are being beaten or shot by police. If you survive, I'll tell you what to do in the hospital before the bandages come off.

My father, Dale Carson, being sworn into office as sheriff of Duval County, Florida, by Judge Shields, January 30, 1958. He cleaned out a briar patch of corruption and instituted standards of education and training that produced a modern police force.

THE HOW-TO AND THE WHY

The book has five parts. Part I deals with the "why"—the reasons you're more likely to get arrested today than formerly. It discusses the major players in the criminal justice system prior to arrest—cops, bad guys, and the clueless horde. (Judges, prosecutors, attorneys, jailers, and probation officers appear later, after you're busted.)

Cops are the major players, and understanding them is essential to arrest proofing. Cops are *not* ordinary people. They are licensed, paid, and trained by the state to hunt the two-legged beast—i.e., you. They enjoy hunting people and making arrests. It's what they do. They're evaluated and rewarded by their superiors almost exclusively on the number of arrests they make. This is no disparagement. Controlling bad guys with hunter cops is essential for civilization. Just think of the next police officer you meet as a polite great white shark with a well-pressed uniform. And you? You're a struggling little fish. This will help you adjust your behavior accordingly. To know them is to avoid them. And that, readers, is the beginning of arrest proofing.

And the bad guys? They're the second group of players. Understanding them is simple. They're career criminals and they enjoy what they do. They don't mind hurting and even killing people who get in their way. They enjoy it. To them, the only thing worse than prison is working a straight job. The worst are the violent offenders. In this book you'll meet several I helped send to the electric chair or prison for life.

OK, readers, get ready for some secret stuff, never seen on TV and unmentioned in the *Daily Fish Wrap* tossed to your front door. Are you seated? Do you have a grip? Here it is: *The criminal justice system does not spend much time arresting and sentencing real bad guys.*

"What?" you say. "That's impossible!" No doubt you want to challenge me. Do not I, like you, watch the news and see that every single day some bank robber, carjacker, or child molester has been rounded up? Of course, but I see what you don't—that for every serious bad guy arrested, *hundreds* of petty offenders go to jail. What the criminal justice system actually does most of the time is process the third group of players, the clueless horde. Clueless petty offenders are by far the most important players in the system because, without their vast numbers, and the money that is extracted from them and their families, cops and judges would be filing for unemployment and all those brand-new police stations, jails, and administrative offices would have "for rent" signs hammered in their immaculate lawns.

Who are these people, the bread and butter—nay, the staff of life—for millions of municipal and state employees? They are people who

>> possess small quantities of drugs

>> get an attitude with police

>> yell at their wives and girlfriends

>> drive with suspended licenses

>> do malicious mischief

>> create disturbances at clubs and parties

>> ride bikes at night without a light (I'm not kidding!)

>> get arrested as accessories during police raids

>> carry medications without the proper labels or prescriptions

>> "loiter," i.e., hang out

>> take pocketknives and nail scissors to school

>> drink alcohol in public

The criminal justice system often acts like a mindless bureaucracy and prosecutes cases that are absurd. For example, I once represented a 12-year-old boy who was arrested, and jailed, for *throwing a pecan at a bus*. A pecan! I took the case in part because, decades ago, my coauthor and I, then 10 years old, stood beneath a bridge and threw mud balls into a bus. We beat feet before the cops arrived. We were lucky.

My client, however, was charged with throwing a deadly missile, which is a third-degree felony. Years ago this was not a serious crime. It became so in the 1960s, when anti–Vietnam War demonstrations and race riots exploded around the country. Legislatures made throwing a deadly missile a felony so police could bring serious charges against the students and black Americans who were tossing rocks and bottles. But a pecan? A freaking pecan!

Today people like this nut-throwing kid are being shoved through the legal sausage grinder. Even though I got him off, he will have an arrest record and will get extra scrutiny from police forever. Had my client known how to behave around police officers, he probably would have received a warning and a trip home to his mother in the back of the cruiser. Instead, he got hammered. Little boys throw things. They poke things, stick things, and kick things. It's what they do. To arrest and prosecute them for doing dopey kid stuff is outrageous.

Other clueless types commit offenses that are more serious but are still misdemeanors or low-level felonies. They are people who

>> drive under the influence of drugs or alcohol

>> do not pay child support or fail to keep up licenses, tags, and insurance; show up for trial; pay restitution; or perform every jot and tittle of their terms of probation

>> are rowdy, drunk, obnoxious, and get in fights

>> buy sex from male and female prostitutes

IS THIS A HOW-TO-BE-A-CROOK BOOK?

No. If it were, the title would be different—something like *Perfect Murders: A Step-by-Step Guide*, or *Your Future in Armed Robbery*. This book deals exclusively with the plight of clueless petty offenders who comprise the overwhelming majority of people who are arrested, jailed, and tried by a criminal justice system that to an alarming degree is operating mindlessly on autopilot. FBI statistics show that violent crimes are down, way down, from what they were in the 1990s, yet the jails are packed and criminal court calendars are hopelessly jammed. Who are all these people getting busted? Let's look.

THE CRIMINAL PYRAMID

At the top are those we fear most—violent criminals. Police are quite competent in arresting murderers, armed robbers, rapists, and child molesters. The more crafty serial killers and sex criminals may take a long time to catch, but police are dogged, and they spend years hunting these guys.

The other occupants of the top perch in crime land are big crooks who operate traditional criminal enterprises such as drug distribution, illegal gambling, loan-sharking, protection rackets, labor union racketeering, etc. These guys are on the police radars but can go for years without being arrested. The reason is simple. Arresting organized crime figures is easy; prosecuting them is not. It requires interagency task forces, wiretaps, 24/7 surveillance, and gobs of government money. The bad guys have the best attorneys money can buy. Worse, they're often connected with politicians and judges who can protect them. When it comes to organized crime, the big heat often turns into the big stink.

Here's an example. In Miami, from 1985 to 1995, the FBI arrested and obtained convictions of

>> the Miami city manager

>> the Miami finance director

>> the Miami chief of police

>> numerous judges

>> various city and county commissioners

>> numerous police officers

These goons were stealing with both hands, running interference for the cartels, *escorting* drug trucks from the Miami River to warehouses in the city, and selling favorable judgments from the bench. Notice, however, that almost all the investigations and arrests were made by the FBI, not local police. The state's attorney (prosecutor), an elected official, seemed not to notice, amid a busy schedule of luncheons, speeches, and fundraisers, that the city was being run by a bunch of hoods.

The other group of big crooks, middle-class criminals, are notoriously *not* on police radars. They run little risk and garner great rewards. FBI statistics show that white-collar crime is booming. Yes, you can steal more with a briefcase than a gun, and insurance fraud, mortgage fraud, identity theft, securities fraud, and confidence rackets such as pigeon drops and bad checks probably gross as much as the trade in illegal drugs. Of course, no one knows for sure, because most of these guys get away with it. I'll discuss this further in the chapter on how to arrest more white people.

The middle group of crooks are career criminals. You can define these guys easily. They make their living in crime. It's what they do, but not forever. Police glom on to these guys sooner or later. Most are arrested, tried, and convicted multiple times and serve long stretches in jail. At some point, usually in their 30s, they give it up and decide that flipping burgers or pushing the broom is better than trying to make a career in crime, or else they go to prison and become permanent wards of the state.

Now gaze at the bottom of the pyramid. Notice that it's huge. It's the base that holds up the entire criminal justice system. It's composed of clueless petty offenders. These poor slobs can be distinguished from other criminals by two crucial characteristics.

1. They don't make their living in criminal enterprise. Rarely do they make any money at all from what they do. They're rule breakers, not money takers. Their lives are a series of infractions, violations, and failures to comply with ordinances, stat-

utes, and rules. They pay dearly for it. The bail bonds, attorney fees, court costs, and probation costs that the system extracts keep them and their families perpetually impoverished.

2. They are rarely violent. Mostly, they're just clueless.

WHY ARE ALL THESE GUYS IN JAIL?

Nobody ever thinks about this. You get caught with a joint, and you go to the joint. Right? Let's consider this for a minute. Why should petty offenders get arrested and jailed *at all*? Let's examine the typical reasons.

FLIGHT RISK. Most people think that petty offenders are jailed so they will show up for trial. This is rarely the case. Most misdemeanor offenders are tossed into the can briefly and then released either on their own recognizance* or on a low bail to free up the cells for the next batch of clueless who are rolling downtown 24/7 in a police cruiser near you. Most of these guys have to show up for their hearings of their own volition, so it's fair to ask why they get arrested in the first place.

In almost all states, police, in lieu of arrest, can issue a notice to appear, also known as a penal citation. This also requires the offenders to show up in front of a judge and get what's coming to them (fines, anger management therapy, drug rehab, restitution, etc.) *without* getting busted and receiving a permanent arrest record and a lifetime sentence on the electronic plantation. To get a clueless weed smoker in front of a judge, do we really need to use jailers, bail bondsmen, prosecutors, and public defenders? In many cases, a citation will do just as well.

Even when the bail is lowered, say to $3,000, the bond, which will be 10 percent of the bail, or $300, can be disastrous to clueless offenders living on

---

* Legalese for a piece of paper that, in the vernacular, goes something like this:

Yo, judge!

I hereby promise, cross my heart and hope to die, that I will show up, bright eyed, bushy tailed, showered, shaved, and tooth-brushed, reasonably rational and not too funky, before Your Honor or Any Other Honor, at the hour herein designated and the place thereunto ordered.

the edge. For someone working for $10 an hour, $300 is one week's take-home pay. When this goes to the bondsman, the electricity and water get turned off, the rent goes unpaid, and child support payments get missed. Of course, before the offender can even get the bond lowered, he has to have a private attorney, and in my state this costs two grand *and up.*

THREAT TO THE COMMUNITY. This is the most important criterion judges use in setting bail or allowing release on recognizance. Petty offenders, however, are generally only a danger to themselves. Once released, what a petty offender is most likely to do is go out and get stoned or drunk to forget all about it. This is stupid but hardly a threat. By arresting clueless petty offenders instead of citing them, police lump them together, in the minds of judges and the public, with career criminals and violent offenders. This justifies arresting them rather than issuing citations.

THEY NEED TO BE "IN THE SYSTEM." By this people mean that police should have records and keep tabs on petty offenders, who sometimes go on to commit serious crimes. I agree, but note that this can be accomplished *without* arresting and jailing clueless offenders and consigning them to the electronic plantation for life. Notice-to-appear citations and police field interrogation (FI) reports place the offender in the local database quite effectively.

CONDIGN PUNISHMENT. Most people think that an arrest and a few days in the sneezer is appropriate punishment for many of these offenses. Don't forget one thing, however. When petty offenders are arrested and jailed, *they have not yet been convicted of a crime in a court of law.* They are presumed innocent. For this reason they're called pretrial detainees. Of course, if it's you in the freezer, you'll be happy to know that even though you're living behind bars; wearing dungarees and flip-flops; eating green baloney sandwiches; and getting handcuffed, ordered about, and yelled at by members of the corrections officers union, you're not actually a prisoner. You're just a detainee.

A BRIEF HISTORY OF ARRESTS

Ever wondered why people get arrested? Years ago arrests were made only for the most heinous crimes against persons, the so-called common-law crimes—night burglary, robbery, rape, assault, battery, mayhem, and murder. The purpose of the arrest was to make time for a thorough investigation. This would include evidence collection and witness interviews. It also included time for prosecutors to decide whether they could get an indictment and prove their case. Historically the arrest was not a matter of public record; only the conviction was.

Nowadays, many misdemeanor arrests are made for crimes for which there is no investigation, and none needed. For example, for possession of small quantities of drugs, what's there to investigate? You've got the dope or you don't. When it comes to fleeing from cops, either you fled or you didn't. For the petty crimes we're talking about in this book, during which there is no investigation and for which you generally get popped loose from jail in a few days, you can reasonably ask why you got arrested in the first place.

It doesn't have to be this way. Let me give you an example. Out to the west of Jacksonville, the sheriff of Bradford County, Florida, does things differently. When his officers cite someone for a misdemeanor, they write a ticket, take an electronic photo, and get a thumbprint. Then they cut the guy loose. That's it. Offenders have to show up in front of a judge on their own and get what's coming to them. Since they have not been jailed and had their funds extracted by attorneys and bondmen, they are more able to pay fines, court costs, and restitution. Bradford County is a conservative and religious place. The sheriff has never been accused of being soft on crime or permissive about drugs. He simply thinks that petty offenders can be punished without raising taxes to build huge courthouses and jails and hiring armies of government employees to process them through these buildings.

Other cities, usually under budgetary pressures, have discovered the same thing. They handle misdemeanors in venues that resemble traffic court. A hundred or so offenders troop in for a session, usually representing themselves, although a few may have attorneys. Judges breeze through the cases at high speed, like this:

"You got caught with two joints in your car and driving with a suspended license. How do you plead? Guilty, not guilty, or nolo contendere?"

"Uh, the third one, your honor, the no-low thing."

"You got your paperwork in order?"

"Yes, sir."

"See the clerk, pay the fine, and don't let me see you in here again." *Bang.*

Punishing petty offenders without jailing them beforehand has the advantage to society of speedy justice at low cost and high volume. For offenders, the advantage is that they do not have to suffer unintended, nonjudicial punishments. Alas, it will take years for this enlightened state of affairs to exist widely. In the meantime, cops are arresting everybody for everything everywhere. The only solution is to arrest-proof yourself right now.

Quite a few clueless people think that keeping a joint or an open alcoholic beverage in the car or yelling at their women is no big deal. Other clueless types are disagreeable, uneducated, and barely literate. A few of them are crazy and should be in state hospitals, not state prisons. Too many clueless people who are arrested are entirely innocent of the crimes for which they are charged.

You are also clueless to some degree, even if you're a millionaire. How could you be otherwise? Unless you're a cop, judge, attorney, probation officer, or jailer, you can't understand the criminal justice system, which is its own world with its own rules. The system is astonishingly powerful. It's backed by courts and legislatures, funded from state and local treasuries, and manned by government employees wearing guns. Its daily mission is to reach out and arrest someone—someone just like you.

Even the most law-abiding citizens can, with one flash of temper, one slip of the tongue, or one wrong move, get arrested and have their lives ruined. The more successful you are, the more damaging an arrest is to your life and career. Real bad guys practically sleep through an arrest. To them jail is just a motel with bland food. To the law-abiding, arrest and incarceration are an unmitigated disaster. Being arrested and incarcerated is always humiliating and expensive. It can be dangerous. You do not want to go there.

This book is the lesson that the teacher, the preacher, and the parents never gave you. Consider this book the ultimate prelaw course. By the time you get involved with the law, my friends, it's too late. You've already been hammered. The best involvement to have with cops and criminal justice is none, as in zip, zero, *nada.*

DON'T KNUCKLE UNDER TO COPS—A 60-SECOND CIVICS LESSON

Every day I see men who helped police arrest them, helped the state prosecute them, and didn't even realize it. They confess for no reason; take pleas when they're innocent; run, resist, and lie needlessly when arrested; screw up their probation; and in a hundred different ways contribute unnecessarily to their personal ruin. There are two things you should never forget when you're by the side of the road in shackles and getting ready to take the long lonely ride to jail. You should remember them whether you're innocent or guilty.

1. You owe no duty to the police to help them arrest you or increase the charges against you by confessing, acting out, or responding to inciters. You *do* have to give police your legal name when asked. You do *not* have to talk to police, answer questions, or agree to a vehicle search if doing so will result in your conviction. The state has lots of money, cops, and investigators. They are quite capable of putting you in jail *without your help*. Think about this. If they had all the information they needed to convict you, they wouldn't ask any questions, would they?

2. You do not cease to be a citizen or to have rights even if you did the crime and are guilty as heck.

The founders of our republic understood, even before strong governments existed, that the power of the state to prosecute and punish was overwhelming. Their first act, after adopting the Constitution, was to amend it to increase the rights and protections of individuals. Here are the famous phrases of the Fifth Amendment that are as valid today as they were more than two centuries ago: " . . . nor shall (any individual person) be compelled in any criminal case to be a witness against himself, nor be deprived of life, liberty, or property, without due process of law."

The founders consciously limited state and police power in the famous words of the Fourth Amendment that stand as law even though they have been attenuated by police tactics and court opinions: "The right of the people to be secure in their persons, houses, papers, and effects, against unreasonable searches and seizures, shall not be violated, and no Warrants shall issue, but upon probable cause, supported by Oath or affirmation, and particularly describing the place to be searched, and the persons or things to be seized."

Of course arrest proofing is not a course in constitutional law. It's a street-smart guide to staying free. Nonetheless, I want you to know that the tactics of staying free would, I think, be looked upon favorably by George Washington, Thomas Jefferson, and James Madison. I hope their spirits were guiding my coauthor and me in this effort.

ARREST PROOFING—THE REAL DEAL

Part II is the nuts and bolts of arrest proofing. It will teach you how to speak, what words to say, and how to hold your body so cops will be less inclined to arrest you. Most arrests have add-on charges—fleeing, resisting arrest, and battery on a law enforcement officer—that upgrade misdemeanors to felonies and result in long sentences and high legal fees. Most of these add-ons can be avoided by knowing how to behave.

Part II discusses why police decide to arrest some people and not others. It has arrestability quotient (Arrest-Q) charts so you can tell whether you and your children are more or less likely to get arrested. It dwells at length on Uncle Dale's Golden Rule #1:

>> **IF COPS CAN'T SEE YOU, THEY CAN'T ARREST YOU.**

Arrest proofing covers how to avoid street stops and traffic stops. It explains how to avoid being apprehended if you're caught in a neighborhood sweep.

Most crimes involve automobiles, and most arrests, whether of bad guys or the clueless, occur during traffic stops. Part II analyzes in-depth your legal rights against search and seizure while driving and tells you how to arrest-proof your car. It has a chart to estimate your car arrestability quotient (Car-Q). There are detailed instructions on how to search your own car after other people drive it and what to do when you find drugs or guns.

A chapter that will particularly offend some people expounds upon Uncle Dale's Golden Rule #2:

>> **KEEP YOUR DOPE AT HOME.**

I abhor the use of drugs, but harbor no illusions that people will suddenly stop using the stuff. Carrying drugs in automobiles and on your person is the *single largest cause of arrests in America*. Observe Golden Rule #2 and you will stay out of jail and have time to wise up, sober up, and become a citizen.

You will find several emergency arrest-proofing procedures. These are last-ditch techniques to use when you're only moments away from being cuffed and stuffed into the cruiser. Some, like asking for a notice to appear (NTA) in lieu of arrest, should be taught in school. Everyone should know what an NTA is. Few do. Some of the emergency procedures, such as vomiting on yourself and pissing and crapping your pants, may seem extreme but are merely practical. Getting arrested is so serious in the age of computers that even outrageous and disgusting expedients are in order.

A short but important chapter explains 'tude, street slang for "attitude." This means arguing and being obnoxious with cops, and it's a sure way to slide into the slammer, usually with plenty of add-on charges to ensure a nice long stay. Too many people confuse attitude with their legal rights, personal style, and ethnic preferences in clothes, music, and behavior. I uncomplicate the issue by advising you simply to be polite for *five freaking minutes* while you're face-to-face with a cop. The rest of the time? Boogie on—go wild—knock yourself out.

Part II is also a workbook. It has credentials that you can fill out, cut out, and carry with you. These "street creds" and "car creds" will answer routine police questions and cut short interrogations so that you will be less likely to fumble, mumble, lie, and act out in front of the cops. These creds contain magic words that you need to memorize so that in the confusion of a police encounter you can say the right thing. In heavily policed neighborhoods, staying free requires practice. Cops train constantly to deprive you of your freedom. Shouldn't you practice how to keep it?

Another feature of Part II is Uncle Dale's Golden Rule #3:

>> GIVE COPS YOUR NAME AND BASIC INFO, THEN SHUT THE HECK UP!

This is the short, easy-to-understand version of the most common advice given by criminal defense attorneys. Defendants pay millions each year for this counsel, generally when it's too late and they're already in jail. I'm giving you this pearl of wisdom absolutely free *before* you get busted. Knowing when to talk to cops, when to remain silent, and *how* to remain silent are crucial in reducing the severity of charges when you do get arrested.

Some definition is in order here. When I say "Shut the heck up!" I mean be quiet. I mean stop babbling, blah-blah-blahing, blathering, bloviating, chattering, kvetching, and going on and on and on. I do *not* mean clamming up and giving cops some attitude that makes them really want to arrest you.

Part III deals with traffic stops. These are the most common way people encounter police and get arrested. Part III describes how stops are made, why police stop one car and not another, and how your car can be searched and seized during an arrest. Another chapter instructs you how to search your own vehicle for drugs and guns that may have been left by friends or relatives. During police searches, *other people's* pistols, weed, pills, powder, and crystal appear under car seats and in the glove compartment with distressing frequency. If contraband is in the car, it's legally yours.

The arrest is yours, too.

Fortunately, Part III also contains information about how to refuse car searches based on recent Supreme Court rulings. Car searches are the single largest source of arrests in this country, so this is the most important chapter in the book. It's filled with all-new, rock-solid advice. Don't miss a word!

Part IV covers the firearms violations that send so many people to prison. It details stupid gun tricks that can hurt you, kill you, or get you busted. It also covers what you *don't know* about firearms laws that can instantly cancel a formerly valid weapons permit and land you in the jug. In this part I will give you my personal recommendations for firearms to use for personal protection, as well as my save-your-life ammo load. Lastly,

I'll discuss Stand Your Ground laws and the horrible consequences that follow when you shoot someone in self-defense.

Part V, "America, Land of the Surveilled," reveals the terrifying ability of police to interrogate your cell phone, computers, and tablets, to dump data from onboard black boxes in your car, to scan your license plate automatically and track your movements, and to use information in the Cloud to arrest and convict you. Big Brother *is* watching you, so watch this chapter—carefully!

GOOFY RHYMES AND STRANGE SCENARIOS

Most chapter titles have goofy rhymes. Here's why:

1. Rap and rhyme are the music of the American street, and this book is a rap and rhyme about avoiding crime.

2. Meter and rhyme have made words easy to remember since the time, 2,700 years ago, when the Greek epic poet Homer sang in magnificent hexameters to rosy-fingered dawn. Of course, most of the rosy fingers I deal with stay busy lifting wallets, easing stereos through windows, or sliding Slim Jims around car door locks. Occasionally I get an artistic type whose rosy fingers can forge a check as pretty as you please.

Another purpose is to communicate the weird humor that pervades criminal justice. Cops, lawyers, and judges witness feats of stupidity that just never happen out in prudent, law-abiding America. Sometimes guys who get arrested leave you speechless with amazement.

Lastly, most authors of how-to and self-improvement books adopt a tone of insufferable moral superiority as they instruct you on your diet, your exercise, your psyche, and your destiny. I have no desire to be a sage. I just want to keep you out of jail, then have a good meal, make love to my wife, take care of my kids, and maybe find a zoot suit and more 'gators* on eBay.

---

* Two-toned, alligator-hide wing tips. In the courts and jails, they're a sensation.

Scattered here and there in the book are scenarios. These are fictional narratives often based on real cases. They demonstrate how the factors discussed in the book come together during an arrest. Most importantly, they illustrate how easy it is for ordinary people to get busted.

AIDS TO LEARNING

Part VI, at the end of the book, is a section that repeats the golden rules for staying out of jail and includes the magic words that keep you free. I suggest you repeat these many times. Just shout them out. Who cares what the neighbors think? Saying things aloud greatly assists memory. Recalling these pages in an emergency will go a long way to maintain your freedom.

POLITICAL INCORRECTNESS

There are things in this book that will make people crazy. I define the major condition that makes you likely to get arrested as cluelessness. This is behavioral rather than racial or ethnic. The more clueless you are, the more *available* you are to be arrested—regardless of color, education, and money. Don't believe this? In a later chapter, I'll discuss South Beach, a place where rich, successful, mostly white people suddenly get clueless and get busted right and left.

There is lingering racism among police and in the courts. Remedies for gross injustices, however, require years of work, litigation, and legislation. You, however, right now, this very day, can make yourself less clueless and less likely to get arrested and jailed by reading this book. Racism is a problem for society. Cluelessness is a problem for you. It's something you can control.

Here are warning signs of cluelessness.

>> You are a little wild and thoughtless or easily influenced.

>> You think the criminal justice system is like what you see on TV.

>> You like black gangsta, Latino gangbanger, or white trash music, clothing, attitudes, and styles.

>> You cannot distinguish gangsta style from the sordidness of criminal life.

>> You enjoy getting stoned and drunk and think that's no big deal.

>> You argue with and beat your family, friends, and sexual partners.

>> You carry marijuana on your person and in cars.

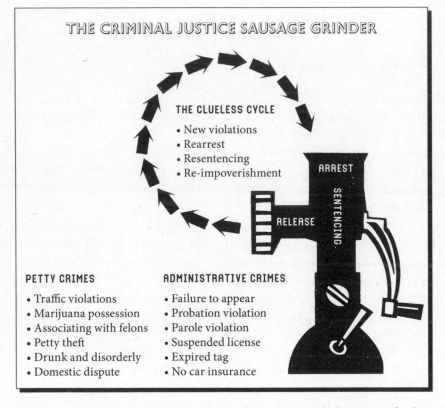

THE CRIMINAL JUSTICE SAUSAGE GRINDER

THE CLUELESS CYCLE

- New violations
- Rearrest
- Resentencing
- Re-impoverishment

ARREST

SENTENCING

RELEASE

PETTY CRIMES

- Traffic violations
- Marijuana possession
- Associating with felons
- Petty theft
- Drunk and disorderly
- Domestic dispute

ADMINISTRATIVE CRIMES

- Failure to appear
- Probation violation
- Parole violation
- Suspended license
- Expired tag
- No car insurance

The criminal justice sausage grinder continually reprocesses clueless petty offenders through the system. Upon release, generally on probation, they continually commit new minor offenses or administrative crimes that get them more time than their original offense.

HEADLINE FROM PLANET EARTH

The criminal justice system is not "as seen on TV" in one crucial aspect—money. On TV, every defendant gets a great (and usually great-looking) attorney who works day and night on the case. TV lawyers work miracles. They persuade judges to free the accused with astoundingly clever arguments and never-before-contemplated motions.

On TV nobody ever discusses who pays for all this. In real life, public defenders are overworked and undercompensated. Except in capital cases, a public defender generally can give you only a perfunctory defense. If you want to fight charges with a top-flight attorney, expect to pay heavy bucks—five- and six-figure bucks—to beat the rap. It's far more economical not to get arrested in the first place. That's what this book is about. The price of this little package of paper is less than the cost of *a few minutes* of a top attorney's time. What a deal!

WHO AM I TO TELL YOU JACK?

I'm a criminal defense attorney. I'm the guy you call at midnight when you're in the can, when your mother's not taking your telephone calls and when the bail bondsman is in your face screaming for cash you don't have. I'm the guy you call when the state's attorney is declaring that what you thought was casual sex is actually capital rape and is recommending 25 years in prison. I'm the guy who gets the midnight ting-a-ling after you gave the cops some attitude that the cops characterized as resisting arrest.

I got my law degree late in life, after three (or was it four?) wives. The jail and the courthouse are my beat. I find getting people out of jail strangely relaxing compared to a bad marriage. Most of my life, however, I spent putting people *in* jail, as an FBI agent and before that as a Miami cop. I've arrested hundreds of people, from millionaires to bums. I've busted white guys, black guys, brown guys, yellow guys, every kind of guy. I was an equal opportunity, bad-guy-busting machine when Miami was one of the most dangerous cities in America. For a period of time I held records for felony arrests.

As a cop and FBI agent, I never thought much about the people I arrested. After they were booked, they became the prosecutor's problem.

That's me on the right, Dale Carson, during the arrest of convicted murderer Wendy Zabel. Desperate to have a child, Zabel faked a pregnancy and abducted a newborn from the obstetrical unit of a Florida hospital. During the abduction she shot the baby's mother and grandmother. The mother died of her wounds. As an FBI instructor, I taught classes on serial killers and sex criminals. I also participated in the arrest and interrogation of Wayne Williams, the Atlanta boy murderer. Photo courtesy of the Florida Times-Union, *1983*

Now, as a criminal defense attorney, I see the other side. I see people rolled over by a gigantic and impersonal criminal justice system. This book is about how the criminal justice system works today in the real world. It's about how you ought to think and act when confronted by police so you can live free and stay out of trouble. Of course, if you insist on being a crook, it's not a complete tragedy, especially if you're a crook in Florida. I need the work.

Here I am in 1978 as a lean, mean, arresting machine, and not as I am today, a warm and fuzzy defense attorney oozing empathy from every pore. The FBI gave me the opportunity to investigate and arrest some horrendously evil people—serial killers, child rapists, and millionaire con men. Most of these perps remain today where they belong, in jail or dead. Note: These credentials have been altered graphically to prevent copying and forgery. Photo courtesy of the FBI

PART I

CRIMINAL JUSTICE PLAYERS:
COPS, BAD GUYS, THE CLUELESS HORDE

NEW PLANTATIONS
FOR NEW GENERATIONS

E verybody knows about the big parts of the system—cops, judges, and state prisons. This chapter is about the parts of the system you don't know about. I call them the plantations, because these hidden parts of the system will keep you in the perpetual servitude of low-wage jobs and constant trouble with police and authorities. Remember, if you're not really a bad guy, just someone who is clueless or has bad judgment, you're not going to spend time in a state penitentiary. You'll land in the local lockup, then shortly be released on probation or placed in the drug-court system. What no one will tell you is that, once the arrest clerk puts your name in the computer, you have just entered the twilight hell of the plantations. Below I explain how it works.

IT STARTS WITH THE ARREST

Most arrests are logged *at once* into the FBI's National Crime Information Center (NCIC). Even if the prosecutor declines the case or you are quickly released or you are ultimately judged innocent and acquitted, you've got an arrest record. This arrest record will *never* go away. It will stay with you and haunt you for the rest of your life. It's your entry to the plantations.

In addition to arrest records, there are criminal court records (local, state, or federal records), corrections records (prison records), and state criminal repository records (statewide records composed of arrest records, criminal court records, and correction records). Certain misdemeanor arrests are not recorded; others are. In addition, there is a second national database of criminal information called the National Criminal File (NCF). But let's keep this simple. Assume that when you get arrested and fingerprinted, your records are going into the computers and they're never coming out. The short version: when you're printed, you're toast.

It doesn't matter that you're a juvenile and that your state arrest record at some point is sealed by a judge (federal arrest records cannot be sealed). You hear all the time on TV about records being "sealed." Have you ever wondered how this is done? What do judges seal them *with*? Tape? Wax? Staples? Chewing gum? Heck, everything is on computers. Do you think a clerk for some local judge whose authority doesn't run past the state line can call the government of the United States of America and tell them to seal your arrest records? Think again.

It gets worse. Here's an actual case that illustrates what happens with arrests and computers. I represented a client who was arrested while driving a vehicle in which police found weapons and narcotics during a traffic stop. None of it belonged to my client, and the state's attorney (prosecutor) dropped all charges. However, for the rest of this guy's life, every time he's stopped for a traffic violation, the police officers will run his license number through the NCIC. When his arrest record appears, it will have a heading that says "armed trafficking." Any cops seeing this will thoroughly search him and his car. They may handcuff him and draw their weapons because they will suspect that he could be armed and dangerous. For the rest of his life, every routine traffic stop will turn into a nightmarish confrontation with police.

The fact that arrest records are computerized, maintained by the federal government, and accessible to local law enforcement, state agencies, and far too many private employers is the reason you need to arrest-proof yourself. To keep from ruining your life at a young age, you need to avoid cops like the plague and never, ever get arrested for anything, no matter how trivial.

Still not worried? Of course not! This is America. You have rights! A good lawyer can get adjudication withheld and the records expunged. The whole thing will be as if it never happened. Right? That *was* right—decades ago. Prior to the invention of the copying machine, the fax, and the computer, criminal records existed only on paper and only in the jurisdiction in which the person was arrested. When records were expunged, a clerk tore a page out of a book or tossed out a file folder, and the records were gone forever.

Even when records remained, anyone wanting to discover whether a person had arrests and convictions had to contact each city or state in which the arrests occurred. To make copies, clerks literally had to photograph paper records, an expensive and tedious procedure. All anyone had to do to escape youthful indiscretions was blow town. Nowadays, that doesn't work. Once you're in the 'puter, my friend, you're there for life.

The federal database, the NCIC, is not your only problem. Every week, another city or county digitizes its arrest information going back decades and dumps everything onto the Internet so everyone, not just cops, can see records anytime, day or night. You can run from your arrests, but you can't hide.

THE CRIMINAL JUSTICE PLANTATION

Guess what? The system *needs* you. It's huge. It's no small chore keeping the jails filled; government employees at work; and those tax dollars, fines, and court costs rolling in. The problem nowadays is that, in many cities, serious crime is way down. The cops are great at arresting the really bad guys, and state legislatures have passed stiff sentencing guidelines that put felons away for decades. What you'll never see, however, is a headline like this: "Crime Down—Judges Laid Off, Cops Furloughed, Jails to Close."

So what to do? If murderers, armed robbers, rapists, and drug dealers are in short supply, the system fills itself with graffiti writers, jaywalkers, petty drug users, drivers with suspended licenses, and clueless types who mouth off to cops. The criminal justice system needs inmates to survive. This bureaucratic imperative to make ever more arrests is never absent from the decisions of cops and judges, and it's never discussed.

You're worth real money when you're busted. For example, if you're arrested for a petty federal offense like making phony IDs (yes, computer-buying moms and dads, Junior can be arrested on a federal charge, as was one of my stepsons, by the Homeland Security Agency and the Secret Service for using the 'puter to make phony IDs to buy beer), the state gets paid more than $150 per day by the federal government for every day you're in custody, since the federal government does not have pretrial detention facilities, i.e., jails. One of my clients was tossed into a cell with 10 other federal inmates. That's 11 inmates at $150 per day, or $1,650 per cell per day. That's as much as the toniest resorts get for presidential suites. Understandably, officials think of jails as hotels that can be profitably filled. All the people around you—cops, guards, clerks, bailiffs, judges, lawyers, probation officers, social workers—are making a good living off *you*.

Once arrested, you enter the criminal justice plantation. You're there to work, or more accurately, to ensure that state and city employees work. All you get is a place to flop and crummy food. Like a slave, you're branded with your owner's mark. Your fingerprints, case number, social security number, photograph, and description (and, soon, DNA) are filed.

Even when you're released on probation, you're still on the plantation. You and your home can be searched at any time. You have to sign away the right to a warrant and judicial review of searches as a condition of probation. If probation officers so decide, they can administer drug tests and strip-search and body-cavity search you at any time. Probation officers are not, repeat *not*, social workers. They're outdoor jailers. And you're paying them! Big dollars monthly in probation charges! Try paying that bill flipping burgers, sweeping floors in a warehouse, or stocking shelves at Wal-Mart.

JUVIE HALL AIN'T NO MALL

Kids, here's a bit of advice from your Uncle Dale: *Stay out of juvenile detention!* You've heard it called cute names like juvie hall. You've heard it's not so bad, sort of a cross between a dormitory and a cheap motel. Forget everything you've heard. Juvenile detention is kid jail—period. It's the criminal justice plantation for kids.

Worse, in many states there're no bail bonds for kids, no notice to appear (see page 14) in lieu of arrest, and no release into your parents' custody. Get busted, and you're going in.

Inside there's generally no rehabilitation, no work, nothing except jail cells and jailers. When you go in, you'll be strip-searched. If the corrections officers think you're carrying drugs, they will force open your mouth and poke around in there. The officers will not be concerned about you as a person. Their job is to process your body through the system. They care only about getting food in, waste out, grunge showered off, and jumpsuits changed as per regulation. Mostly they care about keeping you locked up until a judge decides what to do with you. If you become sufficiently annoying, they will strap you into a detention chair and lock you in a soundproof cell so you can scream your head off without bothering anyone else.

Juvenile detention is one of the most dangerous places in your city or county. Some of the kids there will be stone killers who would very much enjoy cutting out your stomach and intestines with a plastic shiv. Other kids will be florid, unmedicated psychotics, which is medical jargon for saying that they're stark raving mad. Inside, kids yell day and night. They bang on their cells. The stronger ones attack the younger and weaker ones. The only difference between juvenile detention and adult jail is that in juvie the guards are usually not armed and are *somewhat* less likely than adult correctional officers to beat you when you misbehave.

FIELD INTERROGATIONS

With the improvements in computers and data transmission, you can wander into the criminal justice plantation *even without getting arrested!* This is due to something the general public never hears about, a little bit of police routine called the field interrogation reports (FI). Patrol cops are required to make notes about *everyone* they talk to when they respond to a call or make a street stop. They note your name and address, your appearance, what you're wearing, and where you're going. These reports are cross indexed and filed. When a crime is reported in your area, police can review FI cards and instantly know everyone they have encountered in the neighborhood. Back in the old days, FI reports were handwritten on cards. Today, in most cities, they're computerized files and instantly accessible.

As you can imagine, FI reports are extremely useful to police. They might not be so useful to you. Let's say you encounter police. They stop their cruiser, call you over, ask for your ID, and quiz you about where you live and where you're going—all typical questions whose answers go into FI reports. Let's suppose you're wearing a red T-shirt, blue jeans, and a baseball cap. All this gets noted down, and with the miracle of computers and wireless database transmission, the information becomes accessible to every cop in the city almost before the police cruiser gets out of sight.

"So what?" you say. The police didn't arrest you, and you go on your way. But what if a crime is committed later in your neighborhood, by a guy about your size wearing a red T-shirt, jeans, and a baseball cap? You can bet the police will be at your doorstep within minutes. (Remember, you told them where you lived.) Now the cops are not cruising. They're investigating a recent crime and looking for a fleeing suspect. They're tense; they're edgy. They can arrest and hold you as a suspect. Even if charges are later dropped, you will have an arrest record.

Some of the police problems that minorities attribute to racism are actually routine police use of FI cards. You are likely to get arrested if you

>> encounter police and become the subject of an FI card

>> live in a neighborhood where crimes are being committed

>> somewhat resemble the description of a criminal

I'll discuss this further in a section about why you don't want to chat up cops. Remember, the essence of staying free is staying *away* from cops and *out* of the system. The system is designed to arrest you, not to help you.

IT TAKES A VILLAGE? THE SOCIAL SERVICES PLANTATION

Guys, listen up! The worst thing about getting arrested as a juvenile is that an arrest dumps you onto yet another plantation—the social services plantation. In most cases a judge will order you into the custody, or at least the care, of social workers and their contractors. These people can ruin your life trying to help you. Next time you hear someone waxing sentimental about how it "takes a village"—meaning a village of social workers—to raise a modern child, you should run, preferably screaming as you run, as far away as possible. Many well-intentioned people, especially those whose income, education, and jobs mean that their children will never encounter social service workers, imagine that probation officers, juvenile judges, public defenders, guardians *ad litem*, caseworkers, foster parents, and government psychologists are like kindly schoolmarms and wise old preachers who gently guide wayward youth to truth, enlightenment, and the American way.

Wrong. I work with these people every day. They try hard. They want to do the right thing. All of them, without exception, are overwhelmed with cases; underpaid; and restricted by a web of complex, confusing, and frequently contradictory bureaucratic procedures. All of them together, the entire village, cannot care for children as well as the most mediocre parents. Getting into the social services plantation sometimes means getting help. Often, however, it means getting your brain fried with drugs and then being dumped into juvenile detention facilities and foster homes.

Always it means that the state will gather an enormous dossier of information on you. A gigantic file, your "jacket," stuffed with medical reports and "expert" opinions of your neuroses, psychoses, hang-ups, allergies, food preferences, IQ, and personality, will follow you around for life. You'll be officially certified as damaged goods. You'll be in the computer, in the system, for life, even if you never actually get arrested. Juvenile criminal records are generally separated from adult records, but in most states prosecutors *can* get to them. This means that, when you're on trial years later as an adult, a prosecutor can point out to the judge what a loser you've been practically since the day you got the diapers strapped on.

The social services system and its affiliate, the public schools, are obsessed with definitions of what is normal. This definition is narrowed every day by new studies, new expert opinions, and batteries of ever more subtle psychological tests. Anyone outside the acceptable range of behaviors is, by definition, abnormal and subject to state intervention, supervision, and labeling. I call this the tyranny of normalcy.

Let me give you an example. Years ago, children who got distracted, ran around a lot, slept very little, and did several things at once were called jittery, pesky, or a handful. Now such children are defined as suffering from attention-deficit disorder. Supposedly, nearly 10 percent of American children are so diseased. Most are given powerful psychoactive drugs. Some of these, like Ritalin, are related to amphetamines. Others are tranquilizers, antipsychotics, and neurotransmitter inhibitors, which were never approved for use by children and whose long-term effects are unknown. All of these drugs, without exception, are restricted, scheduled narcotics. Many are addictive, and all are sold illegally on the street. Possession of any of them without the prescription *in your possession* will land you in jail. When adults take tranquilizers for a decade or more, they are considered addicts. When children take them, they are considered normal. Of course the kids don't complain. They're drugged.

Now I'm going to say some things that will enrage 52 percent of the population. Ladies, prepare yourselves! Launch your word processors for angry letters and e-mails. Get out the spray paint for protest signs and banners, and dust off those marching shoes. Ready? Here it is: The social services plantation is staffed predominantly by women. Its attitudes are female, and, most importantly, its definition of normalcy is female.

For young men, this is a disaster. The system defines many innate male behaviors as abnormal and sick. For example, the social services plantation's female overseers (teachers, social workers, counselors, psychologists) stigmatize boys for fighting, throwing and kicking things, teasing, resisting authority, etc. Yet these things are what little boys *do*. These behaviors are the play that become, in a man, fighting and hunting skills. Of course, such behaviors need to be socialized and controlled, since we are no longer Neolithic hunter-gatherers, but they are not abnormal or sick. All of us have caveman DNA and behaviors. They require patience and parenting, not drugs and the lockup.

Look at this another way. Do the female overseers ever stigmatize and punish little girls for doing any the following?

>> having too many friends

>> forming overly intense personal relationships

>> coloring too neatly within the lines and failing to be creative

>> being too obedient to authority

>> failing to challenge teachers and think outside the box

>> failing to take risks

>> lacking healthy aggression

>> getting goofy about boys

The social services plantation is the farm team for the criminal justice plantation. Cops, schoolteachers, and social workers are the gatekeepers to this village, but it's a village of the damned. Guys, unless your own home is unbearable, you want to stay out of this place. You want to arrest-proof yourself to stay free and unprocessed until you can grow up enough to figure yourself out. Trust me. I know.

THE ELECTRONIC TATTOO

Every plantation has to inventory its inmates and place its mark upon them. The criminal justice plantation and, increasingly, its social services affiliates use the fingerprint. Everyone is stamped at birth with an indelible identifier, their fingerprints. Advances in computers make fingerprints an outstanding ID, an electronic tattoo.

Fingerprints are manually pressed with ink on paper. Then they are scanned, and their loops, whorls, and patterns converted into a number. This is called the Automatic Fingerprint Identification System (AFIDS). Computers can access records and establish identification quickly. A word here about definitions. Fingerprints lifted from crime scenes are often smudgy partials and difficult to match. What I'm talking about here are the *carefully recorded prints* in law enforcement records.

Police cruisers are already equipped in most cities with portable computers connected wirelessly to government databases. Soon fingerprint scanners will also be portable and wireless. This means that for anyone fingerprinted and processed through the criminal justice system, the fingerprint number will become the one, universal ID that cannot be faked and that can access all records. There will be no way to hide, and no way to lie about identity. Cops (and you can bet employers) will simply say, "Hold out those mitts." One quick scan and they will know everything. Anyone who has been arrested will become a second-class citizen, always subject to police scrutiny.

THE MATRIX UPLOADED—THE EYE IN THE SKY

Sooner than you think, the system will not only know who you are by cataloging information under your fingerprint number, but it will also be able to track where you go and what you do. Remember those thriller movies that begin with a satellite photo of planet Earth, followed by the camera zooming in to show a continent, then a country, then a city, then a city block, then a single person walking on the street? It seems preposterous, yet something similar already exists to monitor the inmates of the criminal justice plantation—global positioning satellite (GPS) locators and mappers. Unlike the movies, no photos are required, only a set of numbers that pinpoint your location by longitude and latitude and are accurate to within 15 meters. Here's a description of the Sky Guardian system from Britain's *Guardian* newspaper: "Unlike tags now used to enforce curfews for general criminal offenders, which communicate on localized radio frequencies, the new device uses global satellite positioning technology. This will allow probation services and police to pinpoint the wearer anywhere in the UK to within three meters.

"The device is capable of providing a detailed diary at the end of every day of where the user has been."

In other words, the state can map where you go all day, every day. If you violate your probation by stopping off to buy a beer after work, or by driving through certain prohibited neighborhoods, the state will know automatically. You can't hide! You can't cut yourself even a bit of slack! The system includes a cell phone so the state can call you and tell you to stop what you're doing, or worse, say, "You're busted!"

GPS chips are here now in a cell phone near you. Law enforcement, with a court order, is able to track your movements as well as record your conversations. Ex-spouses and other enemies, using the civil courts, will not be able to record your conversations, but they will be able to track your movements.

Guess what's happening with those high-end security systems installed in luxury cars, trucks, and SUVs? These systems include microphones and wireless uplinks for voice and data. Law enforcement officers can get search warrants that allow them to turn on the car's microphone and listen and record conversations inside the vehicle without the driver's and passengers' knowledge.

In addition, surveillance drones are becoming smaller, stealthier, and more affordable. These hover overhead, read your tag, and track your movements. License plate scanners mounted on police cruisers and light poles can signal police automatically which vehicles' drivers have warrants, suspended licenses, unpaid tickets, and other administrative offenses. GPS chips located in cell phones, laptops, and navigational systems can be tracked, sometimes with a warrant, sometimes without. Computerized ticketing systems write citations automatically for red light infractions and speeding. No cops are required.

In addition, new vehicles manufactured in the United States and Japan are equipped with "black box" data recorders that track your location, speed, brake use—and much, much more. Law enforcement is now able to interrogate your car. San Francisco wants to require drivers to pull into tax collectors' offices, where their boxes will be plugged in and a "mileage tax" will be levied. None of this has anything to do with traffic safety and law enforcement; it has everything to do with the state sticking its digital fingers into your wallet.

Total monitoring via total telemetry at all times is here now and ready to keep tabs on you. Big Brother *is* watching you!

THE ELECTRONIC PLANTATION

Many poor people do not have computers, do not use the Internet, and have no idea how much they are affected by these innovations. Readers, this is the most important point in this book—computers, high-speed data transmission, and the Internet have changed *everything*. They are the reason you have to avoid cops and avoid arrest more than ever. Because of computers, arrest records follow you everywhere, forever. You can never escape past screwups and start over. There is no clean slate in the era of computers. You can never pay your debt to society because society, with its computers, never forgets and never forgives. This slavery to your past due to computerized record keeping is what I call the electronic plantation.

When you step out of jail and complete probation or parole, you leave the criminal justice plantation. At 18 or so, you get mustered out of the social services plantation. You will, however, remain enslaved in the new electronic plantation. Before you get your first breath of free air, your arrest records will be transmitted to computers around the world. Some of these computers belong to government law enforcement agencies, others to private companies that collect personal information and sell it to prospective employers, lenders, credit card companies, and landlords. The electronic plantation is virtual—everywhere and nowhere. You can't touch it, or ever hope to find it, because it's dispersed among computers, databases, and servers that can be located anywhere in the world yet be in instantaneous communication. Nonetheless, this plantation is absolutely real.

Even if your records are expunged by a judge because your case was dismissed, because an acquittal was entered, or because adjudication was withheld, you can't assume the information is unavailable. The reason? Local courts lack jurisdiction. They can't order the federal government, which maintains the NCIC, or data collection companies in other states to purge information. They also lack funds, technology, or even the inclination to search out and erase expunged records. Preserving the rights of arrestees does not excite judicial officials or arouse the zeal of politicians.

The electronic plantation is less visible than the criminal justice plantation, the social service plantation, or the rice and cotton plantations of centuries past. Nonetheless, it's real. Employers, schools, and government agencies would rather not hire someone who has been arrested or whom the social service system has labeled as "troubled." Lenders would rather not make a loan or a mortgage. Credit cards? Forget about it. Why bother, when other qualified people have clean records? Landlords, ditto. Why entrust rental property to someone who's been arrested?

So you may get back on the streets, breathing free air, but you're on the plantation nevertheless. Only unskilled labor is available, and there's plenty of it—digging holes, pouring concrete, filling boxes, butchering animals, picking fruit, mopping floors, and flipping burgers. Whoopee.

When you're on the electronic plantation, doors close. Opportunities vanish. Years ago background checks were expensive and were used only by large corporations and institutions. Now, via the Internet, any employer, school, or landlord can pay $40 or less and discover that you have been arrested. Major corporations love background checks. They're not only not hiring people who have slipups in their past; they're actually *laying off* employees who have even a returned check or an unpaid traffic ticket. Only Goody Two-Shoes types with perfect church attendance pins can work in the prim corporate America of the future. Yikes!

If you are convicted of a felony, it gets worse. In Florida, felons can never work in any business licensed by the state. That means real estate, securities, health care, law, insurance, and even barbering are out of the question. You can't vote. Don't even *think* about owning a gun. What does it take to get a felony rap? Less than you think. If you're contemplating a life of crime, contemplate this: you'll be washing dishes and dumping garbage for the rest of your life.

THE MAGIC PORTAL

Cops! They're the gatekeepers of the plantations. The door of a police cruiser is a magic portal. Once you go through it, your life changes forever. You lose your freedom and your anonymity. You belong to the state, and whatever it wants to know about you, it will discover. It will fingerprint you, photograph you, and in many states swab the inside of your cheek to map your DNA. It can look down your throat and inside your body anytime it wants. It can force you to spill your guts to psychiatrists and take tests administered by psychologists, who are not, repeat not, working to help you. You're bagged and tagged, and all that information will go into computerized files that are increasingly available to anyone. The magic portal is one-way and leads only to the plantations, where servitude is not limited by indenture and is, in fact, a life sentence. So *don't go through that portal.* Stay out of there! Stay away from cops unless you need them! Run and hide if you must! (More about how to do that in upcoming chapters.)

SO WHO'S IN CHARGE? NOBODY!

The horror of the electronic plantation is that nobody's in charge. Local judges can't do anything because they have no jurisdiction beyond the state line and none whatsoever over the federal government, which maintains the NCIC arrest database. The U.S. Congress, which does have jurisdiction, gives privacy issues more hot air than action. Europe strictly guards data privacy; the United States does not.

Here's another problem. Most lawyers and judges who work in the state criminal justice systems are paper people (in the federal court system, documents are filed electronically). For good and necessary reasons (anyone can say they didn't get a fax or e-mail) judges and court officers do not send documents electronically, but have them served by certified mail or by human process servers. This is the only method so far devised that ensures that people actually receive summonses, complaints, subpoenas, court orders, etc. Most lawyers and judges view computers as glorified typewriters to be pounded by underlings. They are amazingly uninformed about the problems caused by electronic records releases and their use in discriminating against people with arrests but no convictions—and this includes records of false arrests and bad arrests.

Here's something else you need to know that should raise goose bumps of fear. Felony arrests, in many states, can be based solely on the testimony of a credible witness. You say, so what? What's so bad about that?

Imagine one day that your next-door neighbor or your ex-girlfriend or your ex-wife or your ex-boyfriend or your ex-husband who hates your guts calls the cops. He or she says, "Officer, that man threatened me. He beat me and said he was going to shoot me! *Help!*"

You're innocent. You don't like this person, and may have had some sharp words with him or her, but you never touched the person and never made a threat of bodily harm. Nonetheless, you can get arrested, fingerprinted, and dumped into the electronic plantation for life while the cops investigate what's going on. Police are aware that people will lie and make false accusations in order to get their enemies arrested, but cops often err on the side of caution and arrest the person named anyway.

This actually happened to my coauthor. A guy who hates him wrote an anonymous letter to the sheriff's office accusing him of various nefarious deeds. The cops were all over him for *two entire weeks*. Fortunately, as his attorney, I did the talking to the cops, so he was able to avoid interrogation and arrest. As for the poison dwarf who wrote the "anonymous" letter, we sued him.

There's another demon at work here—bureaucratic convenience. Government agencies hate to hire clerks and dedicate office space to fulfilling document requests. They *really* hate records requests from the media, which can give any agency and administrator instant media burn for screwups. And they *really, really* hate records requests accompanied by

Freedom of Information Act and Sunshine Law litigation (with attendant media scorching of all and sundry).

The bureaucratic solution? The light bulb that goes off in every administrator's head? *Dump the whole thing onto the Web!* That's right, put those expensive computer geeks to work. Digitize everything in every file folder. Then dump the whole shebang, now neatly organized into relational databases, into the black hole that is the Internet. This allows schools, colleges, cops, and private and public sector employers to check up on you 24/7 with a click of the computer mouse. It also allows government employees to do what they do best—get the heck out of the office by 4:59 P.M. as God intended.

But let us not unduly excoriate our bureaucratic friends. They get no direction from elected officials who, even if they are aware of the problem, couldn't care less. People who have been arrested but not prosecuted or convicted are not a constituency anyone cares about.

CAN I HAVE YOUR SOCIAL?

Who has not heard a chirpy feminine voice on the phone or over the counter asking for your social security number? Hospital patients might as well have the number tattooed on their heads, since they get asked for it a dozen times a day. Pending perfection of universally accessible fingerprint and DNA identification systems, the social security number has become the de facto universal ID. With this magic number anyone can access an astonishing amount of information about you. The use of this number has created a multi-billion-dollar criminal enterprise called identity theft.

It wasn't supposed to be this way. Look at the illustration of my co-author's social security card (the number has been omitted to keep him out of any more trouble than he's already in). Can you read that last line, printed in uppercase by the government of the United States of America? It says, "NOT FOR IDENTIFICATION." This card was issued in the 1960s. Ah, those were innocent years!

WHAT ABOUT MY RIGHT TO PRIVACY?

The short answer is you don't have a *right* to privacy. You have some federal court opinions that assert that the nation's founders kinda, sorta *intended* that you should have a right of privacy. Alas, these worthy 18th-century gentlemen forgot to actually write anything on the subject in the Constitution and Bill of Rights. Congress and state legislatures are all in favor of rights of privacy, but somehow they keep forgetting to pass bills into law.

Even if privacy laws restricting arrest records get passed, they mean nothing unless enforced. Heck, the right to vote regardless of race, creed, or color is quite clearly written in the Constitution, but until I was a teenager in the 1960s, Southern governors and legislators had difficulty understanding the concept. The sudden appearance of thousands of federal employees with uniforms, helmets, and guns brought about a rapid increase in the understanding of standard English among the Southern lawmaking elite. Here's the bottom line: until privacy rights are enacted into law, and the law is elaborated into rules of criminal and civil procedure, and these laws and rules are upheld by judges and enforced by government employees wearing guns, you don't have privacy rights.

THE RIGHT TO BE LEFT ALONE*

As legislatures and Congress force themselves to contemplate privacy rights, I'd like to respectfully suggest they consider another right—to be left alone. The major problem addressed by this book is this: arrest is

---

* Yes, I know that "left alone" is incorrect and "let alone" is proper. So what? I've got to speak American here.

tantamount to conviction. It doesn't matter that, after you were arrested, your case was "nol prossed" (*nolle prosequi*, Latin for "not prosecuted") or that you were acquitted. Outside the criminal justice system, few people pay attention to such distinctions. Even if you were acquitted, people figure you were *arrested*, weren't you? You must have been doing *something*. In the computer age, that arrest will follow you forever, and become, in essence, a lifetime sentence of shame, lost opportunities, and underemployment.

There are two antithetical trends occurring in this country. The first is the encouragement of diversity. We should understand people of different skin colors, religions, sexual orientations, and social circumstances. We should be less judgmental and cut our fellow beings a little slack. Perhaps we should even decriminalize drug use and think of this as a lifestyle choice, etc.

The second trend, far less discussed, is the enforcement of conformity. Any divergence from a narrow range of behavior is now punished by lifetime incarceration on the social services plantation and the electronic plantation. Arrests, traffic violations, debt payments, notes taken by schoolteachers and counselors and employers, and even malicious gossip contained in law enforcement interviews is subject to being indelibly recorded on computer databases and accessed by way too many people.

These two trends, of diversity and conformity, are antithetical. Advances in surveillance and data transmission make the power to enforce conformity overwhelming, even if its dispersed nature makes it less talked about and more difficult to understand. In an age in which your whereabouts are continuously recordable from GPS chips in your car and cell phone (or, if you are in custody, from your ankle bracelet) and your comings and goings at home and work are recorded by neighborhood and employment security systems that note each time you open gates and doors, privacy is a fiction. Ex-spouses, prospective employers, litigants, personal enemies, and even blackmailers can access this information at any time, sometimes with a subpoena, often without.

In a world where nothing is ever forgotten, nothing is ever forgiven. There is no wiggle room for minor indiscretions. Having a run-in with the cops, getting a traffic ticket, being somewhere you're not supposed to be—

these should not carry the life sentence of a permanent record. Once you're on the electronic plantation, every cop, every government employee, every human resources weenie, every wireless phone company, and every geek with a credit card and Internet access is your judge and critic. As for ex-wives? Let's not even go there! Who can stand such scrutiny? In the Bible the Lord declares, "Judgment is mine." He has a point.

The protection of privacy is advanced in Europe (where even release of employee work telephone extensions is a crime) but practically ignored here. "Privacy issues," alas, are discussed in this country by academic types in the plummy tones of National Public Radio. The issue is an eye glazer. I'm an old cop and not an abstract thinker, so I'm going to stick to the nitty-gritty and propose what I call Dale's Bill of Rights in language everybody understands.

DALE'S BILL OF RIGHTS

1. To have records of arrests not leading to convictions made permanently unavailable to anyone, including judges before sentencing, except law enforcement agencies. Let's make "innocent until proven guilty" actually mean something.

2. To have records of GPS tracking devices, gate security systems, computer monitoring software, and employment telephone recordings made permanently unavailable to anyone except law enforcement agencies. Where you go, who you call, and what you do are your business.

3. To have any and all psychological tests, assessments, job interviews, school interviews, and admissions documents made permanently unavailable to anyone—period. Dissemination of this stuff just speeds your check-in to the social service plantation.

4. To be free from involuntary counseling, psychoanalysis, personality profiling, and use of mind-altering pharmaceuticals. So what if you're a little weird? Stay free.

5. To be left alone. To not have government employees, ex-spouses, enemies, and Nosy Parkers able to know everything you do, day

in and day out, world without end, amen. It's your life. Maybe it's glorious, maybe it's grubby, but it's yours and no one else's, at least not without a court order!

Well and good, you say, but these plantation horrors could never happen to me. Think not? To illustrate how these situations can become real, read Scenario #1 on the next page. This fictional account illustrates how incarceration on the electronic plantation could happen not to a ghetto kid, barrio thug, or trailer trash redneck, but to a nice, hardworking, ordinary guy.

SCENARIO #1

SEÑOR CRANE GOES INSANE

Our hero is a 35-year-old construction crane operator who, thanks to an ability to swim long distances under water, ran into the surf in Santiago de Cuba and swam under a barrage of machine gun bullets from Cuba's Guardia de la Costa. He arrived freezing but unharmed in the Guantánamo Naval Base, considered U.S. territory. Thanks to special immigration laws, he quickly became an American citizen and moved to a large southern city.

Here he was happy for steady work with good pay as a construction crane operator. Every day it was up the high crane with a lunchbox and a jar to pee in, then eight hours lifting loads, then home. He was proud of his safety record of never having dropped a load or caused an injury. He had married a "real American," blonde and blue eyed, and had helped put her through college and law school. She had made partner in a large law firm, and now they lived in a style that allowed him to drive a luxury car that astounded his truck-driving coworkers. He had twin daughters of whom he was foolishly fond.

At first his wife liked the fact that he was big, strong, Latin, and a real working guy, unlike her other boyfriends. After 10 years of marriage, however, her attitude changed. At the last Christmas office party, he had had, as usual, nothing to say to the suits who drank scotch, gossiped about judges, and speculated about who juiced who in the last election. They couldn't understand his accent, and anyway they were uninterested in construction. His wife said that he had embarrassed her, that he was a nobody, and that he was hurting her career.

The next day she served him with divorce papers. He moved out of their magnificent house and into a studio apartment with a chair, a bed, and a TV on cinder blocks. To console him, his construction buddies took him out to a gentlemen's club—really just a glorified strip joint. He had some drinks, ogled the dancers, and had a so-so night. His buddies assured him that the divorce wouldn't be too bad, since this was a "no fault" divorce state.

They were right. The divorce was simple, but the child-custody proceedings were not. His wife's attorney subpoenaed the GPS tracking information from his car and discovered his visit to the strip joint. They also ran a background check and uncovered an earlier arrest. Years earlier, when he first arrived in America, he had had a passionate romance with an American girl. He had been 22 and she 16. The girl's mother, however, had been outraged and had had him arrested. The charge was lewd and lascivious conduct with a minor. He was puzzled. In Cuba, sex is the only activity *not* regulated by government. In many American states, however, it is illegal to have sex with anyone under the age of 18. Fortunately the girl had loved him and refused to testify, so the charges were dropped.

At trial, his wife's attorney described this arrest in detail and kept repeating the words "lewd and lascivious." The lawyer always referred to his former girlfriend as a "minor child." At trial no one mentioned that the girl had refused to testify against him and that the charge had been dropped.

His having been to a strip joint, said the attorney, was evidence of sexual maladjustment and a love of pornography and perversion. The club had a magazine and video rack and sold sex toys, which the attorney described in detail. As a violator of children and a pornography addict, the attorney concluded, our man was an unfit father and should not share custody of the children. The judge ruled in the wife's favor.

Our man was denied access to his daughters, except under strict supervision, and ordered to pay child support, even though his wife's income was many times larger than his. He went into a deep depression and spent weeks on sick leave. His union protected him from being fired, however, and he was able to return to work.

THE MORALS OF THIS STORY

1. The electronic plantation extends even into private civil matters. The assumption that an arrest is the same as a conviction often goes unchallenged.

2. All the whizbang gimmickry of modern life, such as GPS tracking and entry and exit records at gated communities, can be subject to subpoena and used at trial. Do you really want people to be able to know your goings and comings?

3. Construction is the only industry in America that hires large numbers of people with arrest records. Our subject would find it difficult to work elsewhere.

4. Minorities often do not understand how the system works and are more frequently blindsided in courts, both civil and criminal.

2 | TO HUNT AND ARREST IS THE QUEST OF THE BEST

C ops! To stay free, you've got to avoid them like the plague. You've got to stay out of their sight, off their radar screens, and out of their freaking computers. They're the gatekeepers of the plantations. They alone have the power to transform indiscretions, stupidities, and recreational drug use into a lifetime sentence of shame and low wages. This chapter is all about cops, the good and the bad, the noble and the ignominious. In many ways cops are extraordinary people. What's absolutely certain is that they are not at all like you. When you need them, they can be lifesavers. When they need you to make their daily arrest tally sheet look good, they can be life destroyers. To know them is to avoid them, so settle back and learn all about those boys and girls in blue.

Pop quiz. Good police officers spend the majority of their time in which activity?

1. keeping neighborhoods calm by encouraging communication

2. setting an example with courteous, professional behavior

3. serving and protecting the weak and helpless

4. hunting the two-legged beast

The answer is . . . 4. If you selected anything else, you've been listening too much to Officer Friendly, the public relations guy giving smiley speeches in school auditoriums and community centers. To arrest-proof yourself, however, it's important to understand real cops, the guys on the street who can bust you. They are the first group of criminal justice players.

What you've got to understand is this: cops *like* to hunt and pursue. They *enjoy* arresting people. I refer to good cops, not time servers trudging toward retirement or social worker types who decide, after a few bloody scuffles with angel dust–crazed psychotics, that maybe it's time to get that teaching certificate after all. The animal cops hunt is that prince of prey, the two-legged beast. Human quarry are smart and wily. Often they draw guns and knives, or ambush you from inside their cars and their houses. From a cop's point of view, that's real sport.

The above paragraph is one of the most important in this book. Cops are hunters—period. Once you understand this, police tactics will make sense. Cops are the hunters; you are the prey. Avoiding these hunters, hiding from them, and not antagonizing them are the essentials of arrest proofing. As I noted in the introduction, the fact that cops are hunters is not a bad thing. Without intensive policing, our cities would be uninhabitable.

The important thing to understand is that almost all police effort is put into hunting and arresting people. Everything else—serving and protecting, fostering community—is way, way down on the list. To street cops, law and order, peace and quiet, and community understanding are *by-products* of hunting and arresting people.

The way cops think about it is this: toss enough bad guys into the can and—bingo—law and order happen. Peace and quiet break out like roses on a vine. As for community understanding, the community can understand that if they start breaking laws and getting into it with cops, they're going to get hammered. This, ladies and gentlemen and children of all ages, is the cop's point of view.

Confusion results because city police departments and municipal governments are administered by elected sheriffs and mayors. Understandably, politicians downplay the hunt-and-arrest activity and play up the serve-and-protect angles. It's the mayors and police chiefs who show up at community meetings to soothe aggravated and overarrested minorities. The patrol guys, of course, are generally too busy to attend community meetings since they're out on the street arresting people.

Think this isn't so? Here's a reality test. In most big cities, police headquarters have public displays of things cops think are interesting. If you stroll down the display hall in my city and look into the glass cases, will you see photos of black, brown, yellow, and white people standing together in smiling, interracial harmony fostered by sensitive, empathic law enforcement? Nope. How about noble sculptures of little old ladies serving cupcakes to the officers who serve and protect? Nah! What you will see are

>> machine guns

>> revolvers and automatic pistols

>> sniper rifles

>> car bombs

>> gas masks

>> surveillance cameras

>> tear gas grenades

>> switchblades

All this is equipment used to arrest people or weapons captured from serious bad guys in big operations of which the force is justifiably proud. This is not criticism. Cops are all about arresting people, that's all.

When I was a cop, I didn't just like arresting people, I loved it! My favorite activity, and the only thing I've ever considered as good as sex, was breaking down doors. Here's the scenario: You sneak up on a drug house in the dead of night with your partners. In front of you is a steel door studded with locks and barred from the inside. Behind it are bad guys.

Silently two or more cops swing a gigantic iron ram. One, two, three, then whammo! The locks explode, and fragments ping off the floor and walls. The door slams down. People scream. Bad guys reach for weapons, stuff narcotics into toilets, and dive out windows. It's like turning on the lights and watching cockroaches run. Best of all, there are so many guys to arrest! When I was a cop I even stopped smoking. Was this because of health concerns? Heck no! I stopped because cigarettes made me short of breath. I stopped so I could run faster and catch more bad guys.

Police work is not like any other work. Can you name another job in which you are expected to engage in physical combat with people who are trying to kill you? Some of those bad guys are huge, experienced brawlers. Some are psychotics who have superhuman strength from high adrenaline levels caused by brain disease. When psychos flying on adrenaline get extra juice from methamphetamines and angel dust, they can be nearly impossible to stop. My training instructor shot 14 rounds into a maniac he was fighting, and the guy still kept coming.

FLUSHING RABBITS

Cops crave variety and excitement. They never have one shift like another. On slow days they can make their own excitement because they can always find someone to arrest. I call the technique "flushing rabbits." When I was a cop, there were days when even Miami seemed dull. No Jamaican posses were machine-gunning competitors. No Colombian peasants were stubbing out their cigarettes on drums of diethyl ether and vaporizing drug labs in a whoosh of fire. No calls, nothing happening.

My solution was to start pulling over cars that were the same make and model as the number one most stolen car of that year. I'd get behind the car, spin the lights, then give the siren a tap, just a single *honk*. If the car was being driven by a citizen, he'd pull over. I'd pass him and wave him off. I'd do this a few times, then suddenly, the next driver would be a car thief. Instead of pulling over, he'd floor the gas. He'd be off like a shot with me in hot pursuit, siren wailing and lights blazing. My partner would radio in the pursuit and call for backup with that emotion-free, calm voice that is absolutely required to maintain cop cool. (Cops are fanatics about maintaining their cool. It carries over into their prose. Cops can make an account of the most grisly murder sound like a linoleum brochure.)

While you're in pursuit, dispatchers clear the entire network by shutting up every other cop in the city while you call in locations. Nowadays, they'll spin up helicopters. During a pursuit police cruisers are racing ahead of you, behind you, and on every side. A minute earlier you were bored. Now you're leading a cop circus down the highway at 100 miles an hour. Usually the suspect burns out the brakes or crashes. Then there's a foot chase, maybe a fight, then an arrest. Every day cops engage in the primordial male activities—hunting, fighting, and protecting the tribe. They experience thrills that have been honed by a million years of evolution. When a shift gets slow, they just flush a rabbit. Want to be a cop? It's a kick-ass way to make a living.

THE POWER

Cops are backed by courts, jails, judges, and the entire apparatus of the state. They can stop, arrest, search, attack, and even kill. It's The Power. It's The Juice. It's intoxicating, and nobody else has it. Police officers have to train not to let it go to their heads. When the cops show up, the music stops, the party's over, and everybody snaps to attention. It's *la poli*, the po-leece, the fuzz, the heat, the man with the badge and the gun.

In any medium to large city, cops are backed up not only by other officers, but by helicopters, boats, tear gas, explosives, snipers, dogs, SWAT teams, even armored personnel carriers with artillery and high-caliber machine guns. If things get tense, the governor can call out the National Guard, which can muster infantry, cavalry, and armor equipped with mood adjusters like mortars and wire-guided missiles. Yikes!

The funny thing is that the guys who most often get snotty and sass the cops are generally clueless petty offenders. The real bad guys, the stone evil types who hurt people and steal things for a living, give it up when The Man shows. They know who has The Power.

Ever get the *cop stare*? This is a slow, hard, minute examination that gets you filed for future reference. You can almost see the blanks being filled in: hair color, eye color, height, weight, race, distinguishing marks. Cops aren't embarrassed at all to give you the once-over in a public place, even when they're off duty. If you interest or annoy them, you get the stare. This also establishes the pecking order, with the cop, not you, at the top of the food chain. Ever met a waitress who didn't know who's a cop and who's not?

Police are dangerous. They are heavily armed, and unlike any other group in society outside the military, they are trained to fight, maim, and kill. Police officers are better educated and trained than ever, but accidents happen. Anyone who challenges cops, runs from them, hits them, grabs their equipment, or even *appears* to reach for a weapon is risking injury or death. Cops train for hundreds of hours in order to be able to disable or kill people quickly, instinctively, without thinking. When they blow you away, it's not personal, not even emotional. It's just business—cold as ice.

Think law enforcement officers aren't dangerous? This is an FBI SWAT (Special Weapons and Tactics) team. I'm on the bottom row, second from right, holding a CAR-16. This was a fully automatic assault rifle, with a barrel modified by FBI armorers to shoot tight groups in the 75– to 200-yard range common for urban sniping. We spent hours becoming proficient at making the CNS disconnect shot. This is a round fired through a suspect's upper lip. It severs the brain stem and disconnects the central nervous system. The suspect drops immediately, so he cannot fire his weapon or attack other officers or hostages.

In some ways cops are similar to a gang. They have better haircuts than the Hell's Outlaws and use deodorant, but they're still a gang in one characteristic all gangs share: you can't challenge just one member; you always have to deal with the entire gang. With cops, you take on one, you take on all. Even cops who hate each other will stand shoulder to shoulder against outsiders. Cops are always the biggest gang in town, with the most guys, the most guns, and the most money. They show their blue colors with pride, 24/7, every day of the year. Challenging them is insanity. Cops never, *ever*, lose on the street. Whenever challenged, they call up reinforcements until they win.

Later in this book I'm going to advise you to do some things that will really bug you. I'm going to tell you *never* to challenge cops, *never* to try to score verbal points with them, and *always* to be submissive and polite to them—even if this makes you crazy. Worse, you should do these things even if the cops are obnoxious and even racist. The only way to win with cops is to stay free and out of their clutches. So take a deep breath, have a cooling beverage, and read more about cops.

THE BOYS' CLUB FOR MEN

One of the joys of being a professional athlete is that you don't have to stop playing childhood games when you grow up. You even get paid for what you used to do free. Same with the cops. They get to play cops and robbers, cowboys and Indians, and hide-and-seek in the grownup world. To be a law enforcement officer is to join a super-exclusive boys' club.

You get the best toys. Cops have all sorts of high-powered rifles, pistols, and ammunition that are illegal for anyone but law enforcement officers to possess. When I was in the FBI, we used to tool around town in government cars with trunks stuffed with high explosives, rifles, shotguns, pistols, and communication and surveillance gear I still can't talk about—and that was just to go to lunch! Heck, one of my FBI partners, who shall forever remain nameless, had his car, which contained an extra-large arsenal, stolen while he was noshing at a lunch joint. Did he freak out? Worry about getting fired? Heck no! He just commandeered another car (mine) and rolled down to the baddest part of town. He spread the word that his car needed to be returned *at once*. It was, too, with a wash and a wax. The real bad guys know who's boss.

SOVEREIGN IMMUNITY

While on duty, cops have another advantage you don't know about. They are generally immune from lawsuits. "Hey!" you remonstrate. "What about Rodney King, the guy the cops beat up in L.A.? Didn't he sue the police and win millions?" That's right, he did—in L.A., but that's the Left Coast, where tort lawyers are kings.

State and municipal employees generally have sovereign immunity from lawsuits. This means that you can sue the police department, or the city, but not the individual police officer as long as he or she is determined to have been operating within the scope of employment—which is legalese for saying that, as long as cops don't get too far out of line, you can't sue them personally. If you win in a lawsuit against the department or against the city, a cop may get disciplined, fired, or even indicted, but he's probably not going to be writing any checks to you. Most states have strict limits on what you can win in punitive "pain and suffering" damages when you sue the government. If Rodney King had sued in Florida, he would have won lost wages (i.e., zero) and a maximum of $100,000 in damages, which is about what tort attorneys spend on espresso and Danish during a big case.

Sovereign immunity is an amazing power. In law enforcement this makes sense. How could cops work if they had to think "Am I going to get sued?" every time they tackled some whacked-out perp with a gun? Cops don't worry about getting sued—ever. This is astonishing in a society where everyone else is paralyzed by lawsuit fears. Civilians, which in practice means people with insurance, money, and property, can get sued for spilling hot coffee or dropping a banana peel. Fart in an elevator and you can get sued for olfactory pain and suffering. So next time you get stopped by the cops, don't yell, "I'm gonna sue you!" After they quit laughing, they're likely to charge you with stupidity in the first degree.

THE GLORY

Being a police officer is exciting, and not just from the thrill of the hunt. Cops see life and death in the raw. Babies are born in the back of squad cars all the time. When someone gets shot, cops are the first responders and may have to close off an artery and save a life that would otherwise have been lost. They see life at its extremes. During domestic disturbance calls, police intervene between men and women devoured by love and hate, who may be crying, "I love you" even as they pull the trigger or plunge a knife into their beloved. As women wail over dead children and mates, cops are often by their side.

There's much death. Cops hold people and look into their eyes as they bleed out and get cold. They hear the screams of people dying in agony in burning vehicles. They hold epileptics as they shiver in grand mal seizures and their brains fry with electrical discharges. Civilians only infrequently experience life this way. They often know only the gray version of events in the newspapers or the flickering imitation on TV. Cops have a front-row seat, comped by the taxpayers, to life at its most intense.

Media are no substitute for the real thing. Crime reportage is a pale shadow of what it once was. In the 1930s and '40s, police photographers like Weegee photographed murders for the front page. Readers saw gangsters' bodies riddled with bullets in the barber chair or on the restaurant floor. Nowadays, tragedy is masked from view. Crime-scene tape prohibits entry. No photographers and note takers allowed—except cops.

They also routinely see something most people aren't sure even exists— evil. Most cops have looked into the empty eyes of stone killers. They arrest people with no socialization who react with the savage instincts of animals. Such people can exist safely only in prisons, asylums, and graves.

During my FBI tenure, I was a specialist in serial killers and sex offenders. I interviewed Wayne Williams, who murdered 21 boys in Atlanta. I've studied human vampires who drank their victims' blood in Dixie cups. These people are monsters. Cops know monsters personally. Their job requires them to spend hours interviewing them, empathizing with them, understanding what it is to lust for death. Most killers are not insane. They enjoy the crimes they commit.

Surgeons, priests, and executioners know some of these things. Only cops know them all. Sometimes cops *are* the priests and hear appalling confessions. Instead of "forgive me, father, for I have sinned," they listen to gruesome descriptions of murders, rapes, and child molestations. Often a cop will serve as a de facto surgeon, keeping someone alive until rescue comes. Occasionally, they're executioners. Unlike fictional spies, they are indeed licensed to kill.

When my dad was the sheriff of Jacksonville, he used to tell me, "Being a cop brings out the very best in people." What he meant was that cops, more than any other group in society, get called on to supersede themselves and do something truly noble. The cops who were at the World Trade Center on September 11, 2001, may not all have been good cops. Yet when the moment came, they stepped up and did what had to be done, every man and woman of them, knowing they might not survive. They saved a lot of people, and many of them died trying. You can't do that if your job is processing claim forms or pounding the cash register.

Courage is the rarest of human qualities. The sort seen on athletic fields is artificial, and the type portrayed in the movies is phony. The real thing, displayed by ordinary people, is so fine and so magnificently human that it defies description and brings tears to your eyes. Many cops have the real thing, battle tested on the meanest streets in America. They are extraordinary people.

THE FREAK SHOW

When I was a kid, you could buy your way into a freak show for a quarter. You saw Siamese twins, sword swallowers, bearded ladies, midgets, and fire-eaters. This satisfied a universal craving for the bizarre. Today it's crass even to admit an interest in human freakishness. Cops, however, get to see things even the circus would never have displayed.

For instance, cops in North Miami once found the upper half of a woman's body, frozen solid, on an oceanfront condo balcony in 90-degree heat. How could that happen? The corpse was too big to have been in a refrigerator freezer. They finally figured out that the woman had stowed away in the wheel well of a jetliner and become frozen in the minus-50-degree cold of 35,000 feet. When the landing gear was lowered, her frozen corpse split in two and dropped out of the jet while it was coming in over the beach for a landing. Her legs probably fell out first, dropped into the ocean, and became shark snacks. The top half landed in the condo balcony.

In Miami, cops chase voodoo doctors who dig up bodies from graves and sever corpses' heads for use as fetishes. I once investigated a headless face. It belonged to a suicide who had placed a shotgun in his mouth and pulled the trigger. It blew away the skull and brain, but left the face and the front of the skull intact. The face was peaceful; the eyes closed. I've often wondered whether the writer Ernest Hemingway looked like that when he capped himself in Idaho. Only the cops on the scene know.

Of course, there's cop comedy. One of my clients, after complex and clever motions made by yours truly, was released from jail and placed under house arrest with a radio transmitter ankle bracelet. After a few days, however, he just had to get out and get some love, so he sawed off the bracelet. Figuring he would fool the probation officers, he duct-taped the bracelet to the hind leg of his dog! When the cops showed up, they had a laugh, patted the dog, and waited until he returned to arrest him. Many times you wonder not only *what* these guys are thinking, but *whether* they're thinking.

My coauthor talked to a cop in Jacksonville who had just responded* to an arson. When the officer rolled up, the house was ablaze, and the arsonist was stranded—on a second-floor balcony! Turns out the guy got pissed at his girlfriend and decided to burn down her house. He bought a can of gas, set a huge fire on the ground floor, and then *ran up the stairs* to the second floor. What was he thinking? The firefighters and cops had to stop laughing so they could rescue him for immediate criminal justice processing.

To be a cop is to know life's fragility and often its meaninglessness. It can wreak havoc with religious beliefs. Is God a merciful creator, or is blind chance rolling the dice? Cops know courage and cowardice, ecstasy and despair, saintliness and satanic possession. They are fascinating to talk to, fun to make love to, and difficult to stay married to. Just ask my wives.

Now you know a bit about cops. They're hunters, rescuers, observers of the strange and the bizarre. Often they're amused by breathtaking acts of stupidity. You want to treat them the way you do undertakers, which is to stay away from them until they're needed.

---

* "Respond" is the all-purpose cop verb. Cops respond out of the vehicle, respond up the stairs, etc. When a cop feels vitamin deprived, he responds into a doughnut shop.

3 | WHEN YOU'RE LIVING FREE AND TALL, DON'T BECOME A SCORE IN POLICE PINBALL

As hunters of humans rather than animals, cops are at the top of the predator pecking order. All hunters are interested in the number of animals they bag. Cops, however, are obsessed. The most important thing in a cop's life is the number of arrests made—how many each day, each week, each month. Cops get paid, promoted, and earn status and a macho rep almost exclusively by arrest numbers. This is bad news for you, because when cops come up short at the end of the month and have to make their numbers, they'll arrest anybody for anything.

But relax and take a chill pill. If you're reading this book, you're probably not in jail—yet. What you're going to do now is study your hunters and discover what they do, how they do it, and why.

Cops are constantly studying and training how to arrest you. Now you're turning the tables and learning how to avoid them and stay free. What you will discover will astound you. For cops, making arrests and giving out tickets is much like a game, with a point score and a monthly total. I call this police pinball. It's a game you don't want to play.

First, let's discuss basic police patrol operations. Forget what you see on TV—glamorous detectives, undercover officers, and crime-scene technicians. These people exist in big-city departments, and they investigate the most serious crimes, but they make only a small percentage of arrests. The average person, even one who has been repeatedly arrested, may never encounter these types of officers in a lifetime.

The cops who make the most arrests and who fill jails around the nation are patrol officers, the men and women in blue. How does a department know who's a good cop and who's not? Simple. Departmental bosses just count the number of arrests and traffic tickets the cops give out in a month. Is it really that simple? Yep.

On TV, you see police officers having heart-to-heart talks about their careers with (usually) gorgeous psychiatrists. You see concerned captains pondering thick personnel dossiers to which they've given hours of mature reflection. In real life this rarely happens, and it doesn't have to. The best cops give out more traffic tickets and arrest more guys. Period.

Some arrests are more important than others, so there's a rough scoring system. Let's say traffic tickets are worth one point. Misdemeanor arrests then are worth two points, and felony arrests three points. Arrest someone with an outstanding warrant? Extra point! Find guns, narcotics, or stolen property? Score another point.

Police departments deny this and piously proclaim they don't have quotas of traffic tickets and arrests. They're right, in a narrow sense. Departments don't set quotas, but they sure keep score. All police departments value felony arrests more than misdemeanor busts and traffic tickets, regardless of whether they use a formal point system.

So a good cop doesn't hit the street thinking, "How am I going to make America a safer place?" He simply goes out to score points. I set felony arrest records by being assigned to Miami's most dangerous neighborhoods on the night shift. During those hours the place was chock-full of high-value bad guys. It was, as cops would say, a target-rich environment. Many of the guys I arrested had (a) outstanding arrest warrants; (b) drugs, guns, and stolen goods; and (c) automobile violations that required a ticket. So on a traffic stop I could get a traffic ticket (one point), a felony bust (three points), an outstanding warrant (extra point), and recovery of dope, guns, or stolen merchandise (more points). The perfect bust is a jalopy packed with felons wanted on outstanding warrants and with a trunk full of drugs and guns. Yahoo!

To a cop, a patrol is like a game of pinball. He's the player, and he launches the ball onto the table when he starts rolling in his cruiser. Encountering bad guys is like hitting bumpers, each with a different point value. Write a traffic ticket, *bing!* Misdemeanor bust, *bing, bing!* Felony bust, *bing, bing, bing!* Stop a law-abiding citizen? Your ball drops into the hole. *Buzz!* No points.

If a detainee is wanted by police in another jurisdiction, the cop scores double points. If the gods are smiling, the detainee will be wanted by the Secret Service or the FBI. This scores triple points and extra bragging

PUBLIC SAFETY DEPARTMENT — CARSON, D
OFFICER'S NAME

NorthWest DISTRICT - POLICE DIVISION

Oct
MONTH/YEAR

Consolidated Daily/Monthly Employee Activity Report

DAY	TIME INV.	TIME PATROL	CITATIONS HMV	CITATIONS NHMV	ARRESTS FELONY	ARRESTS MISD	ARRESTS TRAFFIC	MSG. RECD	ACCIDENTS INV.	ACCIDENTS CITED	FI CARDS	UNIT NUMBER
1	244	85	2	0	0		0	0	0	0	0	1113
2												
3												
4	251	148	1	0	0	3	0	0	0	0	0	1114
5	334	66	4	0	0	3	0	0	0	0	0	1113
6	228	51	2	0	1	1	0	0	0	0	0	1111
7												
8												
9	354	34	3	0	1	0	1	0	0	0	0	1113
10												
11	107	115	-	-	2	1						1111
12	201	163	14			2						1135
13	149	202	1	0	0	5	0	0	0	0	0	1118
14												
15												
16	315	94	0	0	2	0	0	0	0	0	0	1113
17	278	2	3	0	3	0	0	0	0	0	0	1113
18	306	126	0	0	0	0	0	0	0	0	0	1115
19	254	163	3	0	0	1	0	0	0	0	0	1114
20	343	22	0	0	0	0	0	0	0	0	0	1115
21												
22												
23	288	76	1	0	0	2	0	0	0	0	0	1114
24	254	102	3	0	2	0	0	0	0	0	0	1114
25	264	132	0	0	0	10	0	0	0	0	0	1115
26	169	191	3	0	0	5	0	0	0	0	1	1113
27	277	64	2	0	5	0	0	0	0	0	0	1113
28			0	0	0	4	0	0	0	0	0	
29												
30	243	91	0	0	0	6	0	0	0	0	0	1115
31	130	240	1	0	0	0	0	0	0	0	0	1113
TOTAL	4929	2067	41	0	17	39	1		1	r	1	158

CODE: 0 UNSAT   - WEAK   ✓ SAT   + STRONG   ++ OUTSTANDING

	UNSAT	NEEDS ATTN.	SAT	STRONG	OUTSTANDING
AMOUNT OF WORK COMPLETED ON SCHEDULE					✓
REPORT WRITING TRAFFIC ENFORCEMENT JOB KNOWLEDGE			✓		
ACCURACY EFFECTIVENESS FOLLOW INSTRS. USE/CARE OF EQUIPMENT NEATNESS OF REP/MEMOS				✓	
ATTENDANCE ON TIME APPEARANCE				✓	
SAFE DRIVING HABITS SAFETY PRACTICES					
RELATIONS WITH PUBLIC FELLOW WORKERS/SUPVS ATTITUDE				✓	

REMARKS:
OFFICER CARSON HAS CONTINUED TO DEVELOP & MATURE INTO A VALUABLE ASSET TO THE DEPT. THIS PERIOD OFFICER CARSON LED THE SQUAD & DIST. IN FELONY ARRESTS & NUMBER OF PEOP...

OFFICER'S SIGNATURE	DATE	SUPERVISOR'S SIGNATURE	LTS. INITIALS	CAPT. I...
D. Carson	3 Nov	John A. Buckman	JB	FW

This is one of my tally sheets while I was a patrol officer in Miami. Nobody outside police departments ever sees these things. Now you're looking at one for the first time, and what you realize is that it's all about points. So many traffic tickets, so many arrests, etc. Superior officers can rate a cop in seconds, just by scanning the tally sheet. Note what's not on the sheet—time spent helping citizens. There's no column and no credit for warnings given in lieu of arrest or notices to appear.

rights in the locker room. Of course, there's another level entirely, one with more substantial prizes. If a cop's prisoner is on the FBI's Ten Most Wanted list, or on the terrorist list of the Homeland Security Agency, or if he's being sought in a nationwide manhunt broadcast on TV—*bing, bong, bing, bong*—it's Lotto time! Job promotion? Book deal? A chat with Oprah? Absolutely. Is that the *National Enquirer* calling? FedEx the check and let's talk!

There are three basic patrol activities:

>> responding to calls

>> stopping suspicious people on the street

>> making traffic stops

Cops have to respond to calls, so to score more points, above the level available from calls, they hunt. This means searching for people to arrest by stopping cars and questioning people on the street. This approach seems haphazard, but it works. The reason is that most serious crimes are solved not by dogged detective work, but by street policing by a cop who stops someone suspicious and says, "Hey you, come over here! Got some ID?" That's right. Merely by *pulling over cars and stopping people on the street*, police catch an astounding number of bad guys.

Tim McVeigh, who blew up the Federal Building in Oklahoma City, evaded one of the largest manhunts in history only to be arrested by a Kansas state trooper who noticed that his getaway vehicle had an expired tag. Eric Robert Rudolph, the accused abortion clinic serial bomber, vanished into the Nantahala National Forest and evaded federal, state, and local law enforcement for years. He was nabbed by a rookie cop who arrested him at a convenience store. The cop didn't recognize Rudolph, one of the most wanted killers in America. He simply arrested him because he was dumpster diving for a snack.

Take my old buddy Wayne Williams, the mass murderer. I'd like to say that his arrest was due to the FBI's massive investigation and the nightly stakeouts other agents and I mounted for hours on end, but it wasn't, not directly. Little Wayne got busted because, after dumping a dead body off a bridge, he made an illegal U-turn! Once again, a routine traffic violation ended a major crime spree.

If the basic patrol activities are responding to calls, pulling over cars, and stopping people on the street, how are they accomplished? Police make foot, bicycle, and horseback patrols, but most of them, most of the time, *drive around in cars.*

Here's the lesson: if cops make most of their arrests by driving around in cars, what you need to do to become less arrestable is to be *less visible to car patrols.* Remember Uncle Dale's Golden Rule #1:

>> **IF COPS CAN'T SEE YOU, THEY CAN'T ARREST YOU.**

This also seems obvious, but it's the key to everything. Here's an example. My coauthor was in line to pay some traffic fines in Miami when he saw this Cuban kid with an enormous sheaf of traffic tickets. "*¿Qué tal todo esto?*" he says. Turns out the guy has $3,500 worth of tickets!

This Cuban kid had taken a trip to L.A., where he became wild about Chicano lowriders. These are cars with the springs and shocks removed so they roll only inches above the ground. To make a lowrider you saw off the roof to make the car a convertible, juice the stereo to 500-plus watts, and bolt on enough tweeters and sub-woofers to turn the Rockies into rubble. Finish with a neon paint job, preferably with flames licking up the sides. Some guys even install hydraulic lifts so the car will "dance." Thus equipped, you cruise the boulevards at slow speed and get chicks. Ah, youth!

So this Cuban kid returns home and spends months customizing one of Miami's first lowriders. When the day arrives for his first cruise, he roars out of the garage and, *bang*, he's busted before he goes a mile. He comes home and tries it again. More tickets. And again, ditto. Being a knucklehead, he keeps trying, and gets more tickets. Inevitably he gets short tempered with the cops, who naturally arrest him.

Here's an important point. The kid thought the cops were racist and were picking on him because he's *Cuban*. In Miami, where most cops are Cuban, this is nonsense. He got busted because he was easy to bust. (In Miami and Miami Beach, cops are famous for proving that Miami *ain't L.A.* They have an astounding record of arresting movie stars, celebrities, and professional athletes from the Left Coast. They hate lowriders.) Not only was the car in violation of multiple statutes, it was *visible*, not to mention *ugly*! It gave cops the opportunity to write multiple tickets on a single stop and rack up lots of points, *bing, bing, bing*. To score the same number of tickets at any other time, the cops would have had to stop dozens of solid citizens.

One reason clueless people are arrested disproportionately is that they're more visible to police driving around in cars. They're *available* for arrest. This visibility is based on the "urban outdoorsman" lifestyle. I'll discuss this in an upcoming chapter.

Here's just one example from a guy I interviewed in jail. He and his buddies were driving along and toking some organic hand-raised marijuana, the type with enough THC to topple an elephant with a single sniff. Suddenly, everyone gets the munchies, the insane food craving caused by extra-fine dope. They roll through the drive-through of a barbecue joint, load up on baby back ribs, then suddenly decide they need extra sauce. The driver runs into the restaurant, grabs one bottle of the extra spicy mustard and another of the tomato habanero blend, then butts into the cashier line right in front of a cop! This, of course, violates one of the Cop Commandments:

>> **THOU SHALT NOT ANNOY COPS DURING MEALTIMES.**

The officer is enjoying his digestion, picking his teeth, and getting ready to fire up a stogie when this twerp reeking of dope inserts himself under official police nostrils. Naturally the cop busts the guy, searches the car, finds the weed, arrests the passengers, and impounds the car. He scores three felony arrests, a drug seizure, and a handful of traffic citations. That's a cop's idea of dessert. The moral? Don't make yourself *available* for arrest. Also, it's a good idea to *hide* while breaking laws.

The tally sheet scoring system encourages cops to give out traffic tickets instead of warnings. It motivates them to make arrests rather than resolve problems by conciliation and warnings. Years ago cops might have taken an errant child home to Mama or delivered a drunk to a spouse. Not anymore. Humane alternatives do not score points. Worse, from the cop's point of view, they take up valuable time that could be used to *hunt and arrest more people.* The point system turns arrests into a game rather than a human encounter. It transforms people into points.

The scoring system motivates cops to make arrests rather than issue a notice to appear (NTA). An NTA is a citation that requires you to appear in court. Once there, you can be convicted and sentenced to jail by the judge, but there is one crucial difference: *you are not arrested prior to appearing in court.* Thus if the judge dismisses the case, seals the records, or withholds adjudication (as he or she generally will on a first offense), you do *not* have an arrest record. Your picture and fingerprints are not on file, and you will not be summarily consigned, without your knowledge, to the electronic plantation. This is not an academic point. Police in most states have wide discretion as to whether they make an arrest or issue an NTA for a misdemeanor (at least in Florida, an NTA may not be issued for a felony). A notice, however, scores zero points.

By contrast, federal law enforcement officers' job performances are evaluated not only on the number of arrests, but also on the number and quality of the resulting convictions. This directs them to arrest more serious criminals, and to accumulate more evidence before making an arrest. Generally the concurrence of an assistant U.S. attorney is required prior to effecting an arrest. Municipal police, unfortunately, are generally rated only on arrest numbers. What happens later is irrelevant to the cops. The result is that police are strongly motivated to make an arrest rather than give someone the benefit of a doubt. They tend to "cuff and stuff," which means they make an arrest, dump the detainee in jail, and let a judge and prosecutor sort things out. Even when charges are dismissed, cops get credit for the arrest.

FRUIT PATROLS AND JOHN BUSTS

The rage to make large numbers of arrests affects not only car patrolling, but also undercover operations that might otherwise be devoted to investigating serious crimes. "Fruit patrols" are undercover operations that result in the arrest of gay men for soliciting a sex act or exhibiting lewd and lascivious conduct in public. For a fruit patrol, you get a young, in-shape, male officer in a tight T-shirt to cruise public restrooms. When he gets an offer, he busts the guy.

John busts are similar operations in which female officers impersonate prostitutes. When someone stops and asks, "How much?" he gets arrested. Who are these offenders? They're not bad guys who hurt people, steal things, and sell illegal things. They're schlubs who are too stupid or too ugly to get sex without paying for it. Cops working these units rack up lots of arrests of petty offenders.

PROACTIVE POLICING

The hottest trend in police work is proactive policing. When you cut through the rhetoric, this means making arrests for any and all violations no matter how small. The more people cops arrest, the more likely they are to catch serious bad guys. Proactive policing is a modern version, using computers, radio, and digital communications, of what cops used to call "the big heat."

Think of police patrolling as a large net that's dragged through the city hour after hour. Now and then a huge bad guy gets caught and is dragged flopping to jail. It follows that the faster you trawl, and the finer the mesh of the net, the more bad guys you catch.

There's one little problem, however, that is never officially discussed when police chiefs and mayors proudly announce reductions in crime. For every real bad guy trawled up, hundreds, perhaps thousands, of *other people* get arrested. No one ever mentions these petty offenders and innocent people who get shoved through the criminal justice sausage grinder and dumped onto the electronic plantation in industrial quantities.

If cops are sharks cruising the streets, you are a silvery little fish in danger of getting gobbled up. Little fish, however, are not without defenses. They can hide under rocks or vanish into the shimmering myriads of schooling fish. The arrest-proofing techniques in the second and third parts of this book will show you how to avoid blue-suited sharks and the jaws of justice.

ODE TO DOPE

Marijuana is a cop's friend. "What?" you say. Let me repeat: any sensible cop loves marijuana. As the little ditty goes,

Nothing could be finer
Than marijuana in the liner
Of your
Pickup
Truck!

Dope makes scoring points on the cop pinball machine absurdly easy. Stop a car with a six-pack of beer—no points. Beer's legal. Stop one with a bag of reefer—*bing, bong*—points on the board. Cops know weed makes people careless, so stoned detainees are likely to have other contraband stashed in their cars—more points.

Being confused and limp as wet noodles, potheads are easier to handle than drunks, who are belligerent and want to fight. Marijuana is so great that, when I was a cop, at every dope bust I used to break out in song for sheer joy. As we rolled off to jail I'd put my wasted prisoners on the loudspeaker and lead them in singing:

Heigh ho, heigh ho!
It's off to jail you go.
Under lock and key, never to be free
Heigh ho, heigh ho!

Heigh ho, heigh ho!
It's off to court you go
Under lock and key to be found guilty
Heigh ho, heigh ho!

Heigh ho, heigh ho!
It's off to the chair you go
Under lock and strap to get the zap
Heigh ho, heigh ho!

This is cop humor; it's especially hilarious around 2:00 A.M. in a cruiser packed with happy dopers who don't even realize they've been arrested.

Grass has antinausea properties, so unlike drunks, potheads don't throw up in police cruisers and pee and crap all over the seats. To patrol officers this is incredibly important. In fact, it's so important that, in a later chapter, I recommend doing these things. That's right. In an emergency, when a cop is about to arrest you for a petty offense, I recommend that you *poop your pants, pee down your leg, and barf all over your shirt* rather than go to jail. Timing is crucial. Do this *before* cops decide to arrest you. If you do this after you're arrested, you'll anger the officers and possibly get beaten.

Pot makes people visible, smellable, arrestable, and easy to handle. It's a cop's dream. When I look over my old arrest reports from my days as a Miami cop, most of them are nearly identical:

>> Stopped car.

>> Smelled dope.

>> Found dope.

>> Arrested one and all.

Most of the people in jail are charged with possession of small quantities of drugs.

The war on drugs has been responsible for severe erosions in our liberties. Congress, legislatures, and courts have weakened the protections against search and seizure on the streets and in our cars and vastly extended the government's ability to intercept communications and seize property. This war means, in practice, hoovering up thousands of petty offenders. In any city, big-time drug dealers, with truckload quantities of dope and bags of cash, are arrested *once or twice a year.* The guys with a joint or a rock in their pockets are arrested *every hour of every day,* all over America, by the tens of thousands.

THE CRIMINAL JUSTICE EMPIRE

Widespread use of drugs and proactive policing have created a 30-year boom in jail, prison, and courthouse construction. In every city thousands of people make their livings processing clueless petty offenders. These include judges, bailiffs, attorneys, paralegals, cops, corrections officers, court reporters, file clerks, receptionists, security staff, maintenance workers, cafeteria cooks, jail bus drivers, mechanics, and so on. In my city, for example, the riverfront *skyscraper* that housed the courts was no longer considered sufficient, so a $300 million replacement was constructed.

STATE OF FLORIDA FELONY COMPLAINT AFFIDAVIT AND ALL RELATED CHARGES RESIDENT OF: ☐ FLORIDA
COUNTY OF DADE ☑ Dade County ☐ Other

I swear this statement is correct and true
to the best of my knowledge and belief

Officer's Signature

Ct. ID
No. *1604*

Sworn to and subscribed before me, the
undersigned authority this _____ day of _____ 19___

Deputy of the Court or Notary Public

Arresting Agency ___ (Numeric Code)

OFFICER'S COPY

☐ **Hold for Magistrate's Hearing.**
Do Not Bond Out. (Officer Must Appear)
114.02-142 REV. JAN. 1974 DETACH IF OTHER THAN ADULT FELONY OFFENDER

☐ OUT OF COUNTY/STATE WARRANT

Police Case No. *139106-V*

I.D.S. No. _____ Jail No. _____ Police Case No. *139106-V*

P.S.D. Records I.D. No. _____ Municipal P.D.I.D. No. _____

Defendant's Name XXX XXXXXXXXX Date of Birth *03 17 57*
(Last) (First) (Middle) (Month, Day, Year)

Alias _____ Local Address *20240 N.W. 9CT, MIAMI FLA* Sex *M* Race *W*
(City) (State) (Zip)

Permanent Address *SAME* Phone *653-3171* Hgt. *5 08* Wt *130*
(City) (State) (Zip)

Business Address *20240 N.W. 9CT* Taken to County Station *1* Eyes ___ Hair *BLK*

Soc. Sec. No. _____ Occ. *TOY SALES* POB: *STATEN S.N.Y.* Scars-Tattoos ___

Arrest Date *06 08 76* Time *1 3/4* Location *N.W. 1838 6 AVE*
(Month, Day, Year) (Place of Arrest)

Co-Defendant's Name *CROUSE JON*
(Last) (First) (Middle) / STATUS ☐ AT LARGE ☑ IN CUSTODY
☐ FELONY ☐ MISDEMEANOR ☐ JUVENILE

Co-Defendant's Name *NOWELL MARK*
(Last) (First) (Middle) / STATUS ☐ AT LARGE ☑ IN CUSTODY
☐ FELONY ☐ MISDEMEANOR ☐ JUVENILE

C 1. *POSSESSION OF MARIJUANA* In Viol. of F.S. *893.13* CAPIAS/CIT. #
H 2. _____ In Viol. of F.S. _____ CAPIAS/CIT. #
A 3. _____ In Viol. of F.S. _____ CAPIAS/CIT. #
F 4. _____ In Viol. of F.S. _____ CAPIAS/CIT. #
S 5. _____ In Viol. of F.S. _____ CAPIAS/CIT. #

WITNESSES AGAINST DEFENDANT: see reverse side for additional witnesses
In Viol. of Sec. _____ of the code of _____

1. Name _____ Address: _____ Phone _____
2. Name _____ Address: _____ Phone _____

Arresting Officers *McGRATH, CARSON, HEMLOCK* Ct. ID No. *1604, 1554, 1470* Dept. *30*

The undersigned certifies and swears that he has just and reasonable grounds to believe, and does believe that the above named Defendant
On the *8* day of *JUN*, 19*76* At *1 3/4* *N.W. 1838 6 AVE*
(Time) (Location)
committed the following violation of law: Narrative; (Be specific): *A AND OTHERS STOPPED REF.*
TRAFFIC AT THE ABOVE LOCATION. AS THIS OFFICER
APPROACHED VEHICLE FOLLOWING ARREST OF OPERATOR.
A STRONG SMELL OF MARIJUANA SMOKE EMITTED FROM
VEHICLE. OBSERVED IN VEHICLE BEHIND DRIVERS SEAT
WAS LARGE PLASTIC BAG TORN W/ MARIJUANA. BAG
WAS WITHIN REACH OF ALL OCCUPANTS, AND CONTAINED
APPROX 480 GRAMS MARIJUANA. A WHO HAD SMELL
OF MARIJUANA ON HIS BREATH ARRESTED ADVISED RIGHTS
& TRANSPORTED.

Ever seen a ticket to jail? This is what they look like. The F indicates a felony bust. I've removed the names to protect the guilty. The text indicates that I stopped a car and arrested the driver for marijuana possession. I sniffed some dope in the car and searched the car, for which no warrant was required. I found—surprise, surprise— a 480-gram bag of the magic herb. I arrested everybody in the car, then toodled downtown with a major point score for multiple perps and a nice sack of dope. For every serious offender, I arrested hundreds of clueless people like these.

Half the criminal justice system would be out of business if dope were legalized. You'd see cops on strike holding signs saying, "Bring Back Our Dope!" Defense attorneys in tattered suits, with holes in their hand-stitched Cole-Hahn loafers, would wander down the streets holding pieces of cardboard saying "Will Defend for Food." Dope's not only a moral and public health issue; it's also a jobs issue for city and state employees and us poor little ol' attorneys!

When you're arrested and jailed, the state gives you a job, whether you understand this or not. Your job is to provide state and city employees with work. Think this isn't so? Let me use an example. It's a bit grue-some, but that will emphasize the point. Ted Bundy, "the coed killer," was executed in "Old Sparky," Florida's electric chair. Afterward, a coroner performed an autopsy. This sounds routine, but let's ponder. After an execution, is there any *doubt* as to the cause of death? After the electric chair does its job, *you're toast!* Does it really matter whether you pop up light or dark or a bit charred around the edges? Was it important for a pathologist to discover that Ted had a touch of artery disease or maybe a kidney stone ossifying his nephrons? Basically, Ted was doing his job of providing work for state employees. Even death cannot extinguish this solemn obligation.

Recently a bail bondsman and I were enjoying fine adult beverages in moderation in one of the more elegant riverfront restaurants in my city. My friend looked wistfully across the water to the jail and offered a toast to "the gold mine." The jail a gold mine? Of course it is. For thousands of city and state employees, it's a job, insurance, and a pension. For my friend, and for many attorneys, it truly is an inexhaustible vein of golden ore. My buddy has a 44-foot yacht to prove it.

We'll end this chapter with a fictional scenario that demonstrates just how an upstanding citizen, in a moment of bad judgment, can be swept up in a police dragnet and sentenced to the electronic plantation for life. Moral of story: Getting busted and dumped on the plantations is not just for poor people and minorities. It's an equal opportunity disaster.

SCENARIO #2
BUSINESS WHIZ BECOMES PLANTATION TEMP

Our subject is a successful female executive in a large biomedical manufacturing firm. She has a bachelor's degree in biomedical engineering and a master's degree in industrial marketing. In her mid-30s and engaged to be married, she has just received a promotion to product manager and a substantial raise in her six-figure salary. She dresses fashionably, drives a luxury car, and lives in an elegant, two-story home.

One Friday evening, returning from celebrating her promotion with friends, she is stopped by a police officer. He approaches with a flashlight and asks her to get out of her vehicle. He says he is going to cite her for excessive speed and a burned-out rear taillight, although he appears to be using the flashlight to get a good look at her black cocktail dress, diamond pendant, and matching earrings.

Suddenly the officer leans over and whispers that he might consider not writing the citations in return for a date. Outraged, she slaps him. Her ring cuts his face. He arrests her on the spot. At the police station she learns that she is being charged with battery on a police officer and resisting arrest, both felonies. She spends a night in jail.

The next day, with the assistance of an attorney, she is released on her own recognizance. The state prosecutor reviews a police cruiser videotape which corroborates her story, declines to prosecute and dismisses all charges. She is miffed at the $5,000 bill from her attorney, and annoyed that the officer only received a reprimand. The following Monday she returns to work, but does not mention the incident, which she considers embarrassing.

Six months later, she is called into her boss's office and told that she is being terminated due to an internal reorganization, which has eliminated her job. She is given a small severance. Weeks later, she reads in a national business newspaper that her former company has been running background checks on its employees and firing everyone with an arrest record *or even an unpaid traffic ticket!* She discovers, to her horror, that her arrest record had been picked up electronically by a credit reporting company in another state. She hires a topflight labor attorney and immediately sues for wrongful termination.

There are months of document discovery, depositions, and motion hearings. She finds that, although the company freely admits running background checks, there is no documentation in which her arrest is *even mentioned*, nor any record that background checks were considered in terminating her or any other former employees, all of whom came from different departments with different skills and pay grades.

There is, however, a mountain of paperwork, including lengthy memos and e-mails, regarding a complex personnel reorganization. The company produces multipage spreadsheets and cost analyses. The fact that most, but not all, of the terminated employees had arrest records is, the company insists, just coincidence. Given the documentation, and the company's essentially limitless litigation resources, the woman's attorney persuades her to drop the lawsuit, then presents her with a bill for $75,000. The woman is unable to find work. The biomed corporations to which she applies *will not even give her an interview.* She learns that all have begun to run background checks, and they will not employ anyone with an arrest record. Her education and training have been specific to this industry, and within months, finding herself effectively blacklisted, she signs on with a temp agency doing secretarial work. She is forced to sell her home, and now lives in a studio apartment and drives a battered used car. Her fiancé, a surgeon, has broken off the engagement.

THE MORALS OF THIS STORY

This scenario, about the use of background checks to fire existing employees, is based on news stories of actual events. The woman in our scenario discovered to her horror the following facts of life.

1. Never, under any circumstance, touch a police officer, even when the cop deserves a good swat. Cops rule the streets, with the power of the state behind them. Even when they do wrong, their punishment is limited by civil service regulations and union contracts.

2. An arrest record is tantamount to a conviction. All prospective new employers were alarmed by the fact that she had been arrested, and they seemed not to care that the case was dropped and that she was not prosecuted.

3. The door to the police cruiser was a magic portal through which she passed onto the electronic plantation and a life of low-wage labor. Her arrest record was expunged from state records, but not from the servers and databases of the World Wide Web. It cannot be removed from the NCIC.

4. Large companies and government agencies are astonishingly skilled at obfuscating their intentions and covering their corporate fannies with paperwork that makes it difficult to litigate against them.

5. Lawyers get paid big fees even when they lose.

'Nuf said.

4 | GETTING WISE TO REAL BAD GUYS

Parts of this chapter are going to piss off many readers, especially mothers and sisters of guys who are at risk of getting arrested, and anyone employed by the schools and the social services plantation. I'm going to discuss career criminals and also the attractions of a life of crime. Goody Two-Shoes homilies don't work with young men. In order to choose to become an upstanding citizen, you need to know what real bad guys do and why they do it. Crime is a choice, not an inevitability.

We've talked about cops, who are (generally) the good guys. Now let's discuss the second group of criminal justice players. These are the premium prey, the real bad guys. These are the criminals the cops are *supposed* to spend most of their time pursuing. Bad guys are easy to classify. They

- ≫ hurt people

- ≫ steal things

- ≫ sell things that are illegal

You can add that they *enjoy* crime. It's what they do. As any cop will tell you, crime is not always a bad gig. As a crook, you work when you want to. You don't have a boss, you don't pay taxes, and you thumb your nose at The Man. To choose a life of crime is to shuck off emasculating constraints and return to the primitive world of the barbarian. Here cunning, strength, and violence rule. Men raid alone or in packs, led by an alpha male. Women are seduced and discarded, or taken as booty. You devote every day to rape, pillage, fighting, and fun. Because these are primal male activities, you feel good about yourself.

Taking risks, the prototypical masculine behavior so censured in the schoolmarmy world of education and social work, can be richly rewarded in crime. Can you run dope up the highway without the sheriff getting wise? Or make your women sell their bodies? Can you sneak tax-free smokes into the big cities or smuggle weapons into those outlying burgs with gun laws? Big bucks await if you can.

In Crookland there are no rules. Stay up all night and sleep all day. Do a job only when money runs low. Most bad guys have been processed through the social service plantation, and crime is a welcome change from that suffocating, feminine world of rules, behaving, and taking orders. Crime means escape from social workers, psychologists, and counselors who talk nonsense, scribble in fat files and want to "understand" you.

On the street, bad guys play their music loud, strut their stuff, and tell anyone who annoys them to stuff it. They can wear crazy hair, tattoos, wild clothes, and gang colors that identify them as members of the exclusive Crook Club, or hide behind the finest tailored suits. When people cross them, they take revenge with fists, knives, and guns. There's an enormous thrill in violence.

Bad guys get to see enemies quaver in fear. They savor their panic before sliding in the knife or blowing their brains onto the sidewalk. They dispense life and death like God Almighty. Of course, the cops are always in pursuit. Bad guys have to run, hide, evade, and avoid. Life is an adrenaline rush of intense sensation.

Generally bad guys live off girlfriends, sisters, and their mothers. They get a free crib, so everything they steal is gravy. Let's say they boost a $60,000 car and sell it for $1,000 to a chop shop or underground auto exporter. With that grand they can party, get high, and have sex for days until they have to work again. Bad guys regard working hour after hour for a paycheck with horror. Only squares could be so dumb.

An undercover narc once told my coauthor that *two* marijuana plants, lovingly watered, fertilized, and stimulated with growth hormones and grow lights, will yield $60,000 or more per year—all in the comfort of the home. That's real Miracle Grow. Of course crooks have to do business with other crooks, who will cheat and sometimes kill them, but nobody's got it perfect.

Crooks are innovative. A client told me a story that demonstrates this perfectly. One of his buddies bought a brand-new Chevy Corvette. This guy drives it directly from the showroom to a party in Manhattan. He's not a complete idiot, so once he parks, he gets friends to move their cars and squeeze his car in by touching their bumpers to his. The 'Vette is jammed in tight, and the guy figures he's safe. Wrong. Hours later he finds the Corvette is gone—*poof.* All that's left are two streaks of heavy lubricant. The thieves jacked up his hot rod and slid it out on planks. Smart, huh? "Greased skids" is not just a figure of speech.

Invent computers, and bad guys invent computer crime. Make credit cards universal and voilà, credit card fraud. Cheap 800 lines make possible the phone scams for which South Florida is famous. The Emerald Mine Shares and First Mortgage Certificate scams were works of genius. Con artists love South Florida because it's only 20 minutes by air and a few hours by fast boat from the Bahamas and all those banks whose last name is *Suisse.* They appreciate the skilled services of Miami's identity forgers and the attorneys who know how to make money vanish into a labyrinth of phony corporations. The sun and the nightlife aren't bad either.

Great crime often has a breathtaking simplicity. Years ago, before the coastal setback laws made filling wetlands and waterways illegal, a developer was permitted to create an artificial island in Miami's Biscayne Bay. Similar artificial islands had become some of the most valuable real estate on planet Earth. So this developer borrows $100 million to get started and bangs down a row of pilings to impress visiting loan officers. Once they approve the loan, he just wires the money offshore and vanishes over the Atlantic in his jet. He has never been found. *Adios,* 100 megabucks.

Crooks think they're smarter than ordinary people, and some of them are. Some of the serial killers I arrested while I was in the FBI had studied police procedures and crime-scene investigative techniques. They devoured instructional manuals dense with mathematics, microscopy, and chemistry. These were smart guys who trained to make crime a career.

Unfortunately, pain and misery are not inherent in the life of crime. They have to be applied externally by the criminal justice system. If criminals were victims, society wouldn't need police, just social workers to give solace to crooks weeping in the streets. Fat chance! The bad guys are sassy and full of themselves. They have to be hunted, jailed, and processed by the justice machine.

It's amazing to see the change that comes over bad guys when they do get caught. The swagger is replaced by cowering. The strut becomes a slouch. The mean stare turns into a shifty flickering of the eyes. Jail, for most crooks, is hell. Even if they escape being raped or beaten, the subjection to strict rules is almost unbearable.

For the worst criminals, crime pays off emotionally even while they're in custody. They get fan mail, love letters from women, and flattering media attention. The notorious serial killer Ted Bundy, who was pursued by local police and the FBI in Tallahassee, received fan mail from other serial killers who sought advice on how to avoid being caught. He was the big man in prison until the State of Florida fried his brains in the electric chair.

Wayne Williams, who killed dozens of young boys around Atlanta, had the opportunity during his trial to be the star of the drama of a lifetime. He had perfected the persona of a normal person and was so convincing while testifying in his own defense that he might have been acquitted had he not goofed during a prosecutor's question and let slip the demon within.

A sharp crook indeed was my buddy Wayne. He studied police evidence-gathering procedures and left almost no clues. We never did find out exactly how he killed those boys. All the bodies had a single ligature mark indicating they had been strangled, yet there were never any marks or injuries indicating resistance. Tox screens for drugs were negative. So, Wayne, did you slip a noose around their necks while they slept? Did you give them little teddy bear kisses while they struggled? Your old interrogator would like to know.

MONEYED THUGS

This is a category of criminal more common than people think. I refer here to bad guys who have education and money but choose crime because they get a kick out of it. Some are white-collar crooks whose swindles fill the newspapers. Others use their scientific knowledge to manufacture designer drugs that addict and kill but are not on the narcotics schedule because of small variations in the chemical formulas. Many of the Dilaudid knockoffs and amphetamine derivatives come from these crooks. The first large shipments of ecstasy, a drug that causes irreparable brain damage, were brought into the United States from Europe by Orthodox Jews when it was outlawed. No one suspected that such educated, pious people could be criminals, so they were able to bring tens of thousands of tablets through airport customs without being searched.

Rich bad guys are wily and difficult to catch. They generally drive street-legal luxury cars and rarely get searched or arrested, except perhaps for DUI during traffic stops. Almost never are they dumb enough to carry drugs and guns in their automobiles. When anything happens, they lawyer up fast with the biggest and the best. This makes them nearly impervious to arrest by routine policing methods. When is the last time you heard about your police force making an arrest for a complex multi-million-dollar fraud? Generally the federal government tackles the rich guys, and leaves clueless gorks to the local boys and girls in blue.

Because moneyed thugs have no excuse for criminal behavior, hunting them is particularly satisfying. It has been my pleasure and privilege to arrest and convict several millionaires. Barging into their corporate headquarters is almost as much fun as busting into a crack house. You march in, flash the FBI credentials, and walk right past flabbergasted receptionists. You blow by the secretaries, the flunkies, the flacks, and the mouthpieces. Is Mr. Big in a meeting? Meeting adjourned! Perhaps he's carousing with a young thing in his executive hideaway bedroom? Out she goes, and into jail he goes. Perp-walking these goons out the front door in chains is partial recompense for the drudgery and paperwork that comprise so much of an FBI agent's career. Of course, now that I am a defense attorney, it is my pleasure and privilege to defend the moneyed elite. Life is not without irony, even in the grubby precincts of justice and law.

THE PROBLEM WITH REAL BAD GUYS

Real bad guys share one characteristic: they're hard to catch by cops driving around in cars. Here's my beef with proactive policing as currently practiced. For every big crook caught, thousands of petty offenders get hammered for smoking weed, flipping off a police officer, and playing their stereos too high. Processing these people endlessly through the criminal justice system is abusive, not to mention expensive. Too many people's rights get trampled.

The only way to catch big crooks without filling up stadiums with petty offenders is the hard way—more investigations, more undercover work, more paid informants, more phone taps, more hidden video and sound recording. This is tough, expensive, and dangerous, but it's the only technique that nets big fish only and results in solid prosecutions and long prison sentences. When the prosecutor goes to trial with videos of the bad guys unloading the swag and scooping up the money, not even an attorney as talented as I can get them off!

Let's talk about drug distribution for a moment. Do you really think America's drug habit is supplied by jerks who sneak in a kilo through the airport or wade across the Rio Grande with a bag taped to their bellies? Think again. America gets its cocaine and heroin by the shipload and the truckload. West of the Rockies, drugs are supplied by tractor trailers that roar across the Mexican border. Customs officials on both sides are only too glad to take the cartels' bribes and avoid the hail of bullets that goes to noncooperators. As a Mexican customs officer told my coauthor, "I see these trucks all the time. I just wave them on and say, 'America is over there.' I'm not going to get machine gunned because gringos are drug addicts. Not my problem."

On the East Coast, 44,000-pound containers of dope are off-loaded into the major ports and simply driven away to a town or city near you. Paid-off longshoremen hook up the rigs, and all too often crooked cops provide security. Cops will never catch these guys by busting hip-hoppers with a bag in the glove compartment. How about the really big fish, the billionaire drug lords in Colombia, Afghanistan, Bolivia, Mexico, Pakistan, and Russia? They never set foot in the United States and are beyond the reach of police. All too often, the war on drugs consists of busting people like you in an attempt to clear drugs off the streets one doobie at a time.

This, my friends, is the problem. The biggest criminals share many of the same qualities that bring success in the straight world: intelligence, discipline, persistence, savvy, and the quality of not being clueless.

OK, what's this got to do with you? Simple. A life of crime does have a few problems.

1. You have to live with, and do business with, other crooks. They will cheat you, steal from you, and kill you if you annoy them.

2. Your chances of becoming a rich, super-savvy crook who enjoys the fruits of a life of crime and dies in bed of old age are about as remote as your chances of winning the lottery.

3. Cops are not stupid. The number of career criminals not in jail by the age of 30 is low.

4. Jail stinks.

You want to think about these drawbacks, and think hard, before you embark on a life of crime.

5 | GET ON BOARD WITH THE CLUELESS HORDE

The clueless horde? Say hello to yourself. You're a member. It couldn't be otherwise because, except for cops, prosecutors, judges, attorneys, and other insiders, *everyone* to some degree is clueless about criminal justice. People who are savvy in business can be clueless abut criminal justice. The clueless, regardless of race, education, and income, are the chow that gets processed endlessly through the criminal justice sausage grinder. The clueless are the foundation of the criminal justice empire.

Getting a bit sleepy here? Well, guzzle some strong coffee or a Jolt cola, prop open the eyelids with toothpicks, and grab a pencil. Feel free to scribble in the margins, underline, and make notes.

The bad news? Cluelessness is what gets the overwhelming number of petty offenders arrested. The good news? Cluelessness is not a state of nature. It's a set of behaviors. You can get wise and get less clueless. You can choose *not* to do stupid stuff that sics the cops on you.

First, I'll detail clueless behaviors. Then I'll discuss how to change them. As I said before, everyone is to some extent ignorant about criminal justice. Heck, the cops themselves do stupid stuff that gets them busted all the time. So, as you read this chapter, note clueless behaviors that you have. Think about them. Then get busy changing them. Remember, to stay free you only have to get less clueless for the *few minutes* you're in front of cops, judges, and probation officers. This buys you the years you need to get less clueless about life in general.

While you ponder cluelessness, think about freedom. It's wonderful; it's a narcotic. Imagine how life will be when you don't fear getting busted, when you have a real future that will not be ruined by a sentence on the electronic plantation.

CLUELESS BEHAVIORS

PROBLEM 1: BAD MANNERS. The number one thing the clueless do is to act out in front of cops. They hit cops, curse, run away, or do something else that turns a conversation into an arrest and a misdemeanor into a felony. Cops are the archetypal representatives of the American middle class. They expect people to be reasonably polite and obedient to authority, and they punish those who aren't.

SOLUTION: Get polite in front of cops. You only have to be polite for a few minutes—that's all. Once the cops leave, you're free. It wouldn't be a bad idea to practice being polite to attorneys, prosecutors, judges, and probation officers, but one thing at a time. Remember, just five minutes of polite behavior in front of a cop can free you for life. So how about "yes, officer" instead of "fuck you, motherfucker"? Is that so much to ask?

PROBLEM 2: LOUSY PAPERWORK. Because of illiteracy, depression, obstinacy, or some other cause, clueless people are forever committing the crime of ignoring official paperwork. When they fail to appear in traffic court, for example, a traffic ticket can become, in some states, a bench warrant, which gets clueless types arrested. Showing up in court and complying with the terms of probation are, for the highly clueless, nearly impossible.

SOLUTION: Paperwork is crucial. Start reading your mail. Get someone to read it to you if you do not read well. Get teachers, religious leaders, family, and friends to explain things you do not understand. To stay free in America, you have to pay taxes, obtain driver's licenses, get car insurance, pay fees, show up in court, meet with your probation officer, pay traffic tickets, etc. All of this stuff comes in the mail. Read it.

PROBLEM 3: NO TIME MANAGEMENT. Clueless people don't have watches, alarm clocks, and calendars. They show up late or never at judicial hearings, behavior modification classes, drug court, and meetings with probation officers. This gets them pursued by cops and bail bondsmen and rearrested. Not showing up is often a more serious offense than the one for which the poor devils were busted originally.

SOLUTION: Get a watch, for heaven's sake. The Chinese plastic jobs are five bucks. For a buck more you can get an alarm clock at Wal-Mart. Grab one of the cheapo calendars off the hook while you're there. Think of watches and alarm clocks not as annoyances that spoil your fun but as freedom tools. To stay free, you've got to wake up, dress up, and show up—on time—before judges, probation officers, drug courts, drug test labs, and so forth. Being on time at work, school, and church isn't a bad idea either, but you *have* to be on time before people who can throw you in jail if you're late. Parents, make sure each of your children has a watch, a calendar, and an alarm clock. Don't forget to get a sack of batteries to keep those little boxes ticking. Want to stride toward freedom? Set the alarm!

PROBLEM 4: LOW SOCIAL BACKUP. Clueless people are often alone in the world, with few family, friends, and acquaintances and not much money. They are less able than others to encounter cops without getting arrested and to mount a stout legal defense. They have few if any responsible adults to teach them how to behave. People with sound families and numerous friends are less likely to be arrested and prosecuted.

SOLUTION: Family and friends are everything. Facing the world alone is only heroic in stupid Hollywood movies. In the real world, you've got to have family and solid citizen friends. You can't stand alone and expect to stay free. When the worst happens and you're in jail, who are you going to call? Not the homies and *carnales* and bros you were messing around with—because they're probably in the adjoining cell.

If you don't have a good family, this makes things tougher, but not impossible. Ministers, priests, rabbis, and imams; social club leaders; athletic coaches; and teachers can provide the social backup you need. These solid citizens, even though they may bore you, do have some skills you don't. They know how to

>> work with the system

>> live in freedom unhassled by cops

So next time you're at the family get-together, be sweet to Grandma and laugh at your uncle's corny jokes. Be polite to adults and leaders. Forgive them their hopelessly unhip and uncool style, and soak up some of their know-how and wisdom. Being able to distinguish between style and substance is a sure way to become less clueless.

PROBLEM 5: LOUSY CARS. Clueless people ride around in cop magnets—cars with broken lights and smoking tailpipes; and no valid licenses, tags, and insurance. Too often they have controlled substances in these beaters. Police do not generally need a warrant to search a car, so for the clueless, a traffic ticket becomes a ticket to jail. Because traffic stops are the most important component of the police dragnet that sweeps through your city 24/7, I'm devoting Part III of this book to this important subject.

SOLUTION: Cars have two types of problems that make them cop bait— mechanical and paperwork. You know you have to fix the mechanical and safety stuff—headlights, taillights, turn signals, squealing brakes, smoking tailpipe, bald tires, etc. What you may not know is that, in the computer age, cops can pull up behind you, run your tag through their onboard computers, and instantly discover any paperwork problems (suspended licenses, expired insurance, unpaid tickets) that allow them to stop and search you and your car. You do not want cops doing this. So get your heap street legal and get the paperwork letter perfect with all fines, fees, and insurance premiums paid. This costs money. Get used to it. Freedom isn't free.

PROBLEM 6: NO ADDRESS. The clueless often do not have a mailing address. They "stay at" friends' houses at night and hang out during the day. They can't easily receive official notices, and are forever committing administrative crimes (failing to appear in court, violating probation, driving with a suspended license or expired tag) of which they are often unaware. Administrative crimes recycle them endlessly through the criminal justice sausage grinder. Chomp! Chomp! Chomp!

SOLUTION: Not having an address is an emergency. It means that official paperwork from judges, probation officers, the car insurance company, and the motor vehicle bureau isn't reaching you. Failing to do paperwork can land you in jail and ruin your life. What to do? Get an address—fast. If you have a few bucks, get a post office box either with the postal service or with a private parcel company. If you're absolutely broke, many city missions, churches, and social service agencies will allow you to pick up mail at their addresses.

PROBLEM 7: NO ATTORNEY. Clueless people don't understand how to find, use, and pay for attorneys. They're represented by overworked, underpaid public defenders and naturally spend much time in public jails. Defend that!

SOLUTION: Get an attorney. More precisely, get the name and business card of a criminal defense attorney who could represent you if you're arrested. How to do this without spending money is covered in a later chapter. The trick is to let cops know you have an attorney, so they think twice before busting you. This has to be low key to be successful. What you want to avoid is yelling "Call my attorney!" which annoys cops and makes them want to bust you so you can spend lots of money on your attorney. This delicate maneuver is covered in detail in a later chapter.

Having an attorney is crucial. I'll give you a personal example. One of my former wives is a self-made millionaire. Despite her professional success, she has a chip on her shoulder about being a minority and takes care of this situation in an unusual way—she drives like a maniac. Naturally this attracts the police. When cops stop her, however, they notice at once that she's driving a Porsche that costs more than they make in a year. She always lets them know that her personal attorney is the meanest junkyard dog in the city. Cops realize immediately that giving her a ticket means multiple court appearances, expert witness challenges, appeals, and subpoenas for every piece of paper they've ever possessed on the subject of traffic stops. The woman is prepared, nay, eager, to do whatever it takes to get out of a hundred-dollar ticket. Generally the ticket turns into a warning—no surprise.

PROBLEM 8: THE URBAN OUTDOOR LIFESTYLE. Whether from lack of automobiles and air conditioners or social and cultural factors, clueless people hang out on the streets. There they are visible to, and arrestable by, police riding around in cars.

SOLUTION: Stay out of sight. Remember, if cops don't see you, they can't arrest you. If you must be a thug, at least smoke dope and do stupid stuff *indoors* where police can't arrest you and seize evidence without a search warrant. This buys you time to stay free, grow up, and wise up. Warrants are almost impossible to obtain for petty crimes.

PROBLEM 9: INTOXICANT OF CHOICE. Clueless people prefer marijuana to alcohol as an intoxicant. There are obvious reasons. Dope is tax-free, cheaper than alcohol, and gives a longer-lasting high with no hangover. Unlike beer, it doesn't make you pee every five minutes.

Dope has two problems. First of all, it's still illegal, and second, it dulls emotions and causes you to not care about anything *even when you're straight*. Therefore, you don't care if you miss your court hearing, don't go to drug rehab, and don't call your probation officer. Of course there is another tiny little prob. You have to buy dope from crooks. They often cheat you and steal from you. If you annoy them or fail to pay for dope, they might even kill you. Bang! You're dead.

SOLUTION: Get a legal buzz. Use alcohol in moderation. Never keep an open container in a vehicle or carry alcoholic beverages on the street. Don't drive drunk. Alcohol costs more, but didn't I just mention that freedom isn't free?

PROBLEM 10: BIZARRE APPEARANCE. One thing you notice at the jail is that most prisoners look like crooks. They've got weird hair and wild clothes. The black guys have dreadlocks down to their knees, greasy cornrows, and strange topknots. The Hispanics and white trash have scruffy beards and hair down to their shoulders or shaved heads tattooed fore and aft. The bikers? Let's not even go there. Those leathers that have been soaked in beer, vomit, barbecue, and blood for years without being washed are beyond nasty. As for that fetor wafting its way from the holding cell to your protesting olfactory nerves, it's not just stinky, it's *stanky*. Unfortunately, prisoners don't get mandatory haircuts in jail because, pre-sentencing, they're legally *detainees,* not convicts. So they appear in court, crazy hair intact, before neatly barbered and coiffed judges. This is not wise. I always recommend that incarcerated clients visit the jail barber on their own initiative, trim their nails—especially that pinky-nail cocaine scoop—and wash and deodorize scrupulously. Sometimes they listen.

Petty offenders often get arrested simply because they stand out like neon lights and are easy to spot by cops driving around in cars. If you can't understand that looking like a hoodlum is likely to get you arrested, you're clueless and in need of professional help from attorneys like me, since you're probably already in jail.

Savvy career criminals are aware of this and make an effort to blend in with mainstream America. Mass murderer Wayne Williams wore short, neatly trimmed hair and nondescript clothes, and looked like an accountant. Coed killer Ted Bundy had a movie star smile and wore suits and ties. When not killing young women, he looked like the Republican Party activist that, in fact, he was. As for the big-time white-collar guys, they prefer suits and are always distressed at what handcuffs do to well-starched shirtsleeves.

SOLUTION: Tone it down. Yes, I know your friends and all those music and sports stars are pressuring you to adopt hoodlum chic. But think about this. Your thug friends are on the way to jail. As for those music stars and sports legends, they're millionaires. One of the ways the rich get richer and the poor get poorer is for the rich to sell overpriced, flashy hoodlum clothes to the poor. Forget the superstars. They don't need your money. Consider Wal-Mart and Kmart your clothing friends. Besides, if you don't wear NBA footwear, you're less likely to get beat up by people who want to steal your sneakers.

PROBLEM 11: BEING JUST PLAIN DUMB. Never discount human foolishness, often a factor in who goes to jail and who goes free. Recently I was interviewing an upset bank robber. "How did they identify me?" he wailed. "How did they know it was me?" Well, our robber forgot the first lesson in Heists 101: whenever you rob a place with security cameras mounted every four feet on the wall—*don't forget to wear a hat!*

SOLUTION: If you're born dumb, there ain't one. Of course, if you're that way, you aren't reading this book, so what do I care? The important thing is not to demote yourself from clueless person (curable) to moron (incurable) by doing booze and drugs. Those things shave mucho points from your IQ (intelligence quotient), often permanently.

THE CLUELESSNESS QUOTIENT CHART

To make it easier to figure out how likely you are to get arrested, I've devised the Cluelessness Quotient chart. This chart rates what I call your Clue-Q. Your IQ measures your ability to perform logical analysis, math, and verbal tests. The Clue-Q shows how savvier people are less likely to get arrested and clueless people are more likely to get arrested.

What the Cluelessness Quotient chart makes clear is this: *attitudes, values, and behaviors, not ethnicity and skin color, make people more or less arrestable.* This is one of the most important concepts in this book. For race and ethnic entrepreneurs quivering with rage, hold your horses (and lawsuits), and make a visit to your local lockup on a Friday night. Then tell me this chart is nonsense.

CHANGING CLUELESS BEHAVIORS

First, some truth. Changing behaviors takes a long time. What you're looking at is the short form. Reading is easy; changing is hard. You can, however, start now. Change takes place a bit at a time. Stay motivated by thinking of freedom, of *not* being cop fodder.

You can judge your cluelessness quotient (Clue-Q) from this chart. The higher your cluelessness quotient, the more likely you are to be arrested.

CLUELESSNESS QUOTIENT (CLUE-Q)			
CLUELESSNESS METER	Low — Medium — High	Low — Medium — High	Low — Medium — High
ATTORNEY	Public Defender or pro se (self)	Attorney from Yellow Pages	Attorney on retainer and cell phone speed dial
PAPERWORK SMARTS	None	Minimal	Excellent
TIME MANAGEMENT	Whuzzat?	Some. Have watches and clocks. "There's a calendar around here somewhere."	No problem. Watches, alarm clocks, paper and online calendars, computers
MANNERS	In your face. Obscenity, profanity.	Passable for brief periods. "Well, sir, officer, sir . . ."	Good. "How may I be of assistance, officer?"
ACCENT	Heavy. Cannot speak standard English.	Controllable. Standard English possible for emergency use only.	Standard English
SOCIAL BACKUP	Mama	Mama and my old lady	Family, friends, ministers, doctors, psychologists, etc.
			CONTINUED NEXT PAGE ☞

CLUELESSNESS QUOTIENT (CLUE-Q) CONTINUED

CLUELESSNESS METER			
CAR	Expired tag, broken tail and head lights, smoke—a cop magnet. Four guys ("Crew Cab").	Junker, but street legal. One passenger or none.	Perfection, with showroom shine. One passenger or none except for family outings.
PREFERRED INTOXICANT	Marijuana	Beer	Branded liquor, beer, wine
CONSUMES INTOXICANTS	On street, in car (NO search warrant required)	Indoors (search warrant required)	Indoors (search warrant required)
ADDRESS	None or local bar	Have home address	Home and business
APPEARANCE	Bizarre	Scruffy	Neat
PREFERRED WEAPON	Pistol	Knife	Lawyer
INSURANCE	Huh?	Minimum for automobile	Auto, home, life, health, umbrella
PROSECUTION RESISTANCE	Low	Low to medium	High

SCENARIO #3

CLUELESS AMERICANUS: A PORTRAIT

This is a portrait of one of my legal clients. I'll call him Fred (not his real name). Fred is a young guy. He's handsome and charming in a way that women find endearing. Some of the ladies find him a bit more than endearing, so Fred has several children by various women whom he never seems to get around to marrying. Fred drives a milk truck and lives in a small apartment.

One day one of the women with whom Fred has children became annoyed at what she considered his less than abundant child support, his casual parenting style, his slob appearance, and his easy-go-lucky demeanor. Things got loud, and Fred gave the woman a good whack, which is against the law. When the police arrived, they frisked old Fred and discovered, not entirely to their surprise, that he had some weed in his pocket. So Fred got taken downtown and booked for domestic battery and possession of marijuana.

The judge cut Fred some slack. He gave him a suspended sentence with probation and required that he attend anger-management classes. One day Fred failed to telephone his probation officer as required. He thus violated his probation, and in due course police hauled him back to jail.

THE MORALS OF THIS STORY

1. Fred is not the most upstanding citizen. It's safe to say he won't be elected president of the Rotary Club or the Chamber of Commerce anytime soon, but he's not a career criminal. His crime is that he's clueless about the system.

2. Fred cannot manage time. Working, eating, riding the bus, giving the ladies some love, and watching TV are about all he can do. It's no surprise he missed a call to his probation officer—all day and half the night he's driving the milk truck or riding the

bus to his court-ordered anger-management classes! He can't afford a telephone, and in his neighborhood, pay phones often don't work because they've been whacked with large hammers by guys who hurt people and steal things for a living.

3. Hitting a woman was his first mistake. Not disappearing when the police were on the way, and not getting rid of illegal substances on his person, were his next two mistakes.

4. Fred can't use watches, clocks, and calendars to show up on time at official proceedings. He can barely read and so has no paperwork smarts. He cannot understand the blizzard of notices, court orders, and probation forms he gets. This means he's forever getting into *more* trouble with the system, which defines nonattendance at official proceedings and failure to complete official paperwork as crimes. He doesn't even know that he's been consigned to the electronic plantation, and that jobs better than driving the milk truck may never be his.

5. He has low social backup in the form of family and friends who could help him through his continual legal emergencies.

6. Massive amounts of taxpayer money are being expended to process Fred through courts, jail, and probation, but none of this will teach him what he really needs to know. He doesn't belong in jail but in a life-lessons course that would start with how to read watches and clocks. Such a course would advance to the technique for rolling latex sheaths onto the organ of generation and why this is a good idea. It wouldn't hurt to teach Fred that when arguments with women escalate, the correct response is to *run* out the nearest door or *leap* out the nearest window.*

---

* I've followed this wise policy with all my wives, and I strongly recommend it.

6 | THOSE FREAKING JITS WILL GIVE YOU FITS

This chapter is about the *extreme* form of cluelessness. If you have any of the behaviors described below, you have an emergency. You've got to take immediate action to get less clueless. This chapter illustrates where the extreme clueless life leads—to endless uproars, arrests, incarcerations, and criminal justice processing. Please note that though extremely clueless people are not career criminals, they spend as much or more time in the system as real bad guys. Social scientists call such people "extremely lacking in socialization." Ghetto inhabitants call them jits.* This punchy term refers to young men who grow up without family and friends and who are so unpredictable they're scary. Jits are continually recycled through the criminal justice sausage grinder for the following reasons.

>> Their values affront society and evoke fear and disgust.

>> They're just so darn easy to arrest. What cop can resist?

I've been arresting and defending jits for years. I also have lived among them in a black and white ghetto. Do I know these guys or what?

First of all, they're mostly guys. Because in the barrio, the ghetto, and the trailer park, women earn most of the income, they are less clueless than men. Women do the child rearing, which develops organizational skills and the ability to plan for the future. Women work in service jobs

---

* Originally short for "jitterbug," a slang term for a gang member or juvenile delinquent, the term now encompasses almost all extremely clueless people, especially teenagers.

that require the ability to interact with others, to dress well, to develop good manners, and to speak in standard English. Jits work, when they work, in casual labor. This does not require social skills. Even though there are plenty of bad "girlz" around, the vast majority of jit arrestees are men.

The criminal justice terminology for jits is "disorganized." This is a misnomer. It assumes such people were organized at one time, and subsequently became *dis*-organized. Wrong. Jits are *un*organized from birth and haven't a clue as to what organization is and why it should concern them. They can't spell the word and don't know what it means.

The irony is that the social workers, judges, and cops who come into contact with jits daily almost always overestimate—that's right, *overestimate*—their capabilities. Many assume that ghetto, barrio, and trailer park life are separate cultures deserving respect. The problem is not that jits have a separate culture, but that they have *no* culture.

Jits get few if any values, goals, or skills in childhood and adolescence. They have a precultural mental organization. Essentially they're hunter-gatherers in a *post*industrial age. As sociologists would say, they're ur-humans.

Among educated people, the term "living in the moment" is much in vogue. It's a mantra that really refers not to temporal organization, but to the desire to live more intensely and more in accord with a personal destiny. This is a worthy goal indeed, to be pondered over herbal teas, the better magazines, and the thicker volumes of poetry and philosophy. When educated people say "living in the moment," *they have no idea* that that's what jits actually do.

Let's go down to Jitland for a little taste. These guys, and they generally are men, do not have watches. Why should they? When you're a jit, you go to bed when you're sleepy, wake up when you're not, and eat when you're hungry. There's no planning for the next week, the next day, or even the next meal.

Everything is impulse and satisfaction. You feel something; you do something about it. Life has only one objective, to feel good. Feel hungry? Eat. Bored? Flip on the tube. Horny? Chat up the first female within reach. When women get pregnant, that's their problem, and when they start nagging and finger wagging, you give 'em a swat and walk out the door. Feel bad? Just fire that spliff; shoot that skag, snort, huff; chug-a-lug that beer; and feel better fast. Need money? Steal some or, when you're older, work day labor. When people get in your way, hurt them. If they really piss you off, kill them. Notice there's no moral quality to the jit life. It's all stimulus and response. To themselves, jits are not good or bad. They live in a pre-moral world.

For jits, time is a vast, flowing river that is not divisible into units. Jits don't work much, and nobody other than a probation officer or a judge ever waits for them or expects them to do anything or be anywhere. When a judge tells a jit that he has a hearing before the court on Tuesday, three weeks from today, at 10:30 A.M., the judge generally fails to realize that the guy he or she is attempting to schedule doesn't have a watch or clock and has never paid attention to a calendar except to ogle girls with big breasts on cheap calendars nailed to car repair shop walls. To comply with the judge's request, a jit would have to do the following.

1. Understand that days are temporal units of 24 hours, that each has a specific name, and that days are bundled into larger units called weeks.

2. Project mentally into the future and know to look at a calendar every day for 21 days until the specified day arrived.

3. Be able to read.

4. Have an alarm clock and a watch in order to be able to navigate accurately through time and space on the appointed day.

5. Coordinate bus schedules printed in small type and complicated grids with the calendar and the wristwatch.

6. Have the mental skills we call time management.

This is so complex it exhausts me to write about it. In fact, a jit has no sense at all of days, defined as 24-hour segments of time. There is no "day." There's simply sunup and sundown—wake, sleep, eat, copulate, wander, hustle, hang out, get wasted. Everything is concrete, never abstract. The past is a haze and doesn't matter. The future is inconceivable. The future is neither hopeful nor hopeless; it's simply not there. This is real "living in the moment," and middle-class people find it scary as hell.

There's an upside to this. It's hard to worry when you can't project into the future. When you're clueless, you don't *live* at all in an active sense. Life simply *happens*. It's exciting. People come; people go. There's always a new party, a new woman, a new way to score some cash. Every day there's a new emergency. The lights get turned off, the water gets cut, and the car gets towed by Mr. Repo. What's with the TV? Cable off? Gotta get some money, man! When things get tense, light up, snort up, drink up, and everything is mellow soon enough. That's what's so strange about the jit life. No one has anything to do, but everybody's always busy.

When you say to jits, "It's 7:00. You have one hour to eat and dress. You have to catch the 8:00 bus to be downtown at 9:00 for your hearing," they have only the foggiest idea of what you mean. From their point of view, they don't *have* to do anything. It's not that they don't want to attend their hearing, but that they have no sense of time or urgency. Besides, the electricity just got shut off, there's no food, and the baby is screaming. A bounty hunter just jumped over the back fence. There's lots to do. Gotta go!

Judges misinterpret this. When defendants skip a hearing or miss a call to a probation officer, judges think they're being willfully defiant. They're nothing of the sort. They don't *will* anything. That would presuppose having objectives and a sense of time that extended into the future. To the jit, shit happens, and that's that. When judges feel defied by no-show defendants, they issue bench warrants. What this does is get the jits rearrested and reprocessed through the sausage grinder, thus generating useful employment for thousands. Shit just happens, man.

Before heaping righteous scorn on jits, remember that divisible time (days divided into hours, hours into minutes) has been important in the United States only for about 150 years, and then not for everybody. Divisible time is necessary for factories, where people have to be on time to work together. Trains made divisible time important in rural areas. Wristwatches only became widespread in my lifetime. When I was a kid, most of my city regulated itself Mondays through Fridays by a giant steam whistle called Big Jim and by church bells on Sunday. Big Jim blew for wake-up time, lunchtime, and quitting time, and this was about as many divisible temporal units as were thought necessary. Ordinary people didn't need watches. Until the 1980s, railroads, which require to-the-minute time management, provided employees railroad-certified watches and deducted the cost from paychecks on the installment plan.

In the 1970s, one of the large automobile manufacturers agreed to hire a large number of disadvantaged people—i.e., jits—to work on assembly lines. This is highly compensated, benefit-rich work that requires only rudimentary skills. These are the most highly prized blue-collar jobs in America, and they are frequently handed down from parents to children. Company execs were just starting to feel good about their tender social conscience when they discovered that these jits weren't showing up for work. Horrors! They discovered not only that the workers couldn't tell time, but that they didn't understand what it was or why it was important. The company soldiered on, however, and set up time-orientation classes, where they handed out metal alarm clocks with two ringy-dingy bells on top.

For jits, time management and calendaring have to be external. This makes perfect sense from the jit point of view. If time is important to certain people, let *them* manage it. When the electricity goes off, jits know it's time to pay the bill. When the car vanishes, it's off to the repo lot, cash in hand. When the rent is due, landlords will bang on the door and say "Gimme." Bail bondsmen, defense attorneys, and public defenders are the timekeepers and appointment schedulers of the criminal justice system. Their staffs spend hours on the phone and even comb the streets and search hangouts to get jit defendants to wake up, dress up, and show up.

SUE PEENA? WHO'S THAT?

For the criminal justice system, which lives on paper and notices sent through the mail, the fact that so many defendants can't read is a nightmare. Cops have become the system's paperwork minders. When they stop jits, they often discover that official paperwork, such as outstanding warrants and probation violations, hasn't been received or handled with the required dispatch. They provide a gentle reminder in the form of an arrest, then free transportation down to jail and a judge, where paperwork matters can be attended to promptly. When driver's licenses are suspended and the tags have expired, a traffic ticket, arrest, or vehicle seizure provides the necessary tap to the noggin for the paperwork-challenged and calendar-oblivious. Like time management, document preparation and official permitting for jits are external. Paperwork is done by *other people* to whom such bewildering matters are important. For the jit, paper is something that piles up on tables, swirls around on the floor, and is occasionally useful for firing up spliffs, cigarettes, blunts,* and stogies.

WHERE YOU STAYIN' AT?

Strictly speaking, most jits are not homeless, but they don't really have a domicile. They just stay at places. This is a big topic of conversation. When you live in a crappy neighborhood, you notice that the first thing out of people's mouths is "Where're you staying at?" Whenever possible, guys bunk with women in public housing. They give the women sex and scarf up free food, electricity, and water provided by the government. When the women get testy about unimportant things like being pregnant, the guys move on. Many wander from place to place and never really know where they'll be from one night to the next. It generally works out, however, at least when they're young. There always seems to be a party, a mattress, and a woman somewhere.

Having no address presents jits with unique challenges. First, it causes them to live the outdoor lifestyle. They wander on the streets, where they're visible to, and subject to arrest by, cops riding around in cars. They can never hide their dope and their gun where they're staying because it's full of other jits who will smoke the dope and sell the gun. This means that they carry drugs and guns on their persons, which enables cops to get a felony bust at every encounter.

Being premoral, jits don't feel guilty about what they do, because what they do simply happens to them. It's as natural as rain falling. The police, courts, judges, and jailers out in the world are a vague, amorphous threat to be avoided. If you're a jit, these officials are always bugging you to stop doing what feels good—like hustling, partying, and getting high—and

---

* Blunts are short cigars. Emptied of shredded tobacco and filled with marijuana, they give an excellent high. The THC in the dope is boosted by the nicotine in the tobacco leaf wrapper.

start doing what doesn't—like caring for children and sending women money. When they arrest you, they toss you in jail, then make you sit through hearings where people say bull that doesn't mean anything. If you pay a lawyer, he'll say some magic words back to the judge and maybe you'll get out sooner. Always you have to "sign here" on papers you can't read.

Lest you condemn prematurely, consider that jits are really hunter-gatherers who had the misfortune to be born several thousand years too late. Foraging, hunting, wandering, and raiding are primal male activities. They feel right. To jits, the fact that so many people object to the way they live is puzzling. As for women, you give them protection and money; they give you food and sex. What could be more natural?

PRE-CAVEMAN LIFE—ALPHA MALES ROAMING THE URBAN SAVANNAH

Culturally, jits are at a *pre-caveman* level. Outrageous, you say? Hold your horses and read on. When we encounter evidence of our most distant fore-bears, we see that they were already living in groups. Already there was a social order headed by an alpha male. Other males were subordinate. The pecking order reduced fighting among the men and competition for women. It allowed the men to hunt and face hostile outsiders as a group.

In the city, the caveman stage of social organization is provided by street and motorcycle gangs. As abhorrent as gangs are, their advantages for members are obvious. In the gang, an alpha male enforces a pecking order that protects subordinate males. Lower-ranking men may kill out-siders, but they don't kill each other. Gangs assign women to lower-order males, which also reduces fighting. In the case of motorcycle gangs, the leader decides which women belong to a single male and which are com-munal and can be shared sexually by all. In many motorcycle gangs, the leader will not speak to or look at a woman for purposes other than sex, since women are considered subhuman. (Why women continue to hang with these goons is one of the great mysteries.)

In a city like mine, where there are few street gangs, motorcycle gangs stay out in the boondocks away from police and, thankfully, the citi-zenry. Thus, jits lack even the rudimentary socialization of a small group. Socially, they're *pre*-cavemen.

Worse, they're *all* alpha males, living alone or with a woman. All it takes for someone to become an alpha is a gun. The current favorite is a nine-millimeter automatic pistol, the "nine." All these guys consider themselves the top dog. That's why there's so much random violence. When alpha males collide, they don't know how to subordinate themselves or dominate others, so they fight. This is the reason jits have to carry guns on their persons. If they're not alpha males (men with guns), they're nothing. They can't be subordinate males because they don't know how. Naturally, alpha males strutting on the street or driving beat-up cars are easy pickings for sophisticated hunters like cops. Those illegal firearms turn a traffic stop into a felony bust worth *mucho* points.

HOODLUM CHIC

Here's a really weird thing. "Staying at" places means you always have to have new clothes. It's tough to carry clothes around, and anything you leave behind, like expensive NBA sneakers, gets swiped. Even when you have a long-term crib with a woman, the washing machine is often broken or nonexistent. So you toss dirty clothes. My clients tell me that their women shoplift clothes for them, or that people knock on the door to sell stuff that's "fallen off the truck." This is also known as the Homeboy Shopping Network. Naturally it's hard to get clothes that fit. The solution is to swipe only large sizes, because anyone can tighten the belt. The fad for oversized hip-hop clothes, and athletic pants that have stretch bands and string ties is making a virtue of jit necessity.

INNOCENT SAVAGES

Middle-class people have multiple priorities such as work, family, religion, politics, and so forth. Jits have only one—to feel good. That's it, just feel good. Nothing more. Understand this and you understand all. For example, eating feels good; cleaning up does not. So you eat, then toss the trash over your shoulder. As for those mice and cockroaches that swarm over the mess, as long as they don't crawl over you, they don't matter. They don't feel good or bad; they're just there. Having women give you food and sex feels good; having them get pregnant and nag you about responsibilities feels bad. It's simple. Women spread 'em, you bed 'em; they nag, you walk. Smoking dope feels good; being straight feels bad. Hanging out feels good; working feels bad. You get the picture.

So far I've described jits as violence-prone, lazy, unorganized, irresponsible, and messy, but this misses an innocent quality that is the essence of the jit life. These people have no desire to accumulate money or power; they just want to feel good. They are quite ingenious at doing so. Getting money and resources by theft or living off the public dole seems to them merely making use of the resources at hand. There's no shame in it. It's merely what you do to eat. Selling drugs isn't good or bad; it's what you do to get some for yourself and feel good. Money feels good too. Get some.

What do solid citizens look like to jits? Like space aliens, that's what. They see us rushing around always in a hurry. They see us stressed out, looking at watches, and juggling schedules. We're doing things that don't appear to feel good, so perhaps we're mentally unbalanced. Worse, we're always bugging them. What business is it of ours if jits want to smoke some dope and feel good? Why the emphasis on being here, being there, at this hour or that? There's always money and food around, and places to stay, and you can hunt and gather them after you've had a good sleep, some cigarettes and coffee, and a joint to mellow out the whole process.

The jit solution to dealing with middle-class America is to sleep through it. Jits live at night and sleep during the day. That way they avoid all that bewildering middle-class bustle. Naturally they sleep through court appearances, drug tests, probation meetings, and so forth. Just as naturally they spend years in jails and prisons, where at last they stay awake during the day because The Man controls the food and the lights. One reason the criminal justice system finds pretrial detention so convenient is that, when defendants are in jail, they can always be located, and guaranteed to be awake, 9:00 A.M.–5:00 P.M., as needed.

And the paper! Always paper! Letters, subpoenas, probation notices, license-suspension letters, child-support demands, tag renewal notifications, insurance cancellation notices, and bills, bills, bills. On and on. It's The Man reaching out and hassling someone. When you're Jitus Americanus, all you want is to be left *alone* so you can feel good. Is this too much to ask? Isn't this America?

Sometimes when I'm in the office with the telephone ringing, the cell phone squawking, the fax humming, and the e-mail box filling up, when I'm facing a pile of legal documents that have to be replied to in a timely manner and writing out checks for the car tag, the boat permit, the child support, the mortgage, the health/home/life/car insurance, the credit cards, and *my* attorneys (for heaven's sake), I start dreaming of a simpler life. I think about living on a small boat, with my woman, and sleeping as much as I need to. I want to hang out with my buddies with no place to go and nothing to do. Sometimes I don't want to defend my jit clients; I want to join them.

Of course, I'm not going to do that. Don't you do it either. Get savvy, not clueless. Stay free.

SCENARIO #4

THE DAY-GLO RABBIT

Our subject is an 18-year-old African American boy who lives with his mother in an apartment in a marginal area of town. His mother, an English teacher and staunch Baptist, works hard to support herself and her son, and insists that he attend church at least twice a week. She does not allow him to use obscenity or profanity in the house, and requires that he speak standard English. She calls use of the double negative ("I didn't say nothing") a misdemeanor and the present subjunctive ("I be going") a felony.

She insists that he wear neatly pressed slacks and a button-down dress shirt to school, and she has ignored his protests that this makes him uncool and a wimp. Naturally he is teased by other boys who wear hip-hop slacks, sideways baseball hats, and gigantic sneakers. He is razzed for his high grades. The other students don't understand that making straight As is actually easier than facing his mother with a B. Girls are not impressed by his brains, and they torment him by ignoring his attempts at conversation and by going out with tough guys who've been to jail.

After listening to several thousand repetitions of his mother's insight that "idle hands are the devil's plaything," our subject has obtained a part-time job on weekends at an ice cream store in a suburban mall. He has saved several hundred dollars from his wages and tips and has, after much importunity, secured a promise from his mother that he can spend it on anything he wants "as long as it's legal."

At last his big day has come, and he sets out to shop that mall for once instead of being a worker bee. He buys the coolest Kangol beret to set off an authentic NBA jersey, which is the real thing with the heavy mesh nylon, as worn by the superstars, and not a cheap knockoff from the flea market. He buys giant, below-the-knee pants with pockets everywhere and a crimson nylon windbreaker with the embroidered signature of his favorite NBA center. The topper? Limited edition sneakers (fewer than 5,000 pairs for the entire United States!) that are the signature design of the most famous power forward in the history of the game. The tab is near $600, more than three times what his mother pays for his Sunday suits, but he's proud of how authentic everything is. He knows that many of the kids at school wear clothes that are shoplifted by their girlfriends. These clothes are usually too big. He's proud that his NBA clothes are all the real thing and that they actually fit.

So this Saturday afternoon he's decked out in all his glory back in the neighborhood, and he's sure one of the girls will notice. He's strutting, not on the sidewalk but in the street, just like the tough guys, and making cars slow or stop in order to get around him. This game is called Make Whitey Stop. It's a rush. All the people who generally ignore him in this part of town have to look up and show some respect. They've got to stop! So he's getting off doing the hoodlum strut, with cars swerving right and left, and he's giving the wink to the startled girls who do a double take when they see him and all that money he's wearing.

Suddenly, in a car heading toward him, a driver, distracted by a cell phone, slams on the brakes. The car swerves, then fishtails, and its rear quarter panel brushes our subject before the car slams into a streetlight. The car's front end crumples, oil pours onto the asphalt, and a geyser of green fluid boils out of the radiator. The air bag deploys, and the car alarm starts an ear-splitting wail as the vehicle skids to a stop.

Our hero is momentarily frozen by the crash and doesn't see a police car race around the corner with lights spinning and siren whooping. Two cops jump out. One heads for the car as he calls in the accident on his shoulder microphone. The second officer spots our subject and yells out, "Hey you. C'mere!"

Our guy panics. He just can't get arrested. What would his mother say? So he bolts down the street. He hears a police officer running behind him and shouting "foot pursuit" into his radio just as other cruisers pull up and more cops jump out and run after him. How can the cops get organized so fast? They're coming out of nowhere, cruiser after cruiser, lights flashing, sirens wailing, and beefy guys in blue thundering down the pavement.

He's pulling ahead. Those NBA sneakers have heels like springs, and the cops are wearing crazy leather clodhoppers and dragging around a lot of iron on their belts. Still, he regrets the clothes. All those colors! He's a Day-Glo rabbit with a pack of mastiffs in hot pursuit.

All at once a cop, who had jumped from his cruiser several blocks ahead, is coming toward him! Our hero swerves, trips, and takes a header into the dirt, which grinds into his fancy threads. Now all $600 of clothes, all those thousands of ice cream cones' worth of work, look like they came off a ditch digger. They're torn, filthy, and ruined.

He gets jerked to his feet and surrounded by cops. One of them is shouting at him, something about an ID. All he can think about, however, is the ruined clothes, all that work. He's weeping with shame and anger. One of the cops puts his hand on his chest with fingers outspread. The cop doesn't ask permission, just pokes his hand out and *touches* him! This is too much. Our hero grabs the cop's hand and struggles to get away. Within seconds he's back on the ground, handcuffed, then frog-marched into the police cruiser. He's taken downtown and charged with resisting arrest and felony assault on a law enforcement officer.

Later he is taken to the juvenile detention center, where he is strip-searched. When the corrections officer puts on a glove and touches his scrotum, he starts screaming and struggling. Without saying a word, corrections officers strap him down in a plastic chair and lock him into a soundproofed cell, where he cries for hours. It takes two days for his mother to get money from her church friends and hire an attorney. At a preliminary hearing, after the attorney reviews the facts with the prosecutor and the judge and presents the boy's stellar academic record and character references from teachers and ministers, the charges are dropped. Total cost is about $5,000 and a juvenile arrest record.

THE MORALS OF THIS STORY

1. Here's a kid who has everything going for him—brains, education, and a strict, loving home. He's the kind of minority youth that the best colleges would *throw money at* to get him to matriculate at their institution. In many states lottery funds would pay his tuition at state universities.

2. Like too many bright minority children, he is ostracized socially for doing well in school. The road to freedom is paved with education, but that doesn't mean it's not a hard road.

3. Did he commit a crime? In most states walking in the street is stupid but not illegal. Whether he or the driver is responsible for the car wreck is debatable.

4. The most serious crime the kid committed is panicking in the presence of cops. The number of people who get arrested and jailed for this is astonishing. If our hero had simply stood still in front of the cops, he probably would not have been arrested.

5. Basically this kid is a goofy teenager trying to attract girls, which is hardly a crime. The education this child needs most is arrest proofing, which is not taught in Sunday school or Monday–Friday school.

6. Few people understand police operations. Touching a suspect to check his fight-or-flight status is standard police procedure. Those clunky cop shoes are generally steel tipped for fighting, and although cops are slowed down by their equipment, they generally stay in shape and can run longer, if not faster, than adolescents. Cops practice foot pursuits, so unlike suspects, they do not panic and can think on their feet. Cops hunt in packs and are difficult to elude. Chasing and arresting people is what they do. They enjoy it.

7. It's unfortunate that wearing certain clothes and acting in certain ways predisposes police to consider you a criminal, but if you dress like a crook, strut like a crook, and run like a crook, what else are cops supposed to think?

   Cops spend every day trawling the net through the seething metropolis. All day and all night they round up clueless gorks with drugs and guns in their pockets, stolen merchandise in their cars, and loud clothes on their bodies. Usually the suspects are in some state of drug and alcoholic inebriation and are foulmouthed or incoherent. Cops generally don't make fine distinctions in the heat of making arrests, and may not recognize a straight-A student *pretending to be a thug!* They simply deposit their prisoners, tally the points scored, and let prosecutors and judges sort things out later.

8. The system isn't fair. It's just there.

7 | WHY MINORITIES GET HAMMERED

RACISM

There is lingering racism among police, prosecutors, and judges, but less than at any time in our history. Most big-city police departments now employ black and Hispanic officers at every level, including sergeant, lieutenant, captain, and chief. After years of sensitivity training in police forces throughout America, what has emerged is the modern patrol officer, who is an *equal opportunity* arrest-making specialist. Police like to arrest anybody, of any race, at any time, including people just like you.

So what to do about lingering racism? Nothing. That's right, nothing. When you're in front of a cop, racism is *his* problem. There's nothing you can do about it in the few minutes of a typical police interaction. Your problem is to be less clueless. That's something *you* can control.

When I was a kid, police racism meant that people of color were more likely than whites to be "shot while fleeing arrest." Those evil days are thankfully over. Today police racism means the following:

>> Minorities are more likely than white people to be stopped on the street or in their vehicles.

>> They are more likely to have their IDs checked and their vehicles searched.

This is outrageous, but let's keep things in perspective. Being *stopped* is annoying and insulting. Being *arrested*, incarcerated, impoverished by legal fees, and then dumped onto the electronic plantation is ruinous.

Too many people continue to get stopped for the crime of driving while being black, Hispanic, etc. Nonetheless, if you're not carrying drugs, unlicensed firearms, or stolen merchandise when you confront a cop, and are polite, truthful, and do not touch the officer or flee, it's unlikely you'll be arrested.

Things are changing. Black and Hispanic Americans who drive within the limits with all licenses and tags up to date go years without any interaction with a police officer, just like whites. What cop wants to stop law-abiding, license- and tag-possessing, fully insured blacks and Hispanics? They're savvy, not clueless, and worse, from the cop's point of view, *they're not worth any points.*

Recall that the most important document in a patrol cop's life is the monthly tally of police activity. This records numbers of arrests and traffic tickets. It does not indicate race. There is no column for "black and brown people annoyed and insulted." Racist cops who hassle innocent minorities have low police activity. They generate complaints, internal investigations, lawsuits, and heat from the media and organized blocks of black and Hispanic voters. Racist cops can be politically fatal to elected chiefs and sheriffs.

IN SEARCH OF THE GREAT WHITE DEFENDANT

If anything, police are looking to arrest more white guys. Cops get tired of busting people of color all the time. They welcome what Tom Wolfe calls "the Great White Defendant." If the GWD is not only rich but also a celebrity, this is extra good. Amazingly, there is a place where rich white people get arrested all the time. Where, you ask, is this Mecca of justice? It's South Beach, the 20 or so blocks of south Miami Beach that are the coolest, craziest place to be for the rich, the famous, and the beautiful.

Miami Beach is, notoriously, the celebrity arrest capital of the planet. Millionaire actors, athletes, rock stars, and financial whiz kids fly into town arrogant, snotty, and ready for trouble. They wreck rental cars, punch out patrons in South Beach clubs, get wasted on premium drugs, and slap their women around. Worse, they argue with the managers of upscale hotels and restaurants and leave without paying their bills. In Florida, a tourist state, "defrauding an innkeeper" is only slightly less serious than murder. When stiffed, South Beach hotel and restaurant managers send 300-pound bouncer types to squash Mr. or Ms. Celebrity flat on the pavement until police arrive.

Naturally, local police want to make sure that arrested celebrities are processed by the book, which means very, very slowly. For their *safety*, celebrities generally spend the night in the Miami-Dade County Jail. For their *health*, they get to sample Jailhouse Lean Cuisine, which is to say beanie-weenies, mystery meat with flavored goo, and green baloney sandwiches with mustard dab. Naturally, local judges are concerned that celebrity cases be handled with absolute attention to detail. They often think it necessary for the rich and famous to fly back from L.A. or New York to appear in person even for a traffic ticket. You get the picture.

Let's analyze the South Beach scene in the terms of this book. Why are all those rich white people being busted down there? Simple. As soon as their jets touch down and they cab over to the beach and unpack their hand-stitched luggage with the famous logos, *they get clueless*. That's right. The party scene encourages them to adopt behaviors they would *never* exhibit at home. When they hit the beach, these rich perps suddenly begin to do the following clueless things:

>> Instead of driving, they walk the streets, *where they're visible to police.*

>> They get drunk in public, *where they're visible to police.*

>> They carry drugs on the street, *where they're visible to police.*

>> They smack women in public, *where they're visible to police.*

>> They fight in public, *where they're visible to police.*

>> They get an attitude and curse and shove cops *outdoors in front of witnesses.*

Remember Uncle Dale's Golden Rule #1?

>> **IF COPS CAN'T SEE YOU, THEY CAN'T ARREST YOU.**

The reverse is also true. Do crimes where cops *can* see you and you *will* get hammered, no matter how rich and white you are.

Do these rich white people suddenly become more criminal in South Beach than they are back in New York and L.A.? Nope. They simply become more clueless and more visible. Back home they do their crimes indoors, where cops can't *see* the offense, *hear* the women's screams, or *smell* the dope. If cops are called to a residence, it's generally gated and secured. There's time for rich perps to hide or destroy evidence, speed dial their attorneys, calm down, and sober up. There's time to demand a warrant before allowing a search and to observe Uncle Dale's Golden Rule #3:

>> **GIVE COPS YOUR NAME AND BASIC INFO, THEN SHUT THE HECK UP!**

The point is that behavior, not race, gets people arrested. Being rich, white, and famous doesn't guarantee that someone isn't a clueless idiot when it comes to criminal justice. Rich people can be difficult to *prosecute* because they can afford big-time lawyers, but they're easy to *arrest*—if they're clueless.

Let's consider an example everybody knows: football and media star O. J. Simpson, who was accused, and acquitted, of a double homicide. The fact that he's black was, from a legal standpoint, unimportant. What mattered was his being a savvy multimillionaire. He was easy to arrest, but to prosecute? Fuggedaboudit! He was defended by the best and most expensive attorneys in America. They stomped the prosecutors like so many cockroaches. Here's a clue: the number of multimillionaire murderers convicted in the last hundred years is practically nil. So, if you're charged with murder, your best defense against conviction and extermination is to be worth $5 million or more. I'll need most of that to keep you off the gurney to eternity.

DO WHITE TRASH GET A PASS BECAUSE THEY'RE WHITE?

Let's talk about a group people of color often know little about: poor, clueless white people. Some black Americans have myths, of course, and think poor whites are bogeymen with white Ku Klux Klan hoods in their pockets, always ready for a nighttime lynching. On their part, some poor

Southern whites fly Confederate battle flags at home and on their vehicles to signify a certain disinclination to appreciate the full panoply of America's racial and ethnic diversity.

I live in a neighborhood where poor whites and poor blacks rent rooms in separate rooming houses on the same blocks. Although on paper the neighborhood is a model of integration, the two groups might as well live on separate planets. Since it's been my privilege to arrest people of both groups over the years, and now to defend them, I know them well.

Let's talk about a subset of poor, clueless whites I'll call seagoing rednecks. These guys live along the rivers, seaports, and coasts of the South in an astounding variety of boats and contraptions that float but, lacking propulsion, may not actually make headway in a liquid medium. Some of these guys actually live in truck containers and plywood boxes that bob about on giant blocks of polyurethane foam.

Most of these guys work in fishing boats, boatyards, and marinas. Some of them supplement their income by running offshore to unload mother ships and bring in drugs. This is sometimes referred to as fishing for "square grouper," i.e., marijuana bales and blocks of cocaine. In south Florida, if they can afford full tanks of gas for their boat, they cross to Bahamian outer islands to pick up Haitian and Chinese immigrants, who they carry to the beaches of south Florida and dump overboard just beyond the breakers.

They're fond of the magic herb and can be seen growing their very own shipboard marijuana bushes, which they mist and fertilize lovingly. Nothing, of course, replaces beer. They consider the 24-pack and the kegger to be the most important advances in human convenience in the last century. When in need of jollification, they hie forth to roadhouses and biker bars, where misunderstandings about women sometimes require the intervention of civil authority. When their women are in need of enlightenment, they improve their lady's understanding with a few sharp raps to the head. Their dress code runs to jeans and T-shirts. Their hair is long or shaved off, their beards scruffy, and their skin adorned with tattoos and piercings.

Got the picture? These are petty criminals, but why aren't more of them in jail? Because they're *not totally clueless*. Using the Cluelessness Quotient chart and the Golden Rules for comparison, let's consider manners first.

Although low on the social food chain, these characters don't have a chip on their shoulders about race. They are less likely to act out in the presence of police. Generally they can stifle the profanity during those crucial minutes and mumble "Yes, officer" and "No officer" until the heat has passed.

Most important, they don't adopt the outdoor lifestyle. They're almost never visible walking on streets where they can be seen by cops riding around in cars. When they drive, their cars and pickups may be junkers, but they're street legal, so they have fewer traffic stops. They get wasted indoors, where search warrants are required, and are less likely to carry dope on their persons and in their cars. Often they grow their own marijuana, so they do not buy drugs and fall victim to police stings, undercover cops, and confidential informants. Their dress is scruffy, but T-shirts and jeans blend in better than gang colors and hip-hop gear, so they don't get targeted as quickly by police.

Once they do get arrested, they have some resources. For time management, they generally can muster an alarm clock and a watch, and in emergencies, a calendar. They often marry their women, so they have a wife, the "old lady," in addition to Mama and sisters to pay legal fees and bail bonds. When driving, they get their buzz from beer rather than marijuana. This means that if they're stopped and are not legally intoxicated, they will receive only a citation for driving with an open container—and not even that if they can slide the can out the rear window and into the truck bed before the cop gets close. Rednecks have some knowledge of police procedure. They know that police do *not* like to find guns, so they carry the all-purpose and legal knife. When they do carry guns, they are likely to have a permit.

ARE BLACK AND HISPANIC AMERICANS MORE CLUELESS?

There are entire libraries devoted to black American social problems, so I'll limit myself to two observations. First, black Americans have only been able to vote without hindrance since I was a teenager, with the passage of the Voting Rights Act. Second, black Americans have only begun to hold good jobs and acquire money, real estate, and pristine, street-legal vehicles in significant numbers in the last 30 years. In so doing, they have acquired the armor with which the middle and upper classes gird themselves against the slings and arrows of outrageous fortune—insurance policies, pensions, savings accounts, investments, and attorneys. In the terminology of this book, they have become more savvy and less clueless.

Middle- and upper-class black and Hispanic Americans who drive street-legal cars within speed limits; have nice manners; and avoid carrying drugs, unlicensed firearms, or stolen property in their vehicles can go years without any interactions with police, just like white Americans. They still get pulled over more often than they should, but they do *not* get arrested.

Clueless people, regardless of race or income, get busted because they're *easier* to arrest. They're low-hanging fruit. To a cop, they represent more points for less work. In a cop's world the most important person is his sergeant, and sergeants want only one thing—numbers. Sergeants are great communicators. They're geniuses at crafting pithy sentences in easy-to-understand language. Here's what my old sergeant in Miami had to say about my performance when I first joined the force. I remember it verbatim all these years later: "Carson, if you don't go out there and arrest more of those scumballs, I'll have your job."

Now you know all you need to know, perhaps all there is to know, about police sergeants. When the sarge is busting your chops for stats, the simplest solution is to pull over some beat-up cars stuffed with clueless idiots. You'll get multiple busts fast and soon be back on the sunny side of the guy who hands out assignments and recommends promotions.

STEREOTYPES AND PROFILES—GET USED TO THEM

The following two things make minority Americans insane:

1. **STEREOTYPING**

2. **PROFILING**

Stereotyping means judging individuals according to preconceived ideas. Profiling means choosing whom to stop, question, and search based on stereotypes. Volumes have been written, and bushels of lawsuits filed, to protest police profiling. Cops, however, are not going to stop profiling for a simple reason: it works. Here's why. Humans are in the main con-formists, not individualists. Petty offenders and most real bad guys dress, act, and behave—surprise—like crooks. Let's lay out some examples.

>> Young black and Hispanic men wearing jail tatts (jailhouse tattoos) and gang colors are *more likely* to be arrestable than elderly white guys in suits and ties.

>> Women wearing miniskirts and carrying tiny "condom" handbags are *more likely* to be prostitutes than women in business suits and flat heels.

>> Hell's Outlaws on Harleys are *more likely* to be arrestable than Mormon missionaries on bicycles.

>> Arabs are *more likely* to be terrorists than Eskimos are.

Here's a real-life example. Several years ago a young female customs officer at a lonely Canadian border crossing stopped a truck driven by two Arabs who fit a terrorist profile for the following two reasons:

>> Both were nervous and sweating heavily in freezing weather.

>> Arabs look out of place in snow-covered forests.

The truck was filled with tons of ammonium nitrate and diesel fuel explosive. The guys were heading south to blow up Los Angeles International Airport. Moral of the story: profiling works.

Here's another famous example. The sheriff of Volusia County, Florida, seizes almost as many illegal drugs each year as the entire federal government. He does this by profiling. He knows that the giant containers of dope that arrive in south Florida are split up into car-size loads, then dispatched up I-95, which runs through his county and is the main drug route for the U.S. east coast. He knows that car-size loads are almost always transported by Colombians, and that generally each dope-hauling vehicle will have a driver and a passenger riding shotgun. So he instructs his officers to stop all cars on I-95 that contain two Latins and are being *driven exactly at the speed limit.* Lawsuits have been filed by enraged Latin motorists (including some of the dope haulers!) who were stopped without having committed a traffic violation. Still the sheriff continues to find that an extraordinary percentage of cars he stops are jammed from floorboard to door knobs with pure cocaine.

You get the picture. Profiling by stereotype ignores a person's individuality, but so what? Cops decide whether to pull over a car or stop someone on the street in a split second. When cops stop you, they're not trying to imbibe the wondrous fullness of your being. They're thinking about two things.

1. ARE YOU ARRESTABLE?

2. HOW MANY POINTS ARE YOU WORTH?

Heck, I'm the same way. When I run across you in jail, I'm thinking just two things.

1. DO YOU HAVE A CASE I WANT?

2. CAN YOU PAY MY FEE?

When your check clears there will be plenty of time for us to swap secrets and become best friends.

Profiling is difficult to challenge legally because police departments don't write anything about profiling *on paper* that can be discovered by plaintiffs' attorneys and presented as evidence of discrimination at trial. There's no need. Cops pick up what they know from their partners and training officers and from scuttlebutt in the briefing room and the lockers. Think cops will testify against each other about profiling? Think again. Profiling lawsuits bother cops about as much as a wet kiss from a chubby baby.

Increasingly, profiles are not based on race, but on behavior, dress, and attitude because crooks act alike and look alike to an amazing degree. Check out the Cluelessness Chart again. If you hang out on the streets in view of cops; wear crazy hair and clothes; carry dope, guns, or stolen property; and drive with three hoodlum friends in a car with an expired tag and smoking tailpipe, you're likely to get stopped and arrested. If you address police in an offensive manner, you're likely to get a go-to-jail ticket with the big *F* for "felony" at the top.

If you have no time management and paperwork skills and no address, you're going to get processed through the criminal justice sausage grinder until your life is a soft, bureaucratic mush. You will, however, have provided honest employment to numerous city and state employees who thank you secretly from the depths of their hearts. As for my bail bondsman buddy, he's planning to build a marina, and hopes that you, yes you, will go to jail sometime soon. He needs your money.

We'll end this chapter with an all-too-common scenario of how women are victimized by identity theft and get locked into cruddy jobs and bad neighborhoods by life sentences on the electronic plantation.

SCENARIO #5
CHECK STUB

Our heroine is a young African American woman who has clawed her way out of the social service plantation and the welfare system by doing everything right. When she was younger, she was a heroin addict and a prostitute. Most unusually, she was never arrested. She decided to quit the life and get the drug monkey off her back. Unable to obtain a place in overcrowded treatment centers to kick her habit, she had a friend lock her in a closet and spent three days screaming, vomiting, and having convulsions in order to quit cold turkey. After getting clean, she went through vocational rehabilitation training and received her GED at night school. Her child is in day care, and she has been working as a cashier for a grocery store chain for several years. She attends church regularly, never misses her meeting at Narcotics Anonymous, and will tell anyone who asks that Jesus is her *personal* Lord and Savior who has given her a second chance.

Unfortunately, the grocery store where she works stays open until midnight and is frequented by "jitterbugs" and "rock stars" who smoke crack and shoplift pseudoepinephrine decongestants,

---

which they cook into methamphetamine. Meth makes people crazy, and there have been incidents at the store where street people have attacked shoppers with knives and guns. One meth-head had his veins explode* after he injected the drug, and he bled to death in the parking lot.

Our heroine can't stand the neighborhood and spends every possible moment planning how to get out. She has shared slum apartments with a rotating cast of roommates, but is on a short list to receive a low-cost home from Habitat for Humanity. If everything goes right, she will own her own home in a better part of town, be able to care for her baby properly, and have a piece of the American Dream. The key is a job as a teller at one of the national banks. Such a job pays more than the grocery store and has better hours, nicer surroundings, and a health insurance plan that will allow her to get her baby treated by a real doctor instead of the nurse practitioners at the neighborhood clinics.

One night, while driving home from a church meeting in pouring rain, she drives through a stop sign and is pulled over by a police cruiser. In her vocational rehabilitation classes she learned to always have her license, insurance, and registration handy and to be polite with police officers. She hands these documents to the officer. He goes back to his cruiser and looks her up in the computer. She is shocked when he returns and arrests her for having outstanding warrants for check fraud.

Because it is late, she is unable to get a hearing or make bail, so she has to spend the night in jail with prostitutes and drug addicts who mock her nice clothes and call her "church girl." Some of them wiggle their tongues at her and make lesbian come-ons. The next morning she calls church friends, who raise $5,000 to hire an attorney and get her bonded out of jail.

---

* Grocery store meth has to be injected boiling hot. It cooks the veins going in. Fun, huh?

The attorney discovers that the warrants are really a case of identity theft. A former roommate had copied down her social security number, opened checking accounts under her name, and bounced checks for thousands of dollars all over town. The attorney was able to get the indictments quashed and the arrest records expunged.

A week later she called the bank to ask when she could have her first interview. The human relations specialist told her that all jobs had been filled. She thought this odd, since the bank continued to advertise for tellers in the local newspaper. She called week after week but was always told the same thing. Finally she took a day off from the grocery and drove to the bank and managed to talk her way into the human relations department. There one of the women took pity on her and explained that the bank had discovered her arrest on the bad-check charge. The bank had an ironclad policy of never hiring anyone with an arrest record, regardless of whether the arrest resulted in a conviction.

Devastated, our heroine went back to the grocery store. At church she prays now that one day she can get a promotion to assistant head cashier. This will bring her an additional dollar an hour in wages, qualify her for the Habitat house, and enable her to transfer to a suburban store away from the hellhole downtown. She does not pray for a nice man to marry her, however. She feels this would be asking too much. She thinks God is busy and can attend to her better if she asks for only one thing at a time.

THE MORALS OF THIS STORY

1. Identity theft is a common and growing crime that is devastating for victims. It can result in warrants and arrests since the victim is unaware of the bad checks because the phony checking accounts are set up with fictitious addresses and telephone numbers from stolen "burner" cell phones.

2. It is extremely expensive to clear up arrests and felony charges, even when they are baseless and the arrestee is completely innocent.

3. Banks, other private businesses, and many governmental agencies have, by federal law, been granted access to the NCIC (National Crime Information Center) run by the FBI. All adult arrests, including those for which charges are dropped, and *many juvenile arrests* are recorded by the NCIC.

4. The NCIC is the backbone of the electronic plantation. Once there, you have a life sentence that bars you from working in financial institutions, even if your arrest is not recorded on the data servers of the World Wide Web.

5. Keep social security cards and numbers, bank statements, and driver's licenses under lock and key when they're not on your person. Don't show them to anyone other than officials entitled to see them.

8 | LAW ENFORCEMENT SHOULDN'T GIVE A PASS TO ALL THOSE CROOKS IN THE MIDDLE CLASS

The jails are packed with poor people, mostly black and Hispanic. This is no secret. So why aren't more middle-class people in the pokey? Are all those middle-class types out there solid citizens? Are they all just stoking the machine 40 hours a week, giving the IRS a cut every payday, and raising chubby-cheeked children to become the next generation of Great Americans? Hardly.

Middle-class people are the most exasperating group of crooks because they rarely get caught. There are two reasons.

1. **LOWER CLUE-Q (CLUELESSNESS QUOTIENT).** Even when they indulge in petty crimes and run-of-the-mill thuggishness, middle-class types are harder to arrest and convict because they know the system a bit better. When doing petty crimes, they tend to

   >> keep dope at home rather than in their cars and on their persons

   >> grow their own weed and avoid buying it and falling into police traps

   >> call cops "sir" rather than dirty names

   >> beat women in detached houses rather than apartments, so screams don't get heard and police don't get called

   >> make restitution and talk their way out of petty-theft raps

   >> carry firearms legally

>> sell stolen property to fences rather than peddle it door-to-door in view of police

>> drive street-legal cars, so they are pulled over and searched less often

>> avoid hanging out and living the arrestable, urban outdoor lifestyle (middle-class punks "hang in" and plan and execute crimes indoors, where difficult-to-obtain search warrants are necessary to root them out and arrest them)

>> read their mail, mark their calendars, and set the alarm so they can wake up, dress up, and show up, albeit grudgingly, at court hearings, probation meetings, anger-management classes, and drug rehab

Middle-class thugs, in their scumbag fashion, emphasize the major point of this book. The less clueless you are about the system, the less likely you are to be arrested, even if you *are* a lowlife.

2. **THEY DO CRIMES THAT POLICE CAN'T SEE OR ARE UNTRAINED TO INVESTIGATE.** Middle-class crooks have long ago discovered the obvious—do crimes where there aren't any cops. Better yet, do crimes that patrol cops aren't trained and equipped to *recognize*, much less investigate. Middle-class crooks dominate the following major crime categories:

>> insurance fraud

>> mortgage fraud

>> bank fraud

>> investment fraud

>> securities fraud

>> prescription fraud

>> check fraud

>> Medicare and Medicaid fraud

>> embezzlement

>> identity theft, phishing, pharming*, and Internet fraud

>> money laundering

>> manufacturing of phony passports and IDs

>> mid- and high-level drug distribution

>> manufacturing and distribution of illegal drugs like Dilaudid, LSD, and ecstasy, or "X" (cocaine and heroin are manufactured primarily in foreign countries)

>> fake pharmaceutical drug manufacturing and importation. (Your neighborhood-produced Viagra pills are made of sugar and milk powder. Try getting it up with *that*.)

>> pornography

>> counterfeiting of currency, automobile titles, luxury goods, music, movies, and software

>> immigrant smuggling

>> white slavery** and high-end prostitution

---

* Phishing and pharming are Internet scams. The bad guys send out e-mails directing recipients to phony Web sites that look like the sites of banks or government agencies. There, clueless boobs are encouraged to enter their social security numbers, bank account numbers, and credit card numbers. These are duly harvested by pharmers, who sell the information to identity thieves on a cyberspace version of the black market.

Take a clue here. Your bank already has your account numbers. They don't need to ask for them. As for government agencies, if they want to see you, they'll let you know, and it won't be by e-mail. Set that e-mail spam filter on HIGH! Never open e-mails from people you don't know.

** White slavery is a police term for the illegal transportation and detention of women for the purpose of prostitution. It does not refer to the race of the women.

>> political and ecoterrorism

>> confidence rackets

>> extortion and protection rackets

>> illegal gambling

>> government procurement fraud and bid rigging

>> labor racketeering

>> bribery of judges and elected officials

>> vote fraud

These are enormous criminal enterprises. Thousands of criminals are involved, but comparatively few are arrested. Here's why. All these crimes have one feature in common: *Cops driving around in cars can't see them.* Sounds simple, and it is. No see 'em, no arrest 'em.

Think about this. When your local porn king is making unspeakable child pornography videos, one of the most heinous crimes in America, what do cops driving around see? A warehouse or office building with some cars parked out front—that's all. Cops can't see through walls (yet), so they drive on.

Take bank and mortgage fraud. It happens in offices. Cops don't go there. Even if they drive by and happen to see a fraud artist, what do they see? A guy with a briefcase. That's all. Drive on.

Furthermore, street cops are untrained to even recognize many of these crimes, even if they do see them being committed. Sound far-fetched? Imagine this. A guy is sitting at a table on his front porch committing insurance fraud. He's preparing a phony claim that will net him hundreds of thousands of dollars. This is a major felony. If a cop drives by, what does he see? A guy filling out forms with a ballpoint pen. It doesn't look suspicious. Drive on.

Here's another example. A money launderer is sitting in one of those fancy coffee shops where you buy overpriced java and use the Internet. The bad guy is laundering cash from pornographers who sell kiddie porn on the Internet. He transfers the money to overseas banks. All of this can be done with a laptop computer and an Internet account opened under a phony name and paid for with an untraceable cash card. Imagine that a cop walks quietly into the coffee shop and actually looks over the money launderer's shoulder and witnesses illegal money transfers. All he sees is a guy typing numbers and letters on a computer screen. For all the cop knows, the guy is paying his light bill or ordering a movie ticket. No arrest. Back to the car. Drive on.

Middle-class crime is not small potatoes. The quantities of money are astounding. A middle-class crook perpetrating a single insurance fraud— for example, making a phony disability claim—can make hundreds of thousands of dollars, more than a bank robber could even dream about. For clueless people, the money from crime is hit or miss. Score something here; score something there. There are feast days and famine, but in the end most clueless types who try to make a living from crime end up living in crummy apartments. Sooner or later, they and, generally, their female relatives become impoverished by the criminal justice system, which sucks out their money to pay fines, court costs, attorney's fees, bail bonds, and drug court and probation charges.

Middle-class crime is more like a conveyor belt. Enormous quantities of illegal goods and services move outward to the public, and a never-ending pile of money flows back to the crooks. Ka-ching! Ka-ching! Ka-ching! Every day is a payday and the register never stops ringing.

The FBI is quite good at investigating middle-class crooks. The methods they use—consensual monitors ("wires"), wiretaps, stings, reverse cons, confidential informants, and undercover ops—are the only way to investigate, arrest, and successfully prosecute middle-class crooks. There are, however, two little problems.

1. FBI agents only investigate federal crimes.

2. There aren't many FBI agents. In my city, for example, there are *thousands* of patrol cops riding around in cars and busting people like you. There are only *dozens* of FBI agents. These days, a huge proportion of bureau resources is dedicated to national security. This leaves middle-class crooks more latitude than ever to keep raking it in.

Yes, cops need to arrest many more middle-class people. They can't do it now because their resources are grossly misdeployed. Police department detectives can use many of the same investigative techniques as the FBI, but police departments have nowhere near the numbers of detectives necessary to make a dent in middle-class crime. In any case, most detectives spend all their time, of necessity, investigating homicides, kidnappings, armed robberies, carjackings, and other violent crimes. Often *nobody* is going after middle-class crooks.

Another complication is that middle-class crimes often involve transactions across state lines and national borders and violations of both state and federal law. This means these crimes fall between the cracks of different jurisdictions. Are the cops or the FBI in charge? Maybe the Bureau of Alcohol, Tobacco, Firearms and Explosives; the Office of the Bank Examiner; the Secret Service; the Drug Enforcement Agency; or the Border Patrol should take a hand. Often no one can decide who's in charge. Another interagency task force gets formed, and another SNAFU (situation normal, all fouled up). Ho-hum in Bureaucrat Land.

Police departments are stuck in the last century in regard to their ability to hunt and arrest middle-class criminals. To catch them, police departments will have to become radically different than they are today. They will have to employ, directly or on contract, battalions of the following kinds of people, many of whom can be civilians rather than sworn officers. Many will have job specialties most cops can't even spell:

- fraud investigators

- forensic accountants

- banking investigators

- insurance investigators

- securities investigators

- phone and communications specialists

- Internet specialists

- database specialists

>> computer technicians

>> data-recovery technicians

>> encryption/decryption technicians

>> liaisons to Interpol and federal and state law enforcement

>> undercover investigators and "sting" operations specialists

>> *many more* ordinary detectives

All of this is not—repeat *not*—to encourage you to aspire to be a middle-class crook. The point is to emphasize that cops are massively deployed to catch you at the less sophisticated things you're likely to be up to—carrying weed; driving with a suspended license or expired tag; drinking in public; running from cops; fighting with women; failing to appear at court hearings, probation meetings, and drug court; violating parole; and so forth. Cops often aren't even looking for middle-class crooks laundering money; distributing kiddie porn; and perpetrating insurance, mortgage, and Medicare fraud.

No doubt this gets you steamed. You're hassled by cops right and left, stopped, searched, questioned, and annoyed while all these evil, middle-class perps are stealing money hand over fist with nary a cop around to even slow them down. Their insurance frauds and crapola lawsuits push up the cost of automobile insurance so you can barely afford to drive street legal. Maybe you can't even buy car insurance right now and have to drive outlaw until the next few paychecks. Sweating bullets every time a cop pulls up on your rear bumper and runs your tag on his onboard computer is no way to live.

The system isn't fair. It's just there. What shoulda, coulda, oughta, mighta been is not your problem. Your challenge is to arrest-proof yourself. Want to do something good for America? Stay free. Take a clue here.

I'll close this chapter with a fictional portrait of a master criminal. Note that the biggest criminals have many of the qualities that bring success in the straight world: intelligence, discipline, persistence, and savvy. They are not clueless. This portrait conflates several actual people in Jacksonville and Miami. I've added a dash of James Bond supercriminal as well. Most mid- and high-level drug dealers aren't this smart. They compensate for lack of IQ by blowing out the brains of people who annoy them, such as their attorneys. Details are changed so that the authors of this book don't have to worry about getting bumped off.*

SCENARIO #6

CHEMICAL MAN

Our subject, "the chemist," is in his 40s, the holder of a master's degree in chemistry from a prestigious university. He manufactures a high grade of methamphetamine ("crank") that is sold on the streets under the name crystal lightning. Most manufacturers deliver meth to distributors, who then dilute it for sale at wildly varying dosages with anything from baby powder to laundry detergent. The chemist dilutes his drug with an inert powder, and then packages a pure product, with a standard dosage, in plastic bags with a distinctive lightning flash label. The stuff is wildly popular, since addicts know they can get a good high without being poisoned. The chemist's distributors are similarly upbeat about the product, which arrives packaged and ready to sell and which relieves them of the dangerous chore of "stepping on" the drugs. (To increase profits, street dealers adulterate, or "step on," drugs with any cheap powder they can get their hands on. They have a distressing tendency to use stuff they grab from the kitchen, like Draino, laundry detergent, and rat poison.)

The chemist lives in a luxurious home, and regularly entertains at tasteful dinners presided over by his fashionable girlfriend. They travel together frequently to resorts and spas. On business, of course, he travels by himself.

---

* In south Florida, contract murders are refined to an art form. The preferred method is two taps to the head with a snubby .22. A round from a larger pistol will penetrate the skull, then exit, often allowing the victim to survive. The .22, in contrast, enters the skull, then bounces around, scrambling the brains into mush. Pros appreciate such things.

The chemist has built his enterprise with care. He manufactures his drugs alone and forgoes opportunities to expand in order to avoid the risk of assistants. He moves his lab equipment frequently among warehouses leased under fictitious names and paid for in cash. For business he switches from his personal cars to an ever-changing variety of beaters purchased for cash, then legally insured and tagged. He has never been stopped by police while driving and has never received a traffic ticket.

He has several distributors, none of whom know each other. The chemist never personally delivers drugs or receives money. All sales and payments occur through prearranged drops and electronic transfers to banks. He rarely uses telephones, and never uses mail or computers for business. On the occasions when he meets personally with distributors, he does so one on one, without witnesses, in steam rooms, hot tubs, or on the beach, where bugs, wires, and parabolic microphones are less effective. Outdoors he invariably wears sunglasses and wide-brimmed hats so that he cannot be reliably identified from photographs or surveillance tapes. None of his distributors knows his identity or where he lives.

His minimal financial records are maintained by an accountant and an attorney in a foreign country in the name of several shell corporations. His reported income, which appears in the form of dividends from securities and equities held in offshore accounts, is ample to support his lifestyle. Taxes are paid punctiliously. His girlfriend has no idea he is a criminal; she thinks their lifestyle is funded by investments.

On one occasion police became aware of his operation. After a tip-off from a warehouse manager, they obtained a search warrant and raided his lab. The police were unlucky in their timing. They discovered only the precursors of his drug, all of which, like ammonia, are legal chemicals. Traces of methamphetamine discovered on the meticulously washed glassware proved, after analysis, too minute to support criminal charges. There were no labels or packaging materials discovered, no fingerprints anywhere in the warehouse, and no particles of skin or hair to yield DNA. Police theorize that the chemist used latex gloves, even to open doors, and disposable "clean room" suits, caps, and booties to avoid leaving biological traces.

When questioned, the chemist stood mute and police were not able to make an arrest. Subsequently he sold his house and left his girlfriend, and is thought to have assumed a new identity and resumed operations in another city. When police obtained court orders to investigate his known income, they quickly became lost in a maze of corporations in the Bahamas, the Cayman Islands, and Panama. When they investigated his driver's license, they discovered it had been obtained with a phony birth certificate.

THE MORALS OF THIS STORY

1. This subject is a police nightmare: a savvy crook who works alone and does not discuss business with his women or friends.

2. Because of his general unobtrusiveness and care to drive nondescript, legal vehicles, he is almost immune from arrest by routine policing and traffic stops. Even for police detectives, this guy is a tough nut.

3. Investigating his financial affairs would require the active assistance of the U.S. Departments of State, Treasury, and Justice to enforce treaty obligations with foreign governments. For police departments, obtaining such cooperation is difficult.

4. He could be investigated by the FBI or the Drug Enforcement Administration (DEA), which have more resources than local police, but a successful prosecution would require an enormous investment of agents and resources to keep up with the chemist's frequent moves, changes of identity, and wary business practices that negate the government's most powerful investigative tools: consensual monitors, wiretaps, and confidential informants.

9 | SOME MODEST SUGGESTIONS

This is a save-your-butt book, not a save-the-world book. Nonetheless, I want to suggest several needed reforms of the criminal justice system. These will require years of advocacy, legislation, and court rulings to enact. One suggestion, the court phone, will require an entrepreneur with the money, smarts, and patience to build the phone and then navigate the torturous government procurement process.

1. **ABOLISH PROBATION.** The current probation system was originally conceived as a humane way to lessen prison sentences and prepare inmates for freedom. In practice it's become the funnel back into the criminal justice sausage grinder. The reason? Probation requires *skills* that clueless people don't have, such as time management, calendaring, and good manners in dealing with government employees. It also requires *things* clueless people don't have, such as telephones, reliable cars, and mailing addresses. How would you like to be tossed into jail for failing to show up at a meeting or to return a phone call?

Here's how things go down in real life. A clueless misdemeanor offender will be offered a choice of sentence by the prosecutor such as *either* 90 days in jail *or* immediate release and two years' probation. The clueless gork invariably chooses release and inevitably violates probation. Then he's charged with violation of probation (VOP) and "VOPed" back into the system. This time, however, the offender is charged with a felony and faces a longer sentence, followed by more probation and yet more chances to get VOPed right back into the maw of the machine. Probation is not a stride toward freedom; it's outdoor jail.

2. **THREE CITATIONS AND YOU'RE OUT.** Possession of small quantities of drugs, and annoyances such as acting out in front of cops, should be penalized with a citation rather than arrest. This citation should be given on the spot, with a thumbprint and digital photo for identification. This is different from a notice to appear, which requires the offender to go to court and be liable to conviction, arrest, and jail.

The merits of the citation system are threefold. First, it saves people whose basic offense is being clueless, bad mannered, and stupid from being arrested, incarcerated, and sent to jail and the plantations. Second, it tags clueless people without an arrest. Third, information from this citation does not interface with state or federal systems; it is for in-house use only. If they get three citations, then they deserve to be arrested as chronic offenders. It directs police to arrest real bad guys and deemphasizes vacuuming up clueless people to score arrest points.

3. **DRUG COURTS OUTSIDE THE CRIMINAL JUSTICE SYSTEM.** Drug courts are springing up in jurisdictions throughout America. All sentence drug users to treatment rather than prison. The shortcoming of drug courts is that they still involve arrests, jail, and lifetime sentences on the electronic plantation. Until privacy laws restrict the reporting of arrests that do not result in conviction, drug courts must be administered in a way that is not reportable on the NCIC and the World Wide Web. The presiding officers need to be magistrates rather than judges, and should be people whose main qualification is common sense rather than a law degree.

4. **DECRIMINALIZATION OF SMALL QUANTITIES OF DRUGS FOR PERSONAL USE.** An enormous percentage of people arrested are charged with misdemeanor drug possession, which means possession of small amounts for personal use. In many states, the quantity of drugs that will get you busted is extremely small. In Florida, that amount is 20 grams (less than 3/4 ounce) of marijuana,

and any quantity at all of heroin or crack cocaine. Most drug users are pitiful, clueless idiots, not criminals. Raising the weight limit of drugs that constitutes a misdemeanor would empty the jails of petty offenders.

5. **CLUELESS-PEOPLE MANAGEMENT.** Petty offenders are routinely sentenced to drug courts, anger-management classes, and other nonprison alternatives. I suggest the creation of cluelessness-management courses, which might also be entitled Life Lessons for Dummies.

Even professional social workers often have no idea how socially primitive clueless people are. The clueless urgently need Life 101 training. The first lesson? Time, and why the wristwatch, the alarm clock, and the calendar matter. This will support the imperatives of the Welfare Reform Act, which is forcing millions of clueless people to work. Work is a powerful socializer, and the only mechanism for socialization that can possibly be successful with adults who were raised without effective parents. No one, however, can learn job skills and rudimentary good manners unless they can wake up, dress up, and show up.

6. **SINGLE HEARINGS.** Almost all criminal justice sentencing is via negotiated pleas that avoid the necessity of trial. The problem is that in the course of the plea bargaining, multiple calendar hearings are held, during which the judge inquires about the progress of the negotiations. Defendants are often required to appear at these pro forma proceedings. Given the staff effort and time needed to merely locate, much less awaken, clothe, and transport defendants, these proceedings should be compressed into a single hearing for petty offenses. If hearings were held after 11:00 A.M. it would be helpful. Clueless people cannot, repeat *cannot*, get it together before that hour.

7. **SHRINK THE ELECTRONIC PLANTATION.** The United States urgently needs privacy laws. Reports of arrests that do *not* lead to convictions should be available only to law enforcement and abso-

lutely denied to private companies and individuals. They should also be denied to *judges*. Reason? Judges routinely consider prior arrests, not convictions, in setting sentences. This is an outrage.

8. **ABOLISH POLICE PINBALL.** Cops shouldn't be encouraged to play games with people's lives. Police should be rated, promoted, and compensated the way federal law enforcement officers are—by the quality, not the quantity, of arrests. What counts are arrests leading to convictions, not just the number of dummies vacuumed off the pavement and tossed into the sneezer.

9. **ESTABLISH ON-DUTY PROSECUTORS AND STATE'S ATTORNEYS.** Having prosecutors available 24/7 to consult with police by telephone will allow the state to make a preliminary determination about whether there is probable cause for an arrest, whether there is evidence to make a case, and whether a person stopped by police should be arrested or freed. This enhances the state's ability to protect citizens while safeguarding individual rights and discouraging mass arrests on flimsy pretexts.

10. **COURT PHONES.** This is my own flash of genius-level insight, which I will promote herewith. One thing you can always count on with clueless people is a tendency to vanish. Many have cell phones, but these are often stolen "burner" phones, which are likely to conk out any minute when the free airtime expires and just as likely to be answered by someone who stole the phone a second time or picked it up behind a table at some bar.

My suggestion is the court phone, a specialized cell phone. First, it would have no dial pad, so it could not be used for outgoing calls and would have no resale value to invite theft. Second, only attorneys and court officers would have court-phone numbers. Thus the only callers would be officers of the court, and their only purpose would be to wake up defendants and get them to dress up and mosey on down to court, preferably postbreakfast, postcoffee, and postcigarettes.

The court phone is really just a voice version of the hockey puck beepers that chain restaurants give out that buzz and blink when your table is ready or your food is done. Naturally, the court phone would not have an off switch. It would also have a GPS locator chip so that investigators could periodically sweep through bars and hangouts and scarf up phones that get separated from overly relaxed defendants.

Perhaps the court phone would be better designed as a Dick Tracy wrist radio attached with a titanium steel band and non-pickable lock. It could be removed only by a court officer or someone adept (highly adept) with a torch or diamond drill.

This is it for our brief overview of the criminal justice system. As I've said, the system isn't fair. What matters is that the system exists, and you have to deal with it as it is. So we'll spend no more time pondering reforms and instead concentrate, in Parts II and III, on practical arrest-proofing methods to keep you out of jail *right here, right now!*

PART II

ARREST PROOFING
ON THE STREETS

10 | COP A 'TUDE AND YOU GET SCREWED

People get arrested all the time for copping a 'tude with cops. *'Tude* is short for *attitude*, defined as being defiant, rude, and in your face. Too many people consider attitude to be more "real" than polite behavior. In a perfect world, being obnoxious would not be a crime. Right now, in these United States, attitude will earn you a ride downtown, a strip search, and a diet of beanie-weenies and baloney sandwiches.

When you get an attitude, you're helping the cops, not yourself. Attitude does the following things.

>> It turns a routine inquiry ("Hey you, c'mere!") into an opportunity to make an arrest.

>> It allows police to use "inciters" to make you flee, strike an officer, or resist.

When you're upset, you're vulnerable because your emotions are raging and you can't think clearly. Cops will take advantage of this, intensify routine questioning, and then search you and your vehicle. They may use inciters, such as whispered insults or a quick poke with the baton. If they're successful in provoking you, they can upgrade a simple inquiry, traffic ticket, or misdemeanor into a felony bust. This scores more points for the cops. For you it doubles your legal fees, sends your bail amount soaring, and guarantees a stretch in the pen. It also puts a serious crime header on your NCIC information, so you can count on a lifetime of tough police scrutiny.

Here's an example. My coauthor lives in a condo. Late one night he hears a tremendous crash. Four guys in a convertible have smashed through the security gate and are heading to a party. They're laughing; they're drunk; they're crazy to get laid.

My buddy calls the cops, who break up the good times and round up the miscreants. The lead cop is about six-foot-seven, with 300 pounds of solid muscle. He's got forearms the size of Virginia hams and probably drives nails with his thumbs. Of course the cop has a gun, a baton, Mace, and a partner with more of everything. The four party animals are white, scrawny, and short. These punks think the four food groups are Marlboros, Slim Jims, Juicy Fruit, and Budweiser. So do these guys say, "Sorry, officer. We'll be happy to pay for any damages," and go free?

No! They get an attitude. They direct obscentity-laced insults at the cops. Both cops laugh. They can't believe these midgets are so stupid. Naturally, when the cops recover, they reply, "Gentlemen, face the cruiser, spread your legs, and assume the position I'm sure you're familiar with." The cops hook the four up and head downtown. The giant cop even thanks them! On a slow night, he's suddenly got four misdemeanor busts. His sergeant will be impressed.

Attitude, not a property crime, got these guys arrested. Assuming no serious crime has been committed, attitude determines whether you get busted. If you have committed a crime, attitude determines how you're charged—and whether and how long you'll be in jail. Police have wide discretion. They can choose to set you free, give you a notice to appear, which sends you to court without being arrested, or take you downtown and toss you into the calaboose.

Staying calm and polite in the presence of police is incredibly important, even if you're guilty and have been caught in the act. Attitude with cops increases the number of charges, upgrades charges from misdemeanor to felony, and allows add-on charges. When attitude leads you to resist, it justifies police *beating the living daylights out of you!* Know what kind of medical care is available at most jails? Lousy.

This means that, in the presence of police, you have to act, briefly, like middle-class Americans. Cops themselves are middle class. They respect the middle class and will cut some slack for people who act middle class. If you're poor, uneducated, and have bad manners, you're going to have to tone it *up* and act middle class for at least a few minutes. If you're rich, arrogant, and condescending, you're gonna have to tone it *down* and get humble and polite. Contrary to common opinion, cops absolutely love to bust rich guys.

Now, readers, before you get your cultural hackles up, pay attention. I'm not advising you to jump into the cultural melting pot and emerge transformed into white-bread Americans. All I'm recommending is good manners, common sense, and prudence. These things work for any skin color and culture and in any language. As an attorney I will defend to the death your God-given right to hip-hop till you drop, wave the Confederate battle flag, get down with your *carnales*, or do anything else your multicultural heart desires. I'm merely recommending that you behave like a middle-class American for *five freaking minutes* while you're in front of cops.

OK?

11 | DIRTY COP TRICKS

As discussed in the introduction, police offices are more honest, better disciplined, and better trained than ever. They have computers in their cruisers and excellent radio and cell phone communications with headquarters. This can be a problem for you, since this means that cops can make more arrests, and better arrests, than ever before. Nonetheless cops still use tricks to increase their arrest numbers and to pile on charges that upgrade their arrests from misdemeanor to felony. Some of these are unfair; some are unethical; others are illegal. Most are known as inciters because they get you angry and crazy and goad you to fight or flee. Get to know them all.

THE IN-YOUR-FACE SCREAM-OUT. This is the most common, and *legal*, inciter. During a scream-out, a cop will get an inch or so from your face and start yelling. You'll get covered with spit; your glasses will fog with hot, humid cop breath, and your nostrils will fill with whatever the cop last ate. (Pray it was doughnuts and not pizza with anchovies.) If you raise your hands to cover your face, you're "resisting arrest." If you run, you're "fleeing arrest." If you shove the cop backward, you're committing "battery on a law enforcement officer." Any of these escalates a simple encounter or penny-ante misdemeanor into a felony—more points for the cop, and more grief, expense, and jail time for you.

My coauthor was actually the victim of a scream-out in the cop-infested town of Miami Springs in 2000. He's a fat, balding white guy who was wearing a white shirt and tie at the time. The guy looks like an accountant or a supermarket manager. This is to emphasize that no one is immune from police harassment. There's only one arrest-proofing move when you're on the receiving end of a scream-out. This is a standing defensive position. Here's what you do.

>> Stand straight.

>> Grip your hands to your pants legs. Do not put your hands into your pockets, as this can be interpreted as an attempt to reach for a weapon. Do not raise your arms, as this is considered resisting arrest in many states.

>> Close your eyes and mouth to minimize spit ingestion.

>> Be absolutely silent. Don't react. Don't let the cop know he's getting to you.

>> Hang in there until the cop runs out of breath and stops yelling.

If you avoid responding to this inciter, you have a better chance of going free or avoiding add-on charges.

THE TOUCHY-FEELY. Cops will touch you, often with a hand placed softly on the shoulder, to check your levels of stress and nervousness. They may bore in with the finger or give you a shove to incite you to do something that makes you arrestable. When they search you, they may poke you in the balls or give you a hard squeeze for the same reason. This inciter is unethical, but difficult to use as a legal defense because it's done surreptitiously and is difficult to prove.

You will probably be up against a wall or leaning on the cruiser while you're being searched. No matter what, stay still and do not respond to this inciter. If the squeeze hurts unbearably, *do not run or resist.* Drop to the ground in the fetal ball position. Protect your head. Try to get your head under the cruiser away from batons and steel-capped shoes. Remember, if cops start beating you, they *have* to charge you with resisting arrest. If they don't, they will be admitting to brutality.

PROVOCATIVE WHISPERS, LEWD COMMENTS, RACIAL SLURS, ETHNIC INSULTS, AND VERBAL JABS. When cops use racial and ethnic insults, it's illegal, but difficult to prove. An adroit cop can give you a verbal shot so quietly and unobtrusively that it cannot be heard or seen by bystanders. Many clueless people (and quite a few otherwise savvy citizens) are hot tempered. Cops take advantage to whisper an insult to get you to act out and commit a felony.

There are only two defenses. First and foremost, just stand there motionless and silent. Pocket the insult. Just take it. The only way you win an encounter with police is by staying free. If your brain is operational and the encounter is being video recorded (check for a small camera on the dash of the cruiser) a second defense is to position yourself so that the cop stands full face or in profile to the camera and any witnesses. This means the camera and witnesses will record his lips moving, and either discourage insults or give you a stout defense if arrested.

THE BATON AND FLASHLIGHT POKE. In hand-to-hand combat, police are trained to thrust batons and steel flashlights straight ahead rather than rear back and hit with them. The reason is that these weapons are more difficult to parry when pushed straight into a vulnerable body part, usually the solar plexus beneath the sternum in the center of the rib cage.

They may use this training to give you a discreet poke that will not be visible to witnesses and video cameras. A shot to the solar plexus will double you over and cause you to gasp, choke, move your arms involuntarily, or throw up. A shot to the balls or throat will be even more dramatic.

The only defense is to drop to the ground in a fetal ball position. This will protect you from resisting and battery charges if witnesses and cameras are present, and it will protect your body even if they aren't. This is an illegal inciter, but it is difficult to prove. Try to get your head under the cruiser. You can take quite a few shots to the ribs, but if the cops crack your coconut, you're done.

THROW-DOWN GUNS AND DOPE. Crooked cops can plant guns and dope on you to make a felony bust or to justify having beaten or shot you. This is a high-risk crime for the cops. If a partner squeals, or if the crime-scene guys see something odd about the setup and call for an internal affairs investigation, the cop faces indictment, dismissal from the force, and a long stretch in the penitentiary. If you survive, you can sue the city. Some courts may set aside sovereign immunity and pain-and-suffering damage caps in cases so heinous. You may end up with a pot of money, but you will do some time in jail and the hospital before you get it.

When you are being provoked with inciters, practice Uncle Dale's Golden Rule #3:

> ≫ **GIVE COPS YOUR NAME AND BASIC INFO, THEN SHUT THE HECK UP!**

Of course, some grunts, screams, and a bit of whimpering may be unavoidable. Those flashlights and batons really hurt. If you have to cry, just let those tears flow. I cry, too, when I go to the hospital and the morgue and see what dirty cops have done to my clients.

12 | PEEKABOO! PEEKABOO! DON'T LET BIG BAD COPS SEE YOU

I n this chapter I'm going to discuss how police officers target suspects for questioning and arrest. The more you know about what cops look for, the more you can avoid looking like cop bait. There are three factors.

1. **VISIBILITY.** Cops first have to *see* you to stop and arrest you. Remember, cops are visual predators who drive around in cars and score points by making arrests. This is the basis for Uncle Dale's Golden Rule #1:

   >> **IF COPS CAN'T SEE YOU, THEY CAN'T ARREST YOU.**

   People always ask, "Is it really that simple?" Yep, it is.

2. **THE CROOK PROFILE.** When you look like a crook, strut like a crook, and act like a crook, the police, naturally, will want to know whether you *are* a crook.

3. **INCONGRUITY.** Incongruity is a fancy word that means that you look out of place, like you don't belong somewhere. Remember, cops are not only visual predators, they're curious predators. When you look out of place on the street, cops will stop you merely out of curiosity.

SEARCH WARRANTS AND PLAIN VIEW

Clueless people smoke and carry dope on the street, where cops can see them, stop them, and search them. Savvy people do their drugs in their homes or fenced backyards, and the cops drive by without stopping *because they can't see them.* Not only do the cops not *see* them, they can't *get at* them. Police generally cannot search a house without a warrant. On TV, cops get warrants with a phone call. In real life, it's never so simple, especially for patrol officers. To get a warrant, a patrol cop first has to go to his superiors, and they have to go to department attorneys who then have to present a written request to a judge. This is a lot of aggravation, and no patrol cop is going to get a warrant unless big-time crime is going on. During my years with the Miami Police Department, I only sought a warrant one time.

Most people have exaggerated ideas about their privacy rights and the need for police to get warrants. I'm not going to go into the legal theory and precedent of search warrants because, in practice, it's simple. If you're doing something *in plain view* that makes police suspect a crime, they generally can search without a warrant. If you're inside and *not* in plain view, a warrant is required. The short version is this: if the cops can see you, they can search you.

Most people are under the mistaken impression that police cannot search them on the street. Generally, with a few restrictions, they can. As a practical matter, assume that cops can search you any time they can *see* you. Want to be all right? Stay out of sight.

IDS ON THE STREET

Years ago cops could arrest people for walking around without an ID. Fortunately, courts have ruled that statutes and ordinances requiring citizens to carry an ID when they are not driving are unconstitutional.

Nonetheless, I recommend that you carry an ID at all times. The reason is simple. If you're stopped by police, they will ask for an ID. If you have one, police are less likely to ask follow-up questions. The more questions police ask, the more likely you are to lie, make a mistake, act out, and get arrested. In fact, in another chapter I'm going to recommend that you carry "street creds"—a special form of detailed ID, for police use only, which will address cops' curiosity about who you are and reduce the number of questions they ask you.

Streets are where cops work and where cops rule. The more time you spend on the cops' turf, the more likely you are to be stopped and questioned. The more you're stopped, the more field interrogation (FI) reports about you are entered into criminal justice computers. This occurs even if you're doing nothing and don't get arrested. The more FI reports cops have about you, the more thoroughly you'll be interviewed. The cops are thinking, not illogically, that if other cops are stopping you all the time, you must be up to *something*, right?

To stay free, you have to do the following.

1. Stay out of sight of police.

2. Avoid being stopped and questioned.

3. Avoid having information about you entered into the system—even if the questioning does not result in an arrest.

PROFILING

This word makes people nuts, but it's really just a formalized process for doing what everyone does all the time naturally, which is to give meaning to perceptions by comparing what we perceive to what we know from experience. Minority activists maintain that police profiling is racial. They're usually wrong. It's *behavioral*. Cops know certain behaviors are more likely to result in a valid arrest than others. They talk to bad guys all day, every day. They know what bad guys look like, walk like, talk like, and act like. When they see someone who fits their crook profile, they stop the person and say, "Hey, you. C'mere." Cops are trained to make assumptions about what they see. Have a look at the diagram, taken from police training materials, on the next page. It shows silhouettes of a man talking on the telephone. You can easily guess what the man is doing, based on his posture. In other words, you match the *perception* of the man on the telephone to a *profile* that you have about the way people behave.

LOOK LIKE A CROOK? HOW DUMB CAN YOU GET?

For cops, the crook profile works most of the time. For example, I've arrested numerous guys who were carrying large boxes of stolen goods on the street. Think about this. In contemporary America, legal goods are delivered by truck and brought to the door on a handcart. If you're walking around with a big box and not pushing it on a handcart, cops will want to stop you and peek inside. Why? You fit the crook profile.

Burglars, for example, sometimes put socks over their hands to avoid leaving fingerprints. Amazingly, they then walk down the street still wearing the socks! Every cop will immediately stop sock-handed strollers. This means if you're a puppeteer who performs with sock puppets, you might want to roll those bad boys up and hide them when outdoors. Similarly, toting stereos and TVs on the street, and carrying anything in a pillowcase, gets immediate police scrutiny. In Miami I stopped this guy who was wearing a thick wool peacoat in 90-degree heat. Inside the coat was—drum roll—five pounds of reefer. The guy never could figure out how I knew he had the dope. Moral? In the tropics, it is always best to wear short sleeves while committing crimes.

Here's an example from police training materials I have used myself. These silhouettes of a man talking on a pay phone are generally interpreted as follows: Left figure is a businessman. Middle figure is a guy talking to his wife. Right figure is a man making a suspicious call. Almost without thinking, you make a surmise by comparing the observed behavior to a preconception. In other words, you profile.

Anytime you're visible on the streets and do something that appears furtive or criminal, the cops are going to check you out. When the police cruiser rolls into view and you suddenly pop something into your mouth (as in drugs), pull your hat down to conceal your face, or suddenly change direction, you're going to see the blue lights flash. If you have bulges in your clothing that look like concealed weapons, ditto. When you make a metallic clanking that sounds like a weapon—watch out! Here are some other behaviors that fit the crook profile and will get you stopped:

>> carrying pry bars and hammers without a toolbox or work clothes

>> running on the street and not wearing running clothes and shoes

>> being under 16 and on the streets during school hours

>> crouching in bushes

THE BEAUTY OF INCONGRUITY—IF YOU'RE A COP

Cops profile all the time by matching what they see to their crook profile developed by training and experience. What happens, however, when they see something that doesn't fit a profile? This is an incongruity. Cops react to incongruity differently than ordinary people.

When civilians see an incongruity, it makes them nuts. Let's use a hypothetical example. Suppose you see two attractive women, dressed identically, with identical makeup and hairstyles. They are tied back to back around the middle and at the ankles. They are walking sideways, like crabs, in sync, along a downtown sidewalk. They appear calm and unconcerned. Hmm? When you see something like this, you immediately start to wonder what's up. Are the women actresses? Maybe they're part of a publicity stunt. Why are they tied together? Why do they look alike? In asking these questions you're frantically searching for a meaningful profile but can't find one.

The difference between ordinary people and cops is that police officers don't have to imagine what's going on; they can find out. They're curious predators, trained and paid to be nosy. When they don't understand something, they just spin the lights, stop whatever's going on, and start with the questions.

Cops are incredibly attuned to incongruity. Because they patrol the same areas at the same times day after day, they immediately see anything that doesn't fit in. Then they pounce. This is how many clueless people get swept up into the criminal justice system. Not knowing how to fit into society (or not caring) is the essence of cluelessness. Here are examples of incongruities that would make cops curious and stimulate them to make a stop:

>> beat-up car cruising slowly by million-dollar homes

>> man in tuxedo strolling along loading docks at midnight with no ships at the docks

>> dogs howling uncontrollably

>> yells, screams, doors slamming

>> Daimler Maybach limousine (a $300,000 automobile) cruising the barrio

>> woman in evening gown walking alone on a dirt road

Note that the above activities are not illegal, just unusual. They make curious cops want to stop the people involved and find out more.

THE ARREST-Q

The more you're visible, fit the crook profile, or are incongruous, the more likely you are to get stopped and questioned by police. I call this likelihood your Arrestability Quotient, or Arrest-Q. The following chart indicates the factors that make you arrestable. When you have a high Clue-Q (i.e., you're highly clueless) and a high Arrest-Q, you're meat for the criminal justice sausage grinder.

This isn't fair. In 21st-century America, as long as you're not committing a crime, you should be able to wear the wildest clothes you want, roam the streets when you feel like it, and lean on a light post or hang out at some wild club if it amuses you. TV, the movies, and magazines constantly exhort you to be free and do your thing, whatever that is. Isn't that what life, liberty, and the pursuit of happiness (without the cops butting in rudely) are all about? Answer: theoretically, yes; practically, no.

ARRESTABILITY QUOTIENT (ARREST-Q)		
ARRESTABILITY METER	Medium / Low / High	Medium / Low / High
CLOTHING	Hip-hop, dirty, punk	Neat casual, dress, work
HAIR	Long, greasy, shaved, dreadlocks, Afro, etc	Cut and combed
SMELL	Ripe, "stank"	Low
SOUND	Loud	Quiet or normal
SPEECH	Ebonics, white trash, Spanglish	Standard English
EXPLETIVES	Profanity, obscenity	None or cornball ("Gee!")
ATTITUDE	Angry, defiant, shifty	Cooperative, polite
BODY TENSION	High	Low
EYES	Darting back and forth	Straight ahead
TATOOS & PIERCINGS	Yes	No
POSTURE	Slouched, turned away	Straight, facing officer
GANG COLORS	Yes	No
SWASTIKAS	Yes	No
TRANSVESTITE CLOTHING	Yes	No
CONFEDERATE BATTLE FLAGS	Yes	No

CONTINUED NEXT PAGE ☞

ARRESTABILITY QUOTIENT (ARREST-Q) CONTINUED		
ARRESTABILITY METER	Medium / Low / High (arrow pointing High)	Medium / Low / High (arrow pointing Low)
OUTRAGEOUS T-SHIRTS	Yes	No
PRO-DOPE INSIGNIA	Yes	No
DOPE	Yes	No
ALCOHOL	Carrying	Not carrying
CONCEALED WEAPON	Yes, w/o permit	No, or yes w/permit
SOCKS ON HANDS	Yes	No
CARRYING LARGE BOX	Yes	No, or with handcart
DROPPING SOMETHING SUDDENLY	Yes	No
SUDDEN DIRECTION CHANGE	Yes	No
HAT CONCEALING FACE	Yes	No
METALLIC SOUNDS	Yes	No
CONCEALING SOMETHING IN MOUTH	Yes	No
THROWING SOMETHING AWAY	Yes	No
BULGES IN CLOTHING	Yes	No
WALKING STYLE	Hoodlum strut	Normal walk

The media, which promote this craziness, are not in business to *give* life lessons. Their business is to *sell* carefully crafted illusions in magazines, newspapers, and television. Those gangsta rappers and badass barrio boys strutting down the streets in videos are actually well-educated young millionaires sashaying down soundstages where producers, directors, makeup artists, and lighting technicians tweak the illusion. If you think this is reality, and how you should behave, you'll spend way too much time talking with guys in blue uniforms. One of the ironies of contemporary life is what befalls gangsta rappers when they start to hang with real hoodlums. The entertainers are always shocked—*shocked!*—when actual gangsters cheat them, steal their money, horn in on their businesses, and, if annoyed, shoot them with real bullets. Imagine that! The moral? If you profile like a crook, you're likely to be arrested like a crook.

ARRESTABILITY BY AREA

Common sense says that when you're visible in high-crime areas, you're likely to get arrested. Cops there are keyed up and on the hunt. High-crime districts attract the toughest, wiliest, and most ambitious cops who want to lead their departments in felony arrests, rack up points, and be first in line for promotions. The following chart indicates arrestability by area. You can judge how likely you are to be arrested based on which areas you frequent.

Here's an example of what happens when you hang out in high arrestability areas. Some years ago my coauthor made the mistake of letting some Peruvian buddies convince him to go to a notorious Miami strip joint. People were snorting cocaine and having sex in the bathrooms while the girls boogalooed on stage. Suddenly a door flies open and all sorts of local and federal cops pour in. Pandemonium! My buddy and the Peruvians, fortunately, managed to bolt through an emergency exit and beat feet down an alley while less alert* clubgoers were being arrested. Apparently the feds were after a Russian hustler who was meeting a Colombian

---

* Another reason not to take drugs is that they make you not only stupid, but also slow. The extra half second of reflex time you gain by being straight and sober is useful in emergencies. On that night my buddy was sipping diet cola, since he has deeply felt moral objections to paying $10 for a can of beer.

drug trafficker to sell him a used Soviet submarine so the cartel could ship drugs *underneath* U.S. Navy ships patrolling the Caribbean. Moral: Don't hang out in drug-crazed clubs where Russian mafiosi play footsie with the cartel. On that particular night, that club had the highest arrestability quotient of any place on planet Earth. *¡Caramba!*

Even though certain locations are not high-crime areas, they have a medium arrestability quotient due to in-house security staff and sophisticated video surveillance and antitheft devices. Such places include schools, casinos, airports, sports stadiums, and stores. Locations with the lowest arrest potential are private homes, workplaces, police stations, and courthouses. The last two are so full of cops that committing a crime there is not merely clueless but mentally deranged.

ARRESTABILITY BY AREA

High	Medium	Low
Housing projects	School	Home
"Druggy" apartments	Athletic events	Friends' houses
Gang neighborhoods	Stores	Work
Streets	Airports	Buses & trains
Car	Casinos	Courthouse
Outside Clubs		Police station
Warehouses after dark		
Parks, playgrounds		
Concerts		
Cockfights		
Gambling joints		

HOW THE SHARKS HUNT

Think of cops as sharks with large brains and high-tech enhancements. Their hunting behaviors are almost identical to those of higher predators. They approach everyone as quarry. For prey identification, they utilize all their senses. They look with the edges of their eyes at night to detect motion with the more sensitive rods at the periphery of the retina. They listen for the rustle of grass, the rumble of a car motor, the clank of a round being chambered in an automatic weapon. They can smell guilt and fear when suspects exude a stench derived from proteins and oils excreted during stress.

Cops seek indications of whether a suspect is nervous or guilty. A twist of the head or flick of the eyes tells them the suspect is about to bolt. Often they will touch someone they're interviewing to discover whether the person is tense. Every cop has to decide whether the person encountered is citizen (nonarrestable) or prey (arrestable). If one or two cop/sharks are not sufficient, they will call up reinforcements for cooperative hunts that seal off a block or neighborhood. When their eyes, ears, and noses are not sensitive enough, they can spin up a helicopter with forward-looking infrared (FLIR) scanners that detect the prey's body heat. They can use high-tech microphones to listen and ultra-miniature video cameras and fiber optics to watch, even inside buildings. Once you have been acquired as a target, resistance, as they say, is futile.

So stay away from these predators. Don't annoy or defy them. They *will* get you.

13 | WHATCHA GONNA DO
WHEN THEY COME FOR YOU?*

I t's action time. Imagine that you're on the street. You see blue lights. You hear the siren whoop. You listen to the unmistakable roar of the Crown Vic cruiser. Quick! Whatcha gonna do?

Answer: nothing.

Police are visual predators. Any sudden change in motion, speed, direction, or behavior immediately attracts their attention. It's an incongruity. I can expand this advice by saying: *whatever you were doing before the police appeared, keep doing it.*

>> If you were a hoodlum strutting down the street, keep strutting.

>> If you were leaning on a light pole and staring at the sky, keep staring.

>> If you were arguing with a woman, keep arguing. (Women will help you.)

>> If your shoes were untied, leave them untied.

>> If you were walking the dog, keep the pooch moving.

>> If your hat was on sideways, leave it sideways.

>> If you were dancing, don't let your feet lose the beat.

>> If you were carrying something, keep carrying it.

>> If you were hiding, stay hidden.

---

* This is the famous lyric from the TV show *Cops*. I love the music. Bad boys are my business.

Police watching the scene are aware of a pattern of people, place, and motion. Change triggers the urge to hunt and pursue. This sounds easy to avoid, but it's not. It's natural to feel guilty around police. You immediately start thinking about dumb or illegal things you have done (or are doing). So what things trigger the police's hunting urge?

>> pulling your hat brim down to cover your face

>> slouching low and turning away

>> slowing suddenly

>> stopping to cough, look at your nails, or read a sign

>> picking up something off the street

>> changing direction

>> waving cheerily as the cruiser passes (unless you know the officers personally)

>> starting to talk loudly

>> feeling your pockets

>> shoving your hands into your pockets

>> pulling out the cell phone

For the ladies, here are a few cop stoppers:

>> stopping to dig around in your purse

>> looking around frantically

>> suddenly starting to sing or hum

Of course, some behaviors almost guarantee a stop.

>> throwing something you were holding (as in drugs)

>> putting something in your mouth (ditto)

>> throwing up (as in, those drugs you swallowed didn't go down so good)

>> dropping anything metallic (as in, burglar tools or a weapon)

>> reaching inside your jacket or belt or around your ankles (where pistols are worn)

>> running

>> ducking out of sight

>> flipping the bird

>> dropping your pants to show the full moon

>> silently mouthing insults

You think I'm kidding? No one could be so stupid. Right? Think again! You could not imagine how dumb people can be. Cops are the kings of the street, yet people actually drop their drawers and waggle their fannies at them. They start yelling, heckling, jeering, and flipping the bird. Cops freak them out and make them crazy. All this is a clueless attempt at self-assertion. But enough with the pop psychology. If you want to stay free, don't do this stuff.

The absolutely worst thing you can do is to flag down the officers and attempt to distract them by telling them a nonsense story. All this does is get them interested in you. Here's what you want to do.

>> Don't alter the pattern.

>> Keep on keeping on. Steady as she goes.

>> Keep on trucking.

Got it?

14 | BLUE LIGHT?
       STAY OUT OF SIGHT!

O ne of the most clueless things people do is butt in on police business. Of course it's human nature to do so. You see the blue light, the cruisers, maybe a crime scene van or a K-9 unit. You're curious. You want to know what's going on. Maybe your ego is fragile, and you want to impress yourself and your friends that you aren't afraid of cops. Whatever the motivation, I strongly advise you to stay away from police at all times and in all places except when *you* call them and *you* need them. Then they will be at your service to serve and protect. Otherwise, leave these guys alone.

Consider the obvious. The blue or red light is a warning light. It's telling you to stay away. There is absolutely no advantage to your approaching police, questioning them, or attempting to insert yourself into their operations. First, you won't find out anything. Police are better trained and disciplined than ever, and they will not discuss what they're doing with onlookers, with media, or with anyone except other police or city personnel such as firefighters. On TV shows, reporters get cops to make statements into microphones thrust into their faces. In real life, this rarely happens. Release of police information to the public is generally handled by public information officers, not by uniformed officers on the scene.

The second and most important reason for avoiding cops is that they will immediately wonder what *you* are doing, and why *you* are interested in what's going on. The police have good reason. Arsonists, murderers, and other violent criminals frequently return to the scenes of the crimes they have committed for the thrill of watching the police and wondering if they have outwitted the authorities. In such a scene, cops may question onlookers, ask for IDs, or take photographs or videos of everyone in the vicinity. Even if you're merely curious, it makes no sense to have cops questioning you, filing field interrogation (FI) reports into police computers and in general inspecting your person and asking you questions. If you obstruct an investigation or lie to a police officer, *you have just committed a crime and are subject to arrest.*

Third, if you're driving a car, you're likely to get into an accident as more and more police cruisers zoom around corners and rush to the scene. Worse, if you obstruct an investigation with your vehicle, the cops may inspect it to see if the tag is current, if the tires are good, or if there is a light out. They then will give you not only a ticket, but also an opportunity to act out and get arrested. How delightful.

There's a fourth reason to avoid crime scenes. If the cops are arresting serious criminals—say, drug dealers, armed robbers, or murderers—do you want such people to associate you with their arrests? They may decide that you ratted them out or that you are a police informant. These guys hurt and kill people. You do not want to get involved in any way with their arrests.

The absolute worst thing you can do is hang around a crime scene, get excited by a mob of onlookers, and start to heckle the police. When you yell things like "Why don't you leave this guy alone and go arrest some real crooks," you're saying something cops have heard hundreds of times. If you start with yelling profanities, *you might actually succeed in annoying cops.* This is not wise. Cops are jerk-processing specialists. All day, all night, all year cops deal with disagreeable, annoying people. Handling you will be no problem at all.

Please note, and this is important: The way I advise you to act around an active crime scene is *exactly opposite* of how you should act when the cops are merely cruising by, which was discussed in the preceding chapter. When the cops are patrolling in your area and approach *you*, you want to keep a steady state and make no sudden changes. When *you* approach the *cops*, however, as they're working a crime scene or auto accident, you should change direction, turn around, cross the street, or do whatever it takes to get out of there. Cops *expect* you to clear the area. So when you approach a crime scene or accident investigation, here's what you *don't* do.

>> Ask cops questions.

>> Touch a police officer, his equipment, his dog, or his vehicle.

>> Start talking loudly with other onlookers.

>> Start yelling insults or hollering about police brutality.

>> Jump in front of a television camera, wave, and shout, "Hi, Mom!"

>> Touch crime-scene caution tape or enter the crime scene.

>> Spit on the pavement to show your contempt of authority.

>> Do wheelies on your bicycle to impress the police.

Here's what you *should* do.

>> Stop, change direction, turn around, and get out of there.

>> Walk away slowly. Do not suddenly start running. Do not hide or dart into an alley or backyard.

>> Stop your car, make a turn, and get out of there.

>> Drive slowly and reasonably. Do not screech the tires or speed away.

Simple, huh? Stay free, my friends. Stay free.

15 | IF YOU LIE, THE COPS WILL PRY

The reason I so strongly advise you to make all reasonable efforts to avoid being stopped and questioned by police is that once you're stopped, even if you're completely innocent, you can commit crimes right in front of cops that can get you arrested. You can go from innocent to guilty in minutes by doing things that you don't even realize are crimes.

The most common of these is lying. That's right, lying to a police officer is a crime. It's not a major crime, but it's enough to get you busted, and it's an excellent add-on charge. Remember, once a cop has stopped you, he doesn't score a point unless he makes an arrest. By now you know you don't want even a single arrest.

WHY LYING TO ORDINARY PEOPLE WORKS

When you lie to most people, it often works because ordinary people

>> assume that you are telling the truth

>> do not ask follow-up questions because to do so is rude

>> are busy and generally do not take time to verify what you say

Let's take a hypothetical example of an ordinary lie, no doubt repeated a million times a day between a mother and a teen-aged son.

MOM: Where're you going, Joey?

JOEY: I'm going to play ball with my buddies.
(Mom doesn't say anything more. Joey strolls out of the house with a little weed in his pocket.)

Now, in reality, Joey is not going to play ball. He's going to sneak over to his girlfriend's place, get high, and have some fun. As long as he actually does play ball now and then with his buddies, and is smart enough to wash off the lipstick, perfume, and dope smell before he comes home, he's likely to get away with this little lie. His mother is busy, and she's not going to drop what she's doing and go to the baseball field or basketball court to verify this statement. Also, she doesn't ask follow-up questions because this generates distrust and can start an argument.

WHY LYING TO COPS DOESN'T WORK

Lying to cops is more difficult because

- » cops *assume* that people will lie to them
- » cops always ask follow-up questions
- » cops have resources to verify what you say
- » cops don't mind being rude and nosy because they're paid and trained to be that way
- » the way cops ask questions will cause you to hesitate and give yourself away
- » cops are scary and will exert subtle and not-so-subtle psychological pressure while they question you

Let's take a typical street stop, and an interview with the same hypothetical teenaged guy as he walks down the street and attracts the attention of a police officer.

COP: Hey, you. C'mere.

JOEY: Huh?

COP: You got some ID?

JOEY: Uh, no.

COP: What's your name?

JOEY: Uh, Fred.

COP: What's your last name, Fred?

JOEY: Uh, Smith.

COP: So where do you live, *Fred Smith*? It is *Fred Smith*, isn't it?

JOEY: Uh, yeah. Where do I live? Uh, 123 Main Street. Yeah.

COP: (Writing all this down) Where're you going, Fred?

JOEY: Uh, I'm going to play ball with my buddies.

COP: Where are you and your buddies playing ball today?

JOEY: Uh, well, we play, uh, at Downtown Park.

COP: Hold on a second. Stay right there.

JOEY: OK.
(Cop gets into the cruiser and taps at a notebook computer mounted near the dashboard. A moment later, he gets out of the car, walks right up to Joey, and puts his face inches away.)

COP: Fred, I've got a problem. When I punched your address into that computer over there, it told me that 123 Main Street isn't your home. You want to help me out with this?

JOEY: Well, uh, yeah. I mean, no. I mean, it isn't my home?

COP: No, it isn't. It's a pawnshop, and besides, I drove past Downtown Park just a minute ago and nobody is playing ball there, and Fred isn't your name, and Main Street isn't your home, and pretty much everything you've told me is a lie, isn't it? Why are you lying, *Fred Smith*? Why would you do that? Do you always lie to police officers?

JOEY: Uh, no, I mean uh, yes, I mean no.

COP: (Puts his finger on Joey's chest) What's your real name?

JOEY: Uh, Joey.

COP: Joey, do you have any narcotics on you? Do you have some rock? Some dust? Some weed? You wouldn't be carrying a syringe, would you? Something that would stick me if I put my hand in your pocket? I think I'm going to put my hand in your pockets. (Cop increases pressure of his finger of Joey's chest.)

Joey panics. He runs, but police chase him down and arrest him for lying to a police officer, evading a police officer, resisting arrest, and possession of narcotics. He goes to jail but is sentenced to time served and probation after his attorney pleads the charges down to single misdemeanor. If he misses even one probation call or meeting, he will be arrested and will do serious jail time. He's on the plantation and doesn't even know it.

This is typical of what happens thousands of times a day. If police arrested every young person sneaking out to see a girlfriend or boyfriend with a little happy herb in their pocket or purse, America's high schools, colleges, universities, and—dare I say it?—law schools would be empty. Joey made a mistake in carrying a controlled substance on his person, but he stimulated the police officer to search and arrest him by lying. This fictional dialogue shows why you can't lie to cops.

>> Cops *routinely* apply psychological pressure as they question you. Crowding into Joey's space and poking him with a finger are *legal* inciters. They get the subject emotional so he or she cannot think clearly and lie effectively.

>> Cops ask prying follow-up questions. "Where do you live?" "What's your mother's name?" "Tell me your friends' names and where they live."

>> Cops can verify much of what you tell them. They have cell phones to call anyone you mention. By computer they can verify addresses, licenses, registrations, permits, warrants, criminal records, and much more. Because they constantly drive the neighborhood, they have a better idea of what's going on minute by minute than you do.

>> Because police ask so many follow-up questions, you have to continually make your lies more complex. *It's impossible for most people to elaborate on a lie without hesitating while they think.* The "uhs" and pauses are dead giveaways.

>> Police will ask multiple questions quickly and change subjects within a sentence, confusing you further—if you're lying.

>> Police are adept at reading body language. They often can smell the odor people exude when they are afraid.

>> Pressuring people who lie so that they act out and commit crimes during the interview is how police turn routine stops into arrests that score points.

>> Lying, fleeing, and resisting turn a stop into a big arrest with lots of points. Once the subject flees and resists, dope possession becomes a macho bust instead of a sissy bust. This is important to cops and to their reputations on the force.

Even though our imaginary teenager "Joey" was carrying a controlled substance, he might have avoided arrest if he had simply presented an ID, told the truth, and thereby stopped the officer from asking too many follow-up questions. Here's how it might have worked.

COP: Hey, you. C'mere.

JOEY: Yes, officer?

COP: You got some ID?

JOEY: Yes. (Hands ID to officer.)

COP: So you're Joey Franco.

JOEY: Yes, officer.

COP: You still live at 2435 Elm Street?

JOEY: Yes. I live there with my mom. (Cop goes to cruiser and verifies the ID on the computer and then walks back over to Joey.)

COP: Where're you going, Joey?

JOEY: I'm going over to visit my girlfriend.

COP: Be careful. Be safe. Remember that curfew is 11:00 P.M.

Why do you have a better chance of avoiding arrest, even when you are committing a misdemeanor like carrying a small amount of marijuana, if you tell the truth?

>> When you tell the truth, you do not hesitate, get emotional, or get crazy.

>> When telling the truth, your body language is *congruent* with your story. You do not fidget, slouch, avoid eye contact, or exude the stench of fear.

>> When your story checks out, the officer's incentive is to drive on. Police know that teenagers often carry dope in their pockets, but they generally want something more to make an arrest. Truth does not stimulate the hunting urge.

Truth bores cops. That's a good thing. Remember it.

16 | MAMA WAS RIGHT: STAY HOME AT NIGHT!

Yes, your mother told you, "Don't wander around at night!" Guess what? Mama's right. Every mom and every cop knows there are more bad guys on the streets at night. That's why aggressive cops like I was love the night shift in bad neighborhoods—because that's when and where you make big arrests and rack up lots of points for fast promotion while enjoying the excitement of hunting and capturing the two-legged beast in all his, and occasionally her, nefarious glory.

Nobody has ever done any research on exactly how true your mother's advice is—nobody, that is, except the FBI. As an instructor at the FBI academy, I taught the case of Ted Bundy, the Coed Killer, who began kidnapping and murdering women at Florida State University. The whole country was in an uproar, and the bureau and state and local law enforcement poured people and resources into Florida's capital city. Bundy was an extremely savvy killer and left few clues, so the bureau and local police decided to cordon off parts of the city at night and stop every person and vehicle. It was total shutdown, the big heat. Naturally FBI agents expected to find some fugitives with outstanding warrants and some clueless idiots to be vacuumed up by local police, but what was actually discovered was astounding, even to a former cop like me. Investigators stopped, questioned, and ID checked several thousand people. They found out that, between midnight and 4:00 A.M., *almost everyone interviewed had a criminal record.*

It was incredible. It was a perp parade. Practically every car contained dope, guns, and stolen merchandise. The local cops were going bananas arresting these goons, and the police pinball machine was ringing like a fire alarm as cops made more arrests in an hour than they would normally make in a month and racked up point scores they would never see again in a lifetime.

Tallahassee is a charming small city, the majority of whose inhabitants are state employees and state university faculty, staff, and students. It is not nearly as tough as Miami, New York, Atlanta, L.A., and other big cities. Yet if everyone on the streets late at night in Tallahassee is a present or former crook, the situation in big cities must be the same or worse. It is impossible to study this phenomenon in a scientific fashion because the only way to do so is to stop, question, ID check, and search every person and vehicle. Only law enforcement can do this, and constitutional protection of civil liberties prohibits such actions except under the most exceptional circumstances.

Common sense tells you the same thing. Honest people work during the day. At night they're at home asleep. People who work the night shift are at work at night. The only people wandering around, hanging out or driving in areas where there is no shift work are bad guys. Who else could they be? Law-abiding citizens are all at home sawing logs or on their shift stoking the machine.

TO STAY FREE, STAY HOME

Hanging out at night is one of the biggest items in the crook profile. Solid citizens do not hang out on the streets. They have things to do and places to go. This obvious fact is the reason that, in many jurisdictions, hanging out is a crime called loitering. Hanging out triggers the hunting urge, since cops know that people who hang are likely to be doing something illegal that will enable the cops to make arrests and score points. So to stay out of jail, don't hang out; hang in—out of sight of police.

If you're wandering, hanging out, or driving at night during crook time, generally midnight to 4:00 A.M., police will assume you're up to no good and they'll have an incentive to stop you. Why shouldn't they? You fit the crook profile just by being there. If you're of student age, you're in violation of most cities' curfews. Remember Uncle Dale's Golden Rule #1:

>> **IF COPS CAN'T SEE YOU, THEY CAN'T ARREST YOU.**

As long as you're at home, police not only can't see you, but they also can't get to you without a search warrant. For cops, night transforms the city into a target-rich environment full of high-point-value prey for aggressive, wily nocturnal hunters. So to stay free, stay at home, even if it makes you crazy. Even if your home isn't the best, at least there you can watch TV, play video games, or read a book. In jail, it's lights out at 8:30 P.M.! What a drag.

17 | YOU CAN WIN BY GIVING IN

When you are face-to-face with police, there are two contests going on.

1. **A CONTEST FOR PSYCHOLOGICAL DOMINANCE.** (Who's boss?)

2. **A CONTEST FOR PHYSICAL CUSTODY OF YOUR BODY.** (Do you get arrested or stay free?)

You want to lose the first contest in order to win the second. That's right, lose in order to win. Cops are bosses of the street. They're going to prove it to you anyway, so let them. This costs you nothing. You're in front of the police only for a few minutes. Play your cards right, and you'll win the second contest and stay free. Even if you're carrying dope or have an outstanding warrant, if you let the cops win the psychological game and use other techniques in this book, you're less likely to get searched, ID checked, and arrested. Even if you are arrested, you won't pile up extra charges like resisting arrest, assaulting a law enforcement officer, and lying to police.

In regard to the psychological contest of who's boss, the difference between clueless and savvy people is instructive. Savvy people instantly realize that cops and criminal justice are a separate subculture in which they are *not* players. Whatever power, money, and prestige they have accumulated in their world mean nothing to cops. They acknowledge at once that on the streets cops are boss. In front of cops, savvy people shut up and get polite. They let their lawyers do any arguing that has to be done. They know that the most important contest is staying free. Why get into an argument with a cop and get busted? It's not worth it. So what if the cops prove they're boss as long as the savvy person stays free? As a federal public defender pointed out to me, "Plea bargaining begins on the street."

Clueless people, by definition, do not understand society's games. They do not sense when they move from one social world to the next, and cannot adjust their behavior to fit the circumstances. They try to win the psychological game of Who's Boss. In front of cops, they lie, cuss, and run, and if they're really dumb, they hit the officer. Even if they were innocent when the cops stopped them, they start committing one of those crimes in front of cops.

YES, THIS IS AN INSULT

Being questioned by police is insulting. It makes you feel violated and used. It is, however, less insulting than being arrested. What I'm advising you to do when questioned by police is to pocket the insult. This is difficult and emotionally painful. You must lose the emotional and psychological contest in order to win the custody contest. Trust me. Once the cops leave you alone and you're still free, you'll feel better fast!

A WORD ABOUT SEARCHES

Police are not supposed to search you on the street unless they have reasonable suspicion that you are carrying a weapon or contraband. In bad neighborhoods this rule is a mere formality. Police always have BOLO (be on the lookout) notices for "black male wearing sports clothing," "Hispanic male with tattoos," "white male with facial hair," and so forth. These descriptions fit almost everyone on the street, so on this basis the cops can search just about anybody. In high-crime districts, police can always say they were stopping everyone in the vicinity of a recently committed crime, or that you were acting suspiciously, etc.

Here the wealthy and savvy have advantages. If cops were to stop a rich guy strolling to the first tee at a country club, find some dope, and arrest him, they would get quizzed in court by a highly paid attorney. Did the cops actually have a BOLO for "male wearing Armani jacket and carrying Tiger Woods signature irons and a Callaway Big Bertha driver"? Fat chance. No probable cause. Rich perp gets released to the custody of his buddies at the 19th hole* for some very dry martinis and a thick, juicy steak.

SO WHATCHA GONNA DO?

When cops stop you, you're at bat. Whether you strike out or get a walk (you don't want to get a hit) depends on what you do. Here's what I recommend.

>> **STAND STRAIGHT.** No need to get ramrod stiff and at attention, just straight. This shows respect. Slouching fits the crook profile. Avoid it.

>> **MAKE EYE CONTACT.** Staring at the ground is a suspicious behavior. When police see you flicking your eyes back and forth or twisting your head, they assume you're preparing to flee. Don't do this. Look slightly below the pupil level, not directly into the eyes. Don't smile. Cops don't like smiles.

>> **TELL THE TRUTH.** Lying to police is a crime. Lying is complicated. Telling the truth is simple.

>> **IGNORE INCITERS.** If cops lean into your space and blast you with coffee-and-stale-doughnut-breath, ignore it. If you react, you'll get busted. Even if cops use illegal inciters like racial slurs, ignore it. The game you want to win is your freedom.

>> **BE RESPECTFUL.** Even if you have bad manners, act like a church kid for just a few minutes. It's worth it. The rule is "Cop a 'tude and you get screwed."

>> **DON'T GROVEL OR HUMILIATE YOURSELF.** Some clueless people overcompensate and act like whipped puppies in front of police. You can be polite and maintain your dignity without being disgusting.

---

* For the golf deprived, the 19th hole is the clubhouse, where delicious foods and fine adult beverages are always on the menu.

>> **SAY "YES, OFFICER" AND "NO, OFFICER."** This is polite and shows respect, and will help you avoid saying "Yes, ma'am" to male officers and "Yes, sir" to female officers, which will humiliate and confuse you.

>> **DO NOT RAISE YOUR HANDS, TOUCH THE OFFICER, TOUCH POLICE EQUIPMENT, OR ATTEMPT TO PET POLICE DOGS.** Simply raising your hands ("flailing") is considered, in many jurisdictions, an assault on a law enforcement officer. Keep your hands at your sides. Do not reach into your pockets or bend down to reach for your ankles, which police might consider an attempt to draw a weapon.

>> **DO NOT RUN.** Fleeing police officers is a crime. It also creates reasonable suspicion to justify hands-on contact.

>> **OBEY COMMANDS.** If police issue commands, such as "Come over here and face the car," etc., just do it. Do not argue or question their authority.

In upcoming chapters, I'm going to cover what you say to cops, how to present them with "street creds," and review emergency procedures like crying, throwing up, crapping your pants, etc. What you should remember from *this* chapter, though, is that when you're at bat and the police are pitching questions, be polite, be submissive without being humiliated, and tell the truth. Even if you're naturally snotty and obnoxious, act like a church kid for just a few minutes. If you stay free, you can go back to being your annoying self.

18 | TO AVOID THE TRAGIC, USE WORDS THAT ARE MAGIC

This chapter teaches you words that you can say to police officers that will restrain their impulse to interrogate you and reduce opportunities for you to make a mistake and commit one of those crimes that are done in front of cops. I'm going to ask you to remember and practice some lines, but only a few. Most people are nervous in front of cops, so the words given to memorize will be the fewest possible. In a subsequent chapter I'll provide you "creds" (credentials) to cut out and carry around with you. These have the most important words you need to say printed right on them so you can just read them.

Obviously this advice is for citizens, not crooks. If you're stopped with a nine millimeter shoved into your waistband, a small-caliber automatic holstered on your ankle, boot knives, pockets stuffed with dope, and an overpowering reek of marijuana, just step into the cruiser and have a seat. You're going downtown.

THE QUIZ BEGINS

When cops stop you, they summon you by saying something like, "Hey you, c'mere." Sometimes they spice it up with something more contemporary, like "Yo, player, what's up?" or Chicano slang such as *"Carnal, por aqui."* All this means the same thing: "March yourself over here and face The Man." You know from the preceding chapter what to do. Face the officers calmly, hands at sides, and make eye contact. Here's what you say.

"Officer, have I done something wrong?"

These are magic words. First, they're polite. Second, they're submissive in the proper degree. Third, and most important, they're a question. When you say these words, you toss the ball back to the cops. Now you're questioning them (politely, of course). Often they will tell you why they stopped you. This will let you assess how much trouble you're in and how to react.

Now here's the important part. After you have spoken these magic words, *shut up!* Just stand there and let the cops talk. Do not keep talking yourself, as you will tend to babble, confuse yourself, and start to lie. Here's an example of babbling—exactly what you do not want to do: "Officer have I done something wrong? My God, I was just walking down the street minding my own business. I mean I live around here and was just going to see some guys and why are you questioning me anyhow? Don't you have real crooks to chase? I'm not a crook. I just try to get along here, you know what I mean?"

The technique of responding to police questions is to give them the basic information they ask for truthfully and briefly. Emphasis on briefly. *Do not volunteer information.* This will stimulate follow-ups, verification questions, and requests for information that can be checked by computer.

THE RIGHT TO REMAIN SILENT

You have the right to remain silent. It is not a crime not to talk to police. However, if you have not committed a crime at the time of the stop, I advise you to answer routine questions. Do not assert your right to remain silent because you're annoyed and want to show the cops you have rights. They already know this. Remember, in the preceding chapter I advised you to *lose* the psychological contest so you can *win* the custody contest and stay free. So what do you tell them?

>> your name and address

>> the names of your parents or guardian

>> where you're going

WHAT DO YOU HAVE TO TELL THE COPS?

You have to tell them your name. The Supreme Court has ruled that police may ask you this and that you have to reply except in narrowly defined circumstances. Forget the narrowly defined circumstances. You've got to tell them your name—period.

So tell them. Use your real name; in other words, the name your mother uses. Do not give them a street moniker such as "Bones," "*Carnicerito*" (little butcher) or "Howling Wolf." You do *not* want a street name linked to your real name in police databases via a field interrogation (FI) report. Many street names are common, and whenever a crime is committed and a street name like yours is mentioned, the police will pick you up for interrogation. The whole point of this book is to minimize your contacts with police.

You always want to give cops your basic info: name, relatives, address, and where you are going. The reason not to dummy up completely when you have not committed a crime is that this appears suspicious to police. They will increase the psychological pressure by using legal inciters (touching, crowding, aggressive questioning) and even illegal and unethical inciters (racial and other insults) to get you talking. The cops might even give you a quick jab to the testicles or solar plexus with a flashlight or baton. This will not be seen by onlookers and will be denied by police, but it will leave you curled into a fetal ball and vomiting all over yourself. It will not leave a mark or bruise, so you will not easily be able to sue the city for damages or get the cops disciplined. Once the cops strike you, they will bust you for resisting arrest in order to justify whacking you in the first place. So stay cool, use your head, and do not be a smart-ass with cops. The proper venue for trying civil rights cases is the courts, not the streets.

"WHY ARE YOU HIDING?"

Trespassing is something boys do. It's the nature of the male animal to wander, patrol territory, and take risks. This means that boys are likely to be caught trespassing on private property, where they do not belong. When police patrols pass and you're trespassing, naturally you're going to duck and hide. Remember, if you're hiding when police pass, *stay hidden*. You might get lucky. Once police have you in the spotlight, however, you've got to give it up. When police find you hiding on private property, they suspect two things.

>> You're casing the place for a burglary.

>> You're a Peeping Tom and are looking at women through a window and masturbating.

Regardless of what you're doing, you're going to get asked, "Why are you hiding?" You need to have an answer. I suggest the following.

"Because I'm afraid of police."

This reply has advantages. It's true, it's easy to remember, it's submissive, and it lets the cops start winning the psychological contest from the get-go. Once you've said these words, give the cops the basic information they ask for. If you avoid being arrested, take a huge hint and stay off private property and places you don't belong. Do your wandering and exploring in public areas where it's legal.

PEEPING AT WOMEN

If you are a peeping tom and get pleasure from looking at women through windows, it's time to do some serious thinking about sex. By peeping, you're training yourself to experience sexual pleasure only by doing things that are illegal. To put it bluntly, you're becoming a pervert. If you continue to train yourself to enjoy illegal sex acts, you face a lifetime of arrests and incarcerations. Here's some unsolicited advice. Have faith that there is someone who will love you and have sex with you one day, no matter how dumb and ugly you are. God is merciful in these matters.

ABOUT SHUTTING UP

When you *stop* talking and just stand quietly and politely (even if doing so is making you crazy), the cops will be subtly pressured to *start* talking. They can't help it. On the street they're the bosses, and one of the perquisites of dominance is doing the talking. As long as they're telling you what they're up to, they're not interrogating you. This is a good thing.

The police may ask you if you have any knowledge of a crime that was committed nearby. If you know something, say so, *briefly*. Do not guess or babble. If you don't know anything, just say that, then *shut up*. Act natural and friendly. Do not act arrogant by using too few words. The goal is for you to say the fewest words possible in order to avoid lying, acting out, fleeing, and getting arrested. You can't suck up to cops, so don't try.

WHAT TO DO WHEN THE STUFF HITS THE FAN

If police really lay it on heavy, now what? You're getting crowded, pressured, and blasted with cop breath perfumed with garlic and onions. The questions are coming thick, fast, convoluted, and inside out. "What are you doing?" "Are you lying?" "Why are you lying?" When this happens, and the questions come *faster than you can think*, you have to stop the interview, but in a manner that is respectful and will have the greatest chance of keeping you free. Here are the magic words. The first version is for youth living at home. The second is for adults.

> **YOUTH VERSION:** *"Officer, I'd like to answer your questions, but my mother told me that in a situation like this, I should not say anything unless she and our attorney are present."*

> **ADULT VERSION:** *"Officer, I'd like to answer your questions, but my attorneys told me that in a situation like this, I should not say anything unless they are present."*

Obviously you should make adjustments in accord with your situation. If you're living with someone other than your mother, for example, use the name of your legal guardian. So you might say, "My aunt told me that . . ."

Note that these statements are *respectful* refusals. They are better than yelling, "I want a lawyer," because they tell police that you *already have* a lawyer. How to do this without spending a lot of money is covered in another chapter. What you're also telling police is that you're not clueless. You are not meat for the criminal justice sausage grinder. Last, you're telling them that, if they arrest you to score a point, it will not be an easy point.

At this juncture in the interview, you have not been arrested or searched. Because you have stopped the interview, the cops are on the spot. They have to arrest you or let you go. If you're not carrying drugs or guns, have not admitted to committing a crime, and have not lied or assaulted the officers, they cannot make a good arrest. You have a reasonable chance to go free.

WHAT TO SAY IF YOU'RE GUILTY?

Nothing. If you're caught with drugs, guns, or stolen merchandise, or if you were caught in the act of committing a crime, nothing you say will help you, so say nothing. You are going to be arrested. By saying nothing, you will make it more difficult for the prosecutor to make a case and convict you. The most common advice that criminal attorneys give clients is to *stop talking to police*. You have now received valuable legal advice practically free. This is Uncle Dale's Golden Rule #3:

> **≫ GIVE COPS YOUR NAME AND BASIC INFO, THEN SHUT THE HECK UP!**

MUM'S THE RULE WHEN YOU'RE IN SCHOOL

No doubt you have been taught since childhood to respect teachers, deans, and principals. Nevertheless, I want to remind students of an important matter: school officials are *not* police. They are *not* part of the criminal justice system and they cannot arrest you or put you in jail. If you get grilled by teachers or principals about a criminal matter, you have no legal obligation to answer their questions. School officials are not required to follow any rules when questioning you, or even to be fair. Inquisition without rights is allowed. Thus you should remain silent, say nothing, and exercise *your* options to keep yourself free. But first you should quickly use the magic words found on page 181, merely deleting the word *officer*.

Many city school districts have their own police forces. School cops are sworn officers with the powers of any police. Act with them as you would with any cop. School officials themselves can suspend you or expel you from school, but that's it. Neither of these is a good thing, but neither is half as bad as going to jail and getting dumped onto the plantations. Public school teachers and principals are government employees, but they generally have more limited sovereign immunity than police officers. They work in sensitive, political bureaucracies and are vulnerable to lawsuits when they trample your rights. So when they quiz you about a criminal matter, tell them your name and basic info, then . . .

>> **SHUT THE HECK UP!**

DO AS THE COPS DO

Every year, in every major city in America, cops get arrested. Sex crimes, domestic battery, accepting bribes, and stealing drugs and money from suspects are the most common charges. Many more cops who are not actually arreted are subject to rough internal affairs investigations by their departments. When cops themselves are interrogated or arrested, do you think they babble and make confessions? Heck no! The only answer they give to other cops is the basic info. Then they clam up so tight a crowbar couldn't pry loose another word. They always hire the best *private* attorneys possible. During an internal affairs investigation, they show up not only with the sharpest mouthpiece in the city, but with their union rep as well. It's a tag-team effort that displays legal talent, union muscle, and union money to the investigators on the other side. Cops are super savvy about the criminal justice system. They never give up information for free. They never talk or cooperate with investigators and prosecutors except as part of a carefully negotiated deal to reduce or dismiss charges. When it comes to staying free, you can learn a lot from the cops.

PRACTICE, PRACTICE, PRACTICE

I want you to practice saying the magic words that you read earlier in this chapter. These words defuse suspicion and politely inform police that you already have a lawyer and will not be telling them anything other than your basic info (name, address and where you're going). Practice the magic words with friends or family, or by yourself. I want you to think about what you will do when police question you. Do not assume this will never happen. Almost everyone, regardless of wealth, privilege, or status, is questioned by police at some time or other. So practice talking with police. Practice giving the basic info and being calm, reasonable, truthful, and brief.

19 | STREET CREDS ARE TOPS FOR DEALING WITH COPS

C *reds* is law enforcement slang for "credentials." *Credential* is derived from a word that means "believe," and what credentials do is make you *believable* to other people. They establish who you are. The creds I'm talking about are *not* an official ID, and they should accompany, but not replace, a driver's license or other picture ID issued for legal purposes by your state. The street creds contained in this chapter have one purpose only: to help you deal with police questions and avoid being arrested.

HOW TO USE CREDS DURING A POLICE STOP

1. If police ask you for an ID, hand them your official ID and the street creds at the same time.

2. Even if police do not ask for an ID, you should say, "I'd like to give you my credentials. Is it OK for me to reach into my pocket (or purse) and give them to you?" *Do not reach into your pocket or purse without asking permission*. If cops are on edge, they might interpret this as an attempt to reach for a weapon.

3. Once you've handed your creds to the police, just stand quietly without talking. Let the police read them. Do not interrupt. When police ask you questions based on your creds, answer them politely and briefly.

4. Police officers will not have seen anything like these creds before, and they may be curious. They may also get angry when you hand them your creds. They may refuse to read them, or toss them aside. No matter. Remain calm and polite. If they ask

you what these credentials are and why you have them, just say the following.

"I wanted to write down my basic information so I wouldn't make a mistake when talking to police."

This statement is true, easy to remember, and submissive in the proper degree.

WHAT CREDS DO

The most important thing credentials do is interrupt the interrogation. They stop cops from starting on their barrage of questions. They help you keep cool. Police themselves carry credentials in addition to their badges. They're used to asking for credentials and showing their own. Even though you have just interrupted their interrogation, how can they object? You're being helpful and polite. Showing credentials! Showing respect!

Presenting credentials changes the balance of power during the encounter with police. They help you maintain your dignity. Even though I've advised you to lose the psychological contest with police in order to win the custody contest and keep your freedom, you want to keep your dignity intact.

Never forget that you are a citizen of the United States of America. You have ironclad rights enshrined in the Constitution and elaborated into law by 200 years of legislation by states and Congress. These rights were legislated, and courts were established, specifically to protect you from abuse of power by the states, the federal government, and their agents in law enforcement. These rights are civil rights, which means that they are yours by virtue of your citizenship. They are yours regardless of your success in life and whether you are rich or poor, educated or ignorant. They are yours regardless of the color of your skin or whether you speak English correctly.

I do not advise you, however, to lecture police on your rights. The whole point of arrest proofing is to prevent your having encounters with police and to keep those that do occur as brief as possible. In any case, judges are much better than you at lecturing police.

One of the most important things that credentials tell cops is that you are *not* clueless fodder for the criminal justice system. They show that you have social backup—family, friends, a place of worship. They demonstrate that you have *lawyered up in advance*, and may even have a friend on the police force! These factors influence cops' decisions as to whether they want to interrogate you further, search you, or arrest you. Cops have tremendous latitude in deciding whether to arrest people for petty offenses. You want to tip the scales in favor of their letting you go.

Credentials also change the balance of power by showing police that you understand something about the criminal justice system. Police have a tremendous advantage because they know how the system works and ordinary people do not. That's why even the most solid citizens can get arrested for acting out in front of police. Most people see only the fantasy world of criminal justice portrayed on TV and in the movies, and this has almost nothing to do with the routine police operations that get you stopped and arrested.

The objective of arrest proofing is not that you hand credentials to police and impress them with your preparedness, but that you not have any encounters at all. By taking time to fill in these credentials, you are making yourself aware of police procedures and thinking about encounters with police. This will help you take the important step of staying *out of sight of police*. Off the radars, my friends—that's where you want to be.

FILLING IN THE INFORMATION

Your name and current address are obviously the most important things on the list. If you are a minor and are not living with your parents, list your guardian. If you do not have a legally appointed guardian, fill in the name of the responsible adult with whom you are living. Do the same with information about your school, place of worship, and employer. Look up the telephone numbers in the telephone book. If you are well acquainted with your teachers, supervisors, and religious leaders, ask them for their cell phone numbers. Let them know you will call only in an emergency. If you cannot obtain the information, just leave the line blank. Most important, *do not place false information on these credentials*. Lying to police is never advisable, but lying in writing is even worse. Write clearly. These credentials must be legible enough to read by flashlight at night.

ABOUT LISTING AN ATTORNEY

Most attorneys are specialists, so make sure that you list an attorney with a criminal practice. The telephone listings will tell you this. Your religious leader and family members may be able to make recommendations. You do not want to list an attorney who specializes in family practice, corporate practice, appellate work, admiralty law, personal injury, etc. Most of the lawyers who advertise on TV or with billboards or with big ads in the phone book are personal-injury lawyers, so take time to find a criminal lawyer who works with police, prosecutors, and judges.

Once you have some attorney names, call each office and make sure the attorney is accepting new clients. Then request a brief appointment with the attorney or his or her paralegal assistant, and explain that you do not need an attorney right now, but that if you get into trouble, you would like to be able to list the attorney as your legal representative. Show them the credentials you are filling out. *Get at least three of the attorney's business cards.* One goes with your street creds; one goes with your car creds; and one goes to a parent, guardian, or friend.

The most important thing to remember is that attorneys cost money. Before you talk to an attorney about becoming a client, make sure you understand whether the initial consultation is free, and if not, how much it will cost. You may be able to get the information you want from an assistant at no charge. In my office, initial consultations are free.

Please do not list me on your credentials. I'm a criminal attorney, but I am licensed to practice only in Florida, and I do not generally accept cases outside of Jacksonville. In any case, as a successful author, I will be busy giving media interviews, chatting up beautiful women, drinking fine adult beverages in moderation, lecturing to learned societies, devouring magnificent food prepared at other people's expense, and in general leading the annoying but thoroughly satisfying life of a media superstar.

ABOUT YOUR FRIEND ON THE POLICE FORCE

This is the most important line of the credentials. Cops never want to get into confrontations with other cops. If you have a friend on the force who can vouch that you are a decent person, this is extremely important in making you difficult to arrest. If your friend on the force is a sergeant, lieutenant, or captain, so much the better.

How do you cultivate friends on the force? If you are an adult, you can meet police officers through sheriff's advisory councils or neighborhood watch programs or at your church. For students, the best way to meet police is by participating in the Police Athletic League and the Drug Abuse Resistance Education (DARE) programs. The police officer you list on your credentials does not have to be a close buddy, but he does have to know you well enough to recognize your name if you get into trouble and another police officer calls. For students, this means you have to make an effort to talk with police officers and make sure they know your name. You may want to show them your credentials and explain that you are working to avoid problems with police. Naturally the best arrest proofing is prevention. The more you talk to police officers in social, religious, and service-organization settings, the better. *Ask your police friend for three business cards.* One goes with your street creds; one goes with your car creds; and one goes to a parent, guardian, or friend. In doing this, you'll become more savvy and less arrestable.

Remember, you must find an attorney and develop a friend on the force *before* you get stopped by police. Only then can the police officer who's questioning you and reading your creds realize that you are *lawyered up in advance and have friends in important places*, like the savviest people.

ABOUT THE MAGIC PHRASE

You will note that on one panel of your creds, the magic words you use to end a police interview are clearly printed so you can read them in case you can't recall them. Of course, you'll be nervous in the presence of police. *Everyone* is nervous around police except other cops and people who work in the criminal justice system, such as judges, prosecutors, and attorneys. Police will be curious about this phrase and may ask you what's going on. If they do, just reply with the following statement.

> **"I wanted to be able to read this phrase in case I become uncomfortable talking."**

STREET CREDS / YOUTH VERSION

PLACE IN WALLET OR PURSE

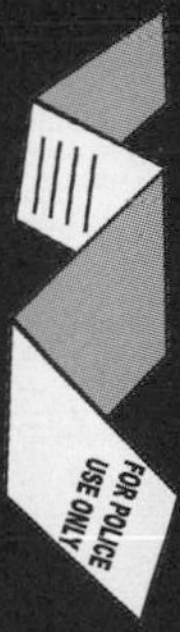

CUT ON DOTTED LINES. FOLD ON SOLID LINES.

Name ______________________________

Address ______________________________

City ______________ State _____ Zip ________

Parent/Guardian ______________________________

Telephone ______________________________

Cell Phone ______________________________

Attorney ______________________________

Telephone ______________________________

Cell Phone ______________________________

Friend in Police Dept. ______________________________

Telephone ______________________________

Cell Phone ______________________________

Church/Mosque/Temple ______________________________

____

Pastor/Priest/Imam/Rabbi ______________________________

____

Telephone ______________________________

Cell Phone ______________________________

School ______________________________

Homeroom Teacher ______________________________

Principal ______________________________

School Counselor ______________________________

Telephone ______________________________

Cell Phone ______________________________

FOR POLICE
USE ONLY

OFFICER, I'D LIKE TO ANSWER
YOUR QUESTIONS, BUT MY MOTH-
ER TOLD ME THAT, IN A SITUATION
LIKE THIS, I SHOULD NOT SAY ANY-
THING UNLESS SHE AND OUR AT-
TORNEY ARE PRESENT.

GLUE OR STAPLE ATTORNEY'S
BUSINESS CARD HERE.

GLUE OR STAPLE POLICE OFFICER'S
BUSINESS CARD HERE.

STREET CREDS / YOUTH VERSION
PLACE IN WALLET OR PURSE

REVERSE
SIDE

Name _____

Address _____

City _____ State _____ Zip _____

Spouse _____

Telephone _____

Cell Phone _____

Attorney _____

Telephone _____

Cell Phone _____

Friend in Police Dept. _____

Telephone _____

Cell Phone _____

Church/Mosque/Temple _____

_____

Pastor/Priest/Imam/Rabbi _____

_____

Telephone _____

Cell Phone _____

Employer _____

Supervisor _____

Telephone _____

Cell Phone _____

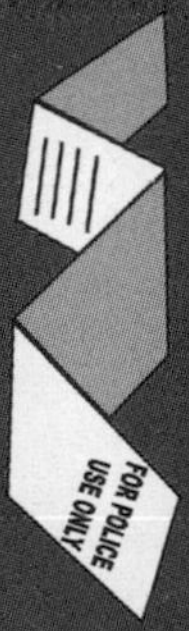

FOR POLICE USE ONLY

OFFICER, I'D LIKE TO ANSWER YOUR QUESTIONS, BUT MY ATTORNEYS TOLD ME THAT, IN A SITUATION LIKE THIS, I SHOULD NOT SAY ANYTHING UNLESS THEY ARE PRESENT.

GLUE OR STAPLE ATTORNEY'S
BUSINESS CARD HERE.

GLUE OR STAPLE POLICE OFFICER'S
BUSINESS CARD HERE.

STREET CREDS / ADULT VERSION
PLACE IN WALLET OR PURSE

REVERSE
SIDE

20 | THERE AIN'T NO HOPE
WHEN YOU CARRY DOPE

H ere's some of the best legal advice I can give you: *Keep your dope at home.* That's it. Keep the magic herb—and any other illegal substance you feel compelled to ingest—indoors where police cannot *see* you, *search* you, and *seize* you without a warrant. Private homes are among the few areas that governments believe are sacred. Take advantage of this legal protection to stay out of jail.

Please note that I never advocate or condone illegal activity. I believe with all my heart that doing drugs is stupid and dangerous. I am a realist, however, and expect that people will continue to mess with this stuff regardless of what I or anyone else says. I will not give my opinion here on the question of whether to legalize marijuana. All you need to know is that, right now, although marijuana is decriminalized to some degree in 18 states, it is still illegal in 32 states. Even in the decriminalized states, possession of larger quantities is a crime, as is sale and distribution except in licensed facilities. Drug violations remain the most common offenses that will get you arrested and tossed onto the plantations.

If that doesn't persuade you, take a tip from the drug cartel—the big boys, not the schlubs who sit on street corners with a bag under a brick. Big-time dope dealers import, transport, warehouse, distribute, and finance drugs. What they *don't* do is stay in physical proximity to the drugs any more than is absolutely necessary. The dope is always in buildings and vehicles that cannot be legally connected to the dealer. It is handled by underlings who take the rap during police raids. The big guys keep their cars immaculate, street legal, and drug free. Take a tip from the drug kings. They know.

If you're wasted at this moment, put your head under the shower, take two aspirin, and have some strong coffee. You need to be awake for the advice that follows.

>> Get wasted at your home or your friends' homes. On the streets cops are kings, and dope provides the easiest way for them to bust you.

>> If you live in a highly clueless situation where family and friends will smoke or sell your dope while you're out, you'll have to devote some sober hours to the problem of hiding your stash. There are books on the subject, but the essential technique involves hollowing out bedposts, lamps, soap bars, books, and so forth as dope depositories. Do this at once. It's work, but less work than getting out of jail.

>> Do not buy your dope on the street, where police can see you.

>> Do not allow dope dealers to make deliveries to your door, as they are often surveilled by police. Some dealers are confidential informants (snitches).

>> Always pay your dope dealer so he will not bounce the fat end of a baseball bat off your head or knees.

>> Do not buy dope at houses or apartments where the stuff is handed out of a window like fast food. These are often police stings.

>> Your friends *will leave* their dope in your car. You will, too, when you're stoned. When sober, clean out the ashtray and thoroughly search under seats, in the glove compartment, and in the trunk. Remove all pills, rocks, weed, and paraphernalia that you or your friends have deposited in your vehicle. See the next section for detailed instructions.

>> Never allow police to search your car. See chapter 26, "No, You Can't Search My Car," for crucial information on how to refuse a search.

Here's how you smoke dope so as to minimize your chances of getting arrested. Basically, when you're at your friends' houses, you smoke their dope. When they're at your house, they smoke your dope. Try to balance it out. Take care to shut the windows and doors while toking those joints and sucking on those bongs. Neighbors will call cops when they smell the stuff. In many states, if police approach the house and catch a whiff, they have probable cause to enter the house and make arrests without warrants. A good alternative to smoking at all is to take a hint from the '60's era hippies and *eat the stuff.* Mix weed with cookie dough, bake it, and toss it down the hatch. You'll mellow out without the smell and the lung damage. In all cases, avoid having marijuana in your possession when you're on the street or in a car where police can *see* you, *search* you, and *seize* you.

Finally, never use dope and drive. DUI means driving under the influence of any substance that would impair your ability to operate a motor vehicle.

This advice sounds cynical, but it's merely practical. The philosophy of this book is that people ought to be able to do a few stupid things in life without getting arrested, dumped in jail, and consigned to the plantations. Most people smoke dope during wayward youth, but years ago the police dragnet was not nearly so thorough as it is today. The World Wide Web and the electronic plantation did not exist. So older generations survived to grow into reasonably sober, lawful, and productive adults. I want you to do likewise by staying free until you wise up, which is to say, until you cease to be a dope(r).

PRESCRIPTION DRUGS AND KIDDIE NARCOTICS

Very few people are aware that it is often illegal to possess prescription medicines *unless you also carry the written prescription with you or keep the pills in the orange plastic container, which contains the prescription on the label.* Pharmacists and physicians are horribly remiss in failing to inform patients of these laws, which exist in many states.

Unless the pills are stamped "aspirin" or are obviously over-the-counter medicines, the officers will assume the tablets are prescription drugs and will arrest you for unlawful possession. Most people find it awkward to carry the orange plastic bottles, so they stuff their drugs in plastic bags and pill dispensers. When you do this, you must carry at least a photocopy of the prescription with you. You will have to make this photocopy *before* you hand the prescription to the pharmacist. These laws apply to all prescription medications, even such routine meds as birth control pills and blood pressure reducers.

Illegal possession of prescription drugs is not a serious crime, but it's enough to get you arrested, and it's a dandy add-on charge.

The new horror story is the mind-altering drugs prescribed for children on the recommendation of school counselors, psychologists, and other devils. These drugs are generally tranquilizers, like Valium, or amphetamine-based stimulants, like Ritalin. *All these kiddie pills are, without exception, scheduled narcotics with highly restricted distribution.* All of these pills will calm kids but get adults high. All have high street value for illegal resale. These pills are prescribed for kids who lose them, sell them, and forget about them. Even if your child does not take prescription drugs, his or her friends may leave their pills in your car. *You* are the one who will get busted. Keep a sharp eye on what's in kids' pockets and purses when they're in your home or car. Periodically search your vehicle and remove any pills you find.

Remember the movie *The Wizard of Oz*? At the end, Dorothy taps her shoes together and says the magic words, "There's no place like home," and the words send her whirling back to safety in Kansas. I want you to repeat similar magic words, which will keep you in safety. Repeat about a thousand times:

Keep your dope at home.
Keep your dope at home.
Keep your dope at home.
Keep your dope at home.
Keep your dope at home.

Got it?

21 | EMERGENCY PROCEDURES

E mergency last-ditch procedures help you avoid arrest when all else fails. These will work only if you have been accused of a *minor* offense, such as possession of small amounts of drugs, disorderly conduct, trespassing, etc. If you have acted out, touched or hit a police officer, lied, or fled, it is unlikely that any of these procedures will help.

ASK FOR A NOTICE TO APPEAR

Most people are aware of notices to appear only when they encounter them in the form of traffic citations, where the police explain that "you've got to go to court with this ticket." Few outside the criminal justice system know that police can issue notices to appear, also called penal citations, for all sorts of offenses, including possession of small amounts of illegal drugs.

A notice to appear requires that you go to court, where a judge will decide your guilt or innocence. However, with a notice to appear, you do *not* get arrested, fingerprinted, photographed, and logged onto the electronic plantation at that moment. Once you sign the citation, you will be set free. Please note: Signing the citation merely indicates that you have received the citation. It is *not* an admission of guilt. So sign the blasted thing. A police officer is doing you a huge favor by giving you a notice to appear and giving up the opportunity to arrest you.

To get a notice to appear, begging and pleading are in order. Tell the officer one or more of the following when applicable. At all times be truthful. One lie at this point will send you to the slammer.

>> You are not a hardened criminal.

>> You have never been arrested before.

>> An arrest will make it difficult for you to get a good job.

>> An arrest might get you fired from your job or suspended from school.

>> You have children and family who need you.

Remember that if you have been arrested before or have an outstanding warrant, the police officers will know it because they will have checked on their police car computer. Do not lie about prior arrests.

If you are fortunate enough to receive a notice to appear and not get arrested, you now have a second chance. You have time to get yourself together, get a lawyer, dress in your Sunday best, trim your outrageous hair, and *look* like a citizen in court. If you are able to hire an attorney, he or she will do the talking, so you won't get confused, act out, or get into trouble because you do not speak English well or cannot understand the proceedings. Not for nothing are lawyers called mouthpieces.

WAKE UP. DRESS UP. SHOW UP.

You must, however, attend your hearing. Nothing short of a serious, well-documented illness will get you excused. *Do not be late.* If you have only a vague grasp of calendars and time, ask your friends or your attorney to help by calling you hours before the hearing. Arrange transportation in advance. If you drive your car, allow plenty of time for parking, which is always difficult to find near big-city courthouses. Bring money for parking and food. Wash, brush your teeth, and use deodorant and mouthwash. Do *not* get wasted before the hearing. The merest whiff of marijuana, booze, or beer will get you hammered for public intoxication. The courtroom is full of police officers and bailiffs who can arrest you on the spot.

Judges have extraordinary power and discretion in their courtrooms. They are extremely offended by defendants who do not appear, and will immediately issue a bench warrant for your arrest if you skip. When you fail to appear, here's what happens.

>> You commit a crime, often more serious than the one for which you were originally charged.

>> You have an outstanding warrant, which will show on every police computer in America.

>> You will be arrested, and you will have a difficult time being set free on bail.

>> Your defense costs will skyrocket.

CRY—TRAGICALLY, COPIOUSLY!

When you're on the verge of being arrested, some humiliation and self-abasement may help. If you feel like crying, do so. Let the tears really flow, especially at night. Toss in some sobs and moans just to be sure. Don't waste time worrying about what your friends will think. Remember, if they're with you, they're getting arrested too. If they aren't, what they can't see they can't know. So let the tears flow. Cops are not inhuman, and they can take pity. As you cry, however, don't beg for police to let you go; *beg for a notice to appear*. This has a much higher chance of success.

BARF, PEE, POOP

If nothing else has worked so far, you can try this last and most extreme measure. Foul yourself so that the police will consider setting you free in order not to get their cruiser nasty. If you've been drinking, throw up all over your shirt, not on the ground. If you're wasted, this may be impossible because of marijuana's antinausea effects. But don't stop here. Pee down your legs and poop—that's right, I said poop—into your pants. After you do it, you must tell the officers what has happened. They can see you vomit, but you'll have to inform them of what else you've done *before* they put you into the cruiser. So say the following, preferably through tears:

"I've pooped my pants and pissed on myself."

In extreme emergencies, this is worth trying. If the police let you go, you can shower off at home. If they do arrest you, you will spend several miserable hours during processing, but ultimately you will get hosed off and issued jail dungarees. Although disgusting, fouling yourself is preferable to going to jail. In any case, feces, urine, and vomit are water soluble and wash out easily. You don't even have to lose a set of clothes. But being arrested is permanent.

POLICE BRUTALITY

Police are better trained, more disciplined, and more honest today, but brutality does occur. Police officers are trained to fight, shoot, and kill, and to become violent instantly if they feel threatened. In a big-city force of tens of thousands of police officers, it would be unusual if a few were not sadists or uncontrollably violent.

By following the procedures in this book, especially by being submissive and polite while police ask questions, you minimize the possibility of brutalization. However, if police start beating you, there is only one thing to do: *curl up into a fetal ball and protect your head with your arms.* If you are already handcuffed with your hands behind you, try to wriggle your head under the police cruiser for protection. You can survive a tremendous beating, but if you are kicked and beaten in the head, you may be killed or seriously brain damaged.

Once you get stabilized in the hospital, get busy. Have yourself photographed, preferably before and after surgery, with and without bandages. *Call your lawyer. Do this at once. Do not delay.* Your attorney may need to file motions with the court to get evidence. You can sue the city and win a substantial amount of money. It will not be easy. The cops and the city will cover their fannies with every trick in the book. City employees will suddenly have difficulty remembering things. Documents will get lost. On the positive side, there are so many people carrying video recorders, digital cameras, and cell phone cameras that it is possible that your beating was recorded or photographed. Some police cruisers are equipped with video cameras. All of this evidence can be subpoenaed and used in your lawsuit and in defense of your criminal indictments.

If you prevail in court, you will get payback. The cops involved will be fired, indicted, and sent to prison. The city will have to pay you big bucks. Abner Louima, who had his intestines ruptured when New York police sodomized him with a toilet plunger, has recovered and returned to his native Haiti. The millions he won in court have allowed him to live a life of luxury in a magnificent home. His donations to charities have made him a local hero.

Yes, there is justice in America. But let me plead with you: *Do not antagonize cops. They are armed and dangerous. Never forget this.*

22 | WHEN GIRLS TELL A TALE THAT SENDS YOU TO JAIL

This chapter is addressed to men. It will infuriate women. Written with a testosterone-dipped pen, it discusses sex and crime from a man's point of view. It advises men *how to defend themselves against women*, but it does so by urging them to be aware of and obey certain laws. Here, as with drug use, society and the criminal justice system are heading in different directions. Society appears to be more tolerant of sex, yet the cops and courts now arrest and prosecute men* for behaviors that years ago were either ignored or considered noncriminal. I'm talking specifically about two offenses that are jamming the jails.

1. **HAVING SEX WITH MINORS**

2. **YELLING AT AND HITTING WOMEN**

Guys, you need to listen up, because either of these offenses can get you hammered with a long stretch in prison and a lifetime on the electronic plantation. As an added bonus, you could get listed, with your very own photo, on bulletin boards of sexual predators so that your neighbors will hate and fear you forever.

The states have their reasons for aggressively arresting men. They have had it with the social chaos caused by unwed mothers. Thus they enforce statutory rape (sex with minor girls) laws with a vengeance. As to strict enforcement of laws against domestic disturbance and domestic battery,

---

* Despite strenuous efforts, women have not been able to get themselves arrested as often as men, who are just better at it.

prosecutors point out that murders of women drop *by half* when these laws are strictly enforced.

Most men have no idea how seriously offenses against women are viewed by cops, prosecutors, and judges. These laws are often enforced by *female* police officers, *female* prosecutors, and *female* judges. Some of these women are on a mission from God to make men miserable. Getting scared yet? You should be.

These laws are vigorously enforced, and you have to deal with them. Ignorance can be disastrous. Getting savvy and arrest-proofing yourself is the only defense.

JAIL BAIT

You may be OK with bopping underage ladies, but legislators, judges, and cops are not. Nothing about this is simple. The age of consent, which in standard English means the age at which a girl can have consensual sex with you without your being at risk of going to jail, varies from state to state. Many states have a "young love" exception, so if you're a year or so older than the girl, you may not be in violation. Generally, however, if you're 20 or older, and your girl is 17 or younger, your young sweetie pie is jailbait.

"But what's the problem?" you retort. "The girl loves me. She's happy. The sex is not only mind blowing, but consensual. Here are her love letters to prove it. Those little hearts she draws above the letter i are as cute as lace pants." Alas, there are problems with all this.

>> Underage girls cannot legally consent to have sex, just as they cannot legally enter into binding contracts or be held liable for debts. Weirdly, many states allow a single exception to the inability of minor girls to give legal consent—abortion. That's right, guys. The girl can consent to *abort* her baby, but she cannot consent for you to *make* her baby!

>> Your young darling, no doubt glowing with love and exuding health and pheromones, generally wants to talk to other women about the rapturous sex she's enjoying. Women have

to share experiences for them to be fully real. Alas, these feminine interlocutors generally are the girl's mother or best friend, and these guardians cannot *wait* to dial 911 and rat you out to the cops.

>> Sex with a minor is a "strict liability" offense. In standard English this means there *ain't no defense* except one: "It didn't happen." The fact that sex was consensual means *nothing* in court. If the girl lies, shows a fake ID, or deceives you into having sex, it's not admissable in court. Likewise, any imputations about her character are inadmissable too. Your only hope of dismissal or acquittal is if the girl lies or refuses to testify.

>> Statutes define sex with a young girl as sordid. Lovemaking becomes statutory rape. Soft caresses and butterfly kisses are called lewd and lascivious conduct. Get the picture?

SHUT UP! SHUT UP! SHUT UP!

Read the following carefully. I'm going to tell you about an old cop trick that gets you to unknowingly confess to statutory rape and dump yourself in the can before you even realize it. Once it is established that the girl you allegedly had sex with was underage, the cops will always ask, in a calm, man-to-man tone, "Well, did she agree to it?"

If you blurt out, "Yeah, man. She dug it!" or something to that effect, *you just confessed to statutory rape.* Years in the slammer! Remember, the only defense allowable in court in most states is that sex never happened—period. So when you're being interrogated about sex with an underage girl, give police your legal name and address, then clam up. Put a sock in it. Shut the heck up! *Speed dial your attorney!* Your butt's in hot water and the popo will be turning up the heat.

GET THE LICENSE—FAST!

You must do two things to arrest-proof yourself. First, find out the age of consent in your state. Make sure you get information on the "young love" exception if you're near the girl in age. Second, and most important, check that your girl is of age in the following manner:

ASK FOR A DRIVER'S LICENSE.

Why a driver's license? Because it's a hard ID to fake. This sounds easy, but it isn't. Imagine. You're in the bedroom. The candles are burning and the cover is drawn. The girl is opening her arms and whispering, "Love me" in musical tones that reverberate to the dawn of time. There's hardly any *thinking* going on. So timing is crucial. You've got to get the ID before the coital avalanche, and the earlier the better.

Often the girl will protest. "Don't you trust me?" The answer is "of course, I do, but . . ." In sex, as in nuclear arms control, the watchwords are "trust but verify." Since it's nearly impossible to think when your blood is boiling with lust—excuse me—love, here are some magic words to say to winkle out the all-important ID. They're sappy, but women love it sappy: "Darling, our love is strong, and we've got to be strong. Showing me your license is the strongest proof that you love me, and that what we're doing is right, so very, very right. If you're too young, we can wait. Our love will only get better, sweeter, and closer over time."

After you say these words, if no license is forthcoming or if she's too young, whisper a sweet goodbye and then *run like hell*. Don't go back. No calls. No letters. No nothing. Do you know what cops call love letters and messages left on answering machines to minor girls? *Evidence.*

Obviously you should know who you're having sex with. Have you considered abstinence?

Here's another suggestion: *older women.* Since you may have missed this in biology class, women reach their sexual peak at the end of their childbearing age.

SMACK YOUR WOMAN AND YOU'LL DO A STRETCH

In centuries past, male "correction" of female behavior was administered with the back of the hand and accompanied by appropriate roars and bellows. In the 21st century, "behavioral correction" of the female has different names. Bellowing is called domestic disturbance. The back of the hand is known as domestic battery. Both will get you arrested and jailed in a hurry.

Tough enforcement has good and bad consequences. On the one hand, many women and men avoid serious injury. On the other, states now intervene early in disputes. Arguments that once might have been resolved by participants now result in arrests and imprisonment. Participants are consigned to the social services plantation. Children are removed from parents and dumped into hellish foster homes. Men are sentenced to anger-management classes, and all and sundry are psychoanalyzed, cataloged, and managed by government employees. The arrests, and all too often the voluminous social services and medical records, get into the electronic plantation, where they are accessed by prospective employers, ex-spouses, and civil litigants. A few yelling matches can rapidly become a criminal, social, psychological, and financial fur ball.

Men and women argue. They yell. It may be a natural occurrence, but it can also be a crime. Here's another problem. Domestic-dispute laws are enforced most strongly against the poor and the clueless for a simple reason—thin walls. In apartments, sounds carry through walls, and neighbors call the cops. In freestanding houses, especially expensive houses with wide lawns and thick, well-insulated walls, shouts and screams are inaudible. Nobody complains. Nothing happens.

DON'T TALK, *WALK!*

Here are arrest-proofing procedures for staying free after arguments with women.

1. When an argument gets loud, assume that the police have been called and are on the way.

2. Shut up. Do not utter any sound whatsoever.

3. Turn on your heel. Walk to the door and leave. Do not be present when police arrive, because in an angry state you'll argue, confess, flee, lie, and otherwise give cops reasons not only to arrest you, but also to pile on charges.

4. Do not get into your car. In an angry state you're likely to get into an accident or get pulled over for a traffic violation. In addition, the woman may describe the car and give the license plate number to police, who will then issue a BOLO (be on the lookout) notice for your vehicle. Cops can find a car more quickly than they can find a person on foot who has a head start. So leave on foot and keep going.

5. Walk quickly, but do not run. Running attracts attention. If possible, go to a restaurant, bar, or convenience store where you can sit down and cool off.

6. Call someone who can take you someplace to stay.

7. Retrieve your car the next day. Do not talk with the woman. Just get in and drive—slowly and lawfully.

8. Do not talk with the woman for at least three days. Let your emotions subside so you can think. Telephone calls, answering machine messages, or notes may be considered stalking, another crime. Avoid all communication.

9. If you merely had a loud argument, you will likely remain free. If you struck or injured the woman, you will be arrested (your attorney can find out if you have an outstanding warrant). Police will take photographs of bruises and injuries, and these and the woman's testimony are enough to convict you in most states. By leaving, you at least avoid confessing to police or committing add-on offenses, so the charges will be less serious and less well documented. This will help your defense.

10. Once you leave a woman after an argument, think seriously about your situation. If you and the woman argue frequently and have to live in an apartment, you almost certainly will be arrested at some point. If you cannot live with the woman quietly, you must leave and stay gone.

Abandon possessions rather than risk an argument that will lead to jail. This is important. I'll repeat it: *Abandon all possessions*. Your crappy stereo, dirty clothes, scratchy CDs, and cheapo fishing rods are not worth an encounter that can lead to prison. Don't get steamed that your soon-to-be-ex has your stuff. Think of it this way. She's now the proud possessor of

>> a crappy stereo

>> scratchy CDs

>> dirty clothes

>> fishing rods smeared with worm goo and rotting shrimp and squid

Say to yourself, but not to her, "Congratulations, honey. Enjoy it while you can. I'm off to Wal-Mart to refit with all new stuff." If your ex insists on holding onto your tighty-whiteys with the tire tracks in the middle, more power to her. She can frame 'em and hang 'em on the wall.

Ladies, this goes for you, too.

Communicate about child custody, real estate, and bank accounts through attorneys. If you are married, file for divorce. Avoid going to hearings, if your presence is not legally required, and let attorneys handle everything. Most important, do *not* be in the woman's presence without a witness. Do not send e-mails or letters that contain threats or that might become evidence against you in criminal and civil proceedings.

You must consider these possibilities when you are subject to arrest for domestic disturbance and battery.

>> The woman might lie and induce others to lie.

>> The woman may injure herself before police arrive so as to increase the charge against you from misdemeanor disturbance to felony battery.

>> The woman might attack and injure you.

>> You might argue with or injure the woman.

This sounds harsh, but it's not. Women can recruit the power of the state to take their side in disputes with men, with disastrous consequences. I myself can testify to the soundness of this advice. One of my ex-wives chased me around the kitchen, knife in hand, shouting. She was easily disarmed. I was not injured. Had the police been called, had she been the least bit injured, without question I would have gone to jail. Luckily, I was teaching about domestic violence at the police academy when this happened. I knew what to do and I did it. I walked out the door, filed for divorce, and have not laid eyes on her since. I abandoned thousands of dollars in new appliances at a time when my wallet was flat as a flounder. Fortunately, I remained free and saved my legal career, which a felony conviction would have ruined.

PART III

ARREST PROOFING
IN YOUR CAR

23 | CITIZEN INSPECTION? REVENUE COLLECTION? OR DRIVER PROTECTION?

To the esteemed governor of your state, to the estimable men and women of your legislature, to the honorable mayor of your fair city, to his honor the police chief of your personal metropolis, and to the immaculately uniformed Officer Friendlies on the boob tube and in the classroom, the primary and sacred purpose of traffic enforcement is citizen safety. We've all seen the message: a concerned, paternal police officer who, after giving a driver a ticket, touches his hat and says, "Drive safely, ma'am."

To the guys in blue driving cruisers, the priorities are different. To cops, the most important part of traffic enforcement is an opportunity to *reach out and arrest someone*. This sounds cynical, but am I ever cynical? Me, a former police officer, now an attorney oozing empathy at every pore and wielding a honeyed tongue in the courtroom for the benefit of learned judges and distinguished juries of your peers? Banish the thought!

Let's be practical. Cops spend months and years in training. Most of this training is devoted to the following subjects:

>> how to find bad guys

>> how to fight bad guys

>> how to shoot bad guys

>> how to arrest bad guys

>> how to convict bad guys

Do you think police officers work and train like crazy to maintain careful, uneventful driving by law-abiding citizens in perfectly maintained automobiles on pristine highways? Heck no! Cops are hunters. They live to arrest bad guys. To cops, citizen safety is not the *goal* of making traffic stops, merely the *by-product*. For cops, the best way to keep the citizens safe is to arrest the maximum number of evil gorks and get them tossed into the jug for the maximum number of years. This will get cops the maximum promotions, the maximum raises, the maximum "attaboys" in the locker room, and the maximum conversations with fascinated and often beautiful women. Remember that top-secret monthly police tally sheet shown earlier in the book? Did you see a score column for "keeping traffic flowing smoothly and safely"? Of course not.

Cops score few points for traffic citations, but citations are crucial to making big arrests. The reason is simple. Serious crimes always require the use of cars. Cars *carry* things—like drugs, guns, money, stolen property, tightly wrapped corpses, and fugitives from justice. Yip, yip, yahoo! When police officers make a street stop, they generally net only a boring misdemeanor arrest. With traffic stops, they make more felony busts. They could even hit the jackpot. I mentioned earlier that some of the worst criminals in American history were apprehended due to traffic stops for routine violations. The law enforcement officers who bagged these monsters are heroes.

DOLLARS FOR CITIES AND ROACH SPRAY FOR CROOKS

All that money from traffic tickets isn't bad, either. In most states there is a revenue split between the state and the municipality where the ticket was issued. For some small towns, traffic tickets are an important source of revenue, and city commissioners constantly remind cops to lay out those tickets early and often. Enough towns have become speed traps that the American Automobile Association tracks and rates them.

Small-town officials are pleasantly aware of another benefit of tough traffic enforcement—it's roach spray for bad guys. The reason is simple. Bad guys are all-around scofflaws. Someone who is prepared to commit armed robbery rarely cares about keeping license plates current. Iron-fisted traffic enforcement can reduce the crime rate in a small, easily patrolled town to an astounding degree.

Let me give you an example. Miami Springs, a small town located in the center of Florida's Miami-Dade County, is famous for some of the toughest traffic enforcement in America. Even *imagining* the speedometer moving over the limit gets you a ticket. And at those stop signs? Full stop and look both ways—or else! Cars with smoking exhaust pipes or broken taillights rarely go more than a few blocks before they're stopped. If four males are in a car and wearing anything other than business suits and ties, they get busted automatically. Miami Springs is so safe it's eerie. It's like Smallville. You expect Superboy to fly overhead and say, "Have a nice day!" Meanwhile, just blocks away in Miami and Hialeah, murder, mayhem, robbery, and rape are the order of the day. Those are Batman towns.

YOUR CAR AS A FREAKING EASTER EGG

When a cop sees a car speeding or weaving between lanes, he doesn't say to himself, "Aha! There goes an errant vehicle operator in need of firm but oh-so-gentle correction." What he actually says is, "I wonder if there's somebody in that heap I can arrest?" Stopping cars is exciting because, as a cop, you never know what you're going to find. Dead bodies? Duffle bags of pharmaceutically pure cocaine? Shrink-wrapped, neatly bar-coded blocks of hundred-dollar bills? Machine guns? Plastic explosives? One of the Al-Qaeda Top Ten? Anything is possible, and the ordinary patrol cop knows that a traffic stop is the most likely way to make the once-in-a-lifetime arrest. The more traffic tickets you write, the more felony arrests you make. Quantity has a quality all its own—for cops.

So to a cop, your vehicle may *look* like a car or truck, but it *feels* like a big, brightly colored plastic Easter egg, the kind with a prize in the middle.

Traffic stops are fun for other reasons. As a cop, every now and then you flush a rabbit and start a chase that can go all across town, even to other counties and states. Frequently the fugitives toss dope and guns out the windows, which makes evidence gathering easy. When the bad guys freak out or burn their brakes, they bail, so you get an exciting foot chase down alleys and across backyards. (Watch out for those aluminum clothes lines!) This is often followed by a good, old-fashioned street scuffle, with lots of punching, kicking, gouging, and yelling. A quick blast of Mace to the face of an oversized offender can equal the odds, and a Taser jolt will leave the thug vibrating like a marionette on a

Your car—the Easter Bunny's gift to law enforcers.

string. What a way to begin the day—felony and misdemeanor charges; drugs, guns, and money recovered; traffic citations up the wazoo; and a full tally sheet for the sergeant! *Bing, bing, bing!*—points and more points. If the bad guys land a few blows during the scuffle, you get to go to the hospital and have the rest of the day off. This is traffic enforcement from the cops' point of view. Remember, police *enjoy* chasing people and making arrests.

Traffic stops are dangerous. Bad guys have a distressing habit of poking pistols and shotguns out car windows and opening fire. To see what's going on, drivers will swerve off the road and crash into police cruisers and run over cops. For these reasons police have developed specific techniques to minimize traffic-stop risks. I'll discuss these in upcoming chapters.

THE UNIFORM ARREST CODE

Every aggressive cop has a policing bible that stands in the place of honor on his or her bookshelf, beside the hand-to-hand combat guides, weapons manuals, police-procedure books, and evidence tomes. This is the Uniform Traffic Code. Every state has one. Their titles may vary, but these volumes have one thing in common. They're huge! Most have well over a thousand pages of dense, two-columned text that lists thousands of traffic infractions for which you can be stopped and receive citations. Why bureaucrats require more words to regulate driving than God needed to reveal His Creation in the Bible is a mystery even a lawyer can't explain.

Many of these laws are incredibly petty. Others are catchalls, such as "careless driving," which cover anything. The upshot is that it's nearly impossible for even the most upstanding citizen to drive a vehicle in 100 percent compliance with the law. Aggressive cops study the traffic code with religious fervor, not because they want citizens to drive safely, but because they want to stop more cars, write more tickets, perform more searches, and make more arrests. These blasted books should be called the Uniform Arrest Code.

Here are some examples. In Florida it's illegal to do any of the following.

>> Get run over by a car. Should you survive, you might wake up in intensive care with a citation taped to your bandages.

>> Coast, i.e., disengage the transmission and roll. So every time you push in the clutch and cruise, you're in violation. Fortunately, Florida is flat as a pancake, so nobody coasts much.

>> Follow a fire truck or emergency vehicle closer than 500 feet (one and a half football fields, if you count the end zones). Does this ever happen in rush hour? Fuggedaboudit.

>> Mount a light on the side of a vehicle that is any color except amber. For cops in need of a Great White Defendant or celebrity felon, the solution is easy. Just stop a limousine!

They have white side lights. Cops will have to work their way through a thicket of newlyweds, but they'll strike gold sooner or later.

>> Carry a combustible fuel in a bladder or other nonapproved container. Obviously the state has an interest in the safe transport of inflammables, but in Florida this is a third-degree felony!

This last infraction suggests the following to any cop who has committed the serious violation called insufficient police activity and needs to make some quick arrests to score points and keep the sarge happy.

1. Drive to an area of high arrestability.

2. Hide the cruiser near a gas station until some clueless type pulls in and fills a milk jug with gas for the lawn mower or kerosene for the space heater.

3. Make felony arrest and enter same on monthly tally.

It's important to note that most traffic codes were enacted by legislatures solely for the purpose of making driving safe. The use of traffic codes to make more arrests is an unintended consequence.

"YOUR PAPERS, PLEASE": THE CITIZEN INSPECTION SYSTEM

The primary purpose of driver's licenses, vehicle registrations, and license plates is not to help you drive safely, but to allow the government to check on you and collect fees and fines. How can standing in line in a government office each year in order to get a sticker for your license plate have anything to do with how you drive? It has everything to do with the government having an opportunity to check where you live and whether you have outstanding traffic tickets or warrants. A huge proportion of traffic tickets are for the infraction of "failure to complete government paperwork and pay government fees."

All this paperwork ensnarls the clueless in never-ending complexities since they lack organization, reading skills, a sense of time and urgency, and a permanent address at which to receive government notices. Minor traffic violations quickly escalate. Fail to pay traffic tickets and your license is suspended. Get stopped with a suspended license and you get arrested or receive a notice to appear in court. Fail to appear and you get a fine, bench warrant, and another arrest, this time with incarceration. Fail to meet with your probation officer after you get out, and it's back to jail or state prison. And on it goes for the human meat processed over and over through the criminal justice sausage grinder. Please note that none of these violations is a crime against people or property. These are paperwork and procedural crimes. They do not hurt citizens; they only annoy government.

ABOUT THAT PAPERWORK

Let's be blunt here. Don't even *think* about driving outlaw with a suspended license, unpaid traffic tickets, and no insurance. It's not happening in the age of police cruiser computers. Cops run vehicle license tags all day, every day. When they find your paperwork out of order, it's cop time, with vehicle search, vehicle seizure, and maybe a trip to jail. To keep that car insurance paid, settle those outstanding traffic tickets, and get your suspended license reinstated, *do whatever it takes*. If this means getting a second job or borrowing money, do it. It may mean cutting spending for cell phones, the Internet, club hopping, mall shopping, bar crawling, cigarettes, beer, and the products of your favorite neighborhood drug dealer, who is probably a police snitch anyway. But how bad is that? In jail, there's no fun. As for jailhouse sex, we won't even go there.

Helpful hint: Cops in need of writing a few tickets and making some cheap busts sometimes hang around motor vehicle bureau offices to catch people with suspended licenses. Cops can bust you anytime before you pay up and get your license cleared. So when you get the cash to clear your license, park your car *across the street* from the motor vehicle bureau office and stay away from cops until your paperwork is squeaky clean. Once it is, keep the paperwork in your car. Don't assume that cop computers are 100 percent accurate and have instantly updated information.

The lesson here? To avoid cops and stay free you've got to drive street legal. This means you must do the following.

1. Make sure your driver's license is current—not expired, not suspended, and not, for God's sake, revoked.

2. Make sure all traffic fines are paid, including parking tickets.

3. Keep your insurance paid up and current.

4. Keep onboard copies of prescriptions for pills you may be carrying and for insulin and syringes if you're diabetic. Cops do *not* like to find syringes without a prescription.

5. Keep receipts for all this stuff in the car where you can reach them quickly. In a later chapter I'll provide some car creds that help you organize all this paper.

6. Make sure you have no smoking tailpipes, broken headlights or taillights, or other gimmes that make you cop bait. More about this later.

7. Wear your seat belt. Consider your seat belt cop repellant. In many states, not wearing one gives cops an easy reason to stop and search you.

8. If you carry a firearm, make sure you are carrying it legally. Each state has different laws concerning firearms. Memorize these laws.

9. You've got to drive safely and slowly, even if this makes you crazy. If you feel the need for speed, save up your cash and go to a race track that rents time to ordinary people. There, after receiving a driving lesson and signing a waiver of liability (a "you can't sue" letter), you can roar 'round and 'round with the pedal to the metal until your motor explodes. No cops, no probs.

SUSPENDED LICENSES

Do you know if your license is suspended and you're driving outlaw? If you've been moving around, "staying at" different places, or if you're sloppy about reading your mail, you may not know. You don't want to be cop bait, so find out. Here's how. In some states, you can check your license status through the Internet or over the telephone. If this isn't possible, you can generally go to an automobile insurance agency. They can go online with their computers and find out if your license is valid or suspended. Auto tag agencies also can do this, as well as motor vehicle bureau offices. Remember, the people you're talking to are clerks, not cops. They can't arrest you, so ask for their help. If you don't know how to use computers or are confused when talking to government and insurance clerks, get a friend, family member, or social worker to help.

If you discover your license is suspended, get busy paying the fines and fees necessary to have your license reinstated. In the computer age, your ability to drive with a suspended license in a city for any length of time is approximately zero.

TRAFFIC COURT

Traffic court is a bit more relaxed than circuit court, but don't be fooled. Those traffic judges are real judges. They've got *the power*. They've got *the juice*. If you annoy them they can, with a snap of a finger, have you arrested. So here are the rules.

1. Show up! Skip traffic court and, in many states, judges will issue a bench warrant for your arrest. Once you're on ice, the judge can summon you at his or her discretion, which means after you've been locked up for a few days and are fully nourished by a diet of beanie-weenies and green baloney sandwiches. Before your court day, wind up those alarm clocks and get friends and family to help you wake up, dress up, and show up. Bring all paperwork. If you need copies, get them the day before at motor vehicle bureau offices.

2. Be respectful, even if this is not your style. Say "Yes, your honor" and "No, your honor." No cussing, no arguing.

3. Spit out gum and chewing tobacco before you talk to the judge.

4. Turn off pagers and cell phones. These things make judges nuts when they go off.

5. No ranting about racism. Judges, many of whom are black, Hispanic, Jewish, or Asian, will not be sympathetic. Keep on topic, i.e., explain how you're going to pay all fines and fees and get your license reinstated. If you annoy judges sufficiently, they can keep you in custody while they ponder, slowly, the evidence of your case. So behave.

OUTSTANDING WARRANTS

Traffic stops are the way most people with outstanding warrants get arrested. To deal with this, you've first got to know *whether you have a warrant*. Sounds obvious, but many people don't know.

One of my neighbors at the condo I own in Jacksonville missed some drug-court appearances. She assumed a warrant had been issued for her arrest, so she took off on the lam and spent a year hiding in Georgia and working under assumed names. A year later, her boyfriend got arrested during a traffic stop (he *did* have an outstanding warrant), but she was released. Turns out the prosecutor had never pursued her case, and she never even knew it. Her car, alas, was seized and impounded. Moral of story: Read that mail! And don't allow people with outstanding warrants to drive *your* car.

So how do you find out if you have an outstanding warrant, unpaid traffic ticket, or suspended license? Google it. Many courts list warrants, tickets, and civil and criminal cases on their Web sites. For example, if you live in Jacksonville, you would Google "Duval County Courts." Once on the official Web site for the Duval County Clerk of Courts, you'll find a prominent link for "Online Services." When you search your name, you will find civil and criminal cases in which you are involved, plus warrants and tickets. Other jurisdictions have less information, so in those instances you should visit the courthouse and ask a clerk to look up your name. Get copies of any cases or citations in the database. Usually there is a small fee, so bring cash. Some counties have a telephone "warrant line" so you can safely, and anonymously, inquire about warrants and detainers. Always be courteous to court clerks. Courthouses are chockablock with cops and usually have a holding cell ready and waiting for the obstreperous.

If you find tickets and suspended licenses, stay off the roads until you get everything paid up. Beg and borrow the cash if necessary. If you have an outstanding criminal warrant, retain an attorney, who will advise you whether it is possible to quash the warrant. If not, the attorney will arrange your surrender, avoid a public arrest, and assist you in making a statement to police or maintaining silence. This costs money. Freedom isn't free.

Now you have some basics of how traffic laws really work. For government, it's all about paperwork, fees, and citizen inspection. For police, it's all about making arrests. Amazingly, traffic safety still happens.

24 | MIRROR, MIRROR IN THE CAR, WILL THE COPS STAY NEAR OR FAR?

Who hasn't had this experience? You're rolling down the road, happy as a clam. Suddenly, in the rearview mirror, there are blue lights, red lights, strobes popping, blinding searchlights, sirens, radio antennas, and heaven knows what else bristling from the cruiser rack. It's the cops! If you committed some obvious infraction, you know why they're behind you. When the blue lights are spinning and the siren is whooping, there's nothing to do but pull over.

But what if the lights are not flashing? What if the cops are just hanging behind your bumper or driving alongside or standing in the median with or without a radar gun and facing oncoming traffic? Now what? The situation is tense. What you do in the next few seconds will determine whether you get pulled or whether the police vanish. The emphasis of this chapter is how *not to get stopped*. The next chapter will cover what to do when you do get stopped so that a traffic ticket does not become an arrest.

Police have wide discretion in deciding which cars to stop. Absent an obvious infraction, what makes them decide to pull one car and not another? Recall that the major purpose of traffic stops is to reach out and arrest someone. The uniform traffic codes list so many violations that, for practical purposes, police always have a reason to stop a car. Whether to stop you or let you go therefore depends on your perceived *arrestability*, just like it does when you walk the streets. Clueless people are more arrestable; savvy people are less arrestable.* You can judge your risk by rating your

---

* Drivers of Ferraris and Maseratis get stopped anytime, anywhere, because if the cops are lucky enough to find enough dope in these handmade hot rods, they can, in many states, seize the vehicle, get title to it, then slap some blue lights and a siren on top. Cruising in a cop Ferrari is as good as it gets for the boys and girls in blue.

car arrestability quotient (Car-Q) on the handy chart in this chapter. The higher your Car-Q, the more likely you are to be pulled over by police.

Cops have an uncanny ability to slide in behind you before you notice them. The benefits of closing in on your rear bumper are twofold.

1. It allows police to run your license plate on their computers and check for unpaid tickets and outstanding warrants.

2. It pressures you into clueless behaviors that make you arrestable. If you turn rabbit and step on the gas, the cops will get a chase and a treasure trove of felony charges and points when they arrest you.

Think of streets as oceans in which vast schools of traffic fish are constantly swimming. Sedans, pickup trucks, and SUVs are ordinary fish; VW Beetles and MINI Coopers are tiny, colorful reef fish; and semitrucks and limousines are whales. Cops are sharks. Clueless drivers exhibit prey behaviors that stimulate the hunting response. Believe me, these decisions truly are stimulus-response. They happen instantaneously, with no thought necessary. At most, a cop will say to his partner, "Wow! Look at that. Let's go!" Here are some clueless behaviors that stimulate cops to stop you even when you have not committed an obvious traffic violation.

>> **THE HEAD BOBBLE AND GOOSENECK STRETCH.** When you suddenly start bobbing your head and stretching your neck to watch the cops in the rearview mirror, police may stop you to find out why you're so nervous.

When you need to sneak a peek at the cops, flick your eyes up toward the mirror without *turning your head. This will avoid the head bobble that stimulates police to stop you.*

>> **REACHING.** Any unusual motion inside the vehicle by driver or occupant will cause police attention. Cops will presume you are hiding contraband or acquiring a weapon.

>> **HITTING THE BRAKES.** If you suddenly hit the brakes, cops in front of you will see your front end dip, a tip-off that you were speeding. If you're truly unfortunate, or just plain stupid, and slam on the brakes while police are *behind* you, the cruiser will crash into your vehicle. Once cops disentangle themselves from deployed airbags and bent metal, they may emerge somewhat less cheerful than before.

>> **PERFECT DRIVING.** Nobody drives perfectly. When cops see anyone driving perfectly, they get curious. They may stop you just to see what's up.

>> **DOPE FLYING OUT WINDOWS.** Clueless people think that if they toss the bags, the cops cannot arrest them for possession. Wrong.

>> **CREW CAB.** When cops see four young males in a car, they immediately wonder if this is a crew of criminals out to do a job. They also know that with four guys in a car, they are four times more likely to discover outstanding warrants, dope, guns, or stolen property.

>> **LOAD TILT.** When cops see a car heavily loaded and low on its springs, or tilted backward from something heavy in the trunk, they want to stop the car and have a look. Perhaps there's a dead body in there, or some square grouper* just unloaded from a mother ship offshore.

>> **DARK-TINTED WINDOWS.** When cops can't see inside a car, they like to stop the vehicle and have a look.

>> **DRIVER SLOUCH.** People slouching in seats appear to be *hiding from cops*. Since hide-and-seek is what police work is, cops

---

* Cop slang for bales of marijuana and blocks of cocaine and heroin.

always like to check anybody who appears to be hiding. By the way, cops like to see your hands on the wheel. They like this a lot.

>> **OVERLY SCRUPULOUS USE OF TURN SIGNALS.** See "Perfect driving."

>> **BRAKE SQUEALS.** Many brake linings have metal studs embedded in them that squeal when the brake pads wear to the point of needing replacement. When police hear these squeals, they will pull you over for an extra-thorough equipment check, with document perusal and contraband search tossed in at no charge. At the first brake squeak, run, don't walk, to get those pads replaced.

>> **INAPPROPRIATE VEHICLES.** Police are extraordinarily attuned to incongruities, and one of those that most attracts their attention is drivers whose visible status is different from that of the cars they're operating. If you're dirty and wearing scruffy clothes while driving a Mercedes Benz, expect police attention.

>> **DRIVING TOO SLOW.** Because drunks often drive very slowly, cops will pull a slow-moving vehicle in a heartbeat.

>> **GIVING THE FINGER TO POLICE.** Yes, people do that. Cops love it. The constitutional right to be an idiot was established by Adam at the clap of Creation and has been upheld by courts ever since.

A PRAYER FOR POLICE

Every thinking person is grateful for police and all their hard work. Perhaps you'd like to join me in a famous prayer, paraphrased somewhat, for police.

LORD, BLESS THEM AND KEEP THEM—*AS FAR AWAY FROM ME AS POSSIBLE!*

Why do you want to make sure this prayer comes true? After all, a traffic ticket is not such a big deal. It's not, as long as it's just a ticket. But cops aren't interested in tickets; they're interested in arrests. Even the most upstanding citizen can have too much to drink and be in danger of incarceration. Countless solid citizens don't realize they're driving around with drugs and guns left by passengers. How many carpooling soccer moms are tooling around in vans and SUVs in which a child has dropped kiddie narcotics? So here are some tips to help you drive safely past the police/sharks swimming along the highways and byways of America.

>> **JUST SO YOU KNOW, GO WITH THE FLOW.** Just as on the street, make no sudden changes in driving, as police are visual predators who are ultrasensitive to such changes. Whatever you were doing (except violating traffic laws), keep doing it.

>> **IF YOU REACH, YOU'LL BE ON THE BEACH.** No reaching for anything inside the vehicle.

>> **EASE THE GAS TO GET A PASS.** If you were speeding, ease off the gas *without* touching the brakes.

>> **DON'T EVADE IF YOU WANT TO FADE.** Make no sudden turns or lane changes that make you appear to be evading police.

>> **SLOUCH DOWN AND BE A CLOWN.** Straighten up—slowly. Ease those hands up onto the steering wheel where cops can see them. You don't want to look like a crook.

>> **BLEND IN TO HIDE OUT.** Wild paint jobs, Confederate flag plates, football team flags, bumper stickers, nation-of-origin flags, fuzzy dice, CDs, baby shoes, stuffed Garfields on sucker feet, "baby on board" signs, plastic Jesus statuettes, custom rims and pipes, fog lights, rear bumper propellers, and undercarriage neon lights all make you stand out in traffic. By removing these vehicle identifiers, you can hide in plain sight by blending in.

>> **DON'T DARE WITH A BIG STARE.** Don't stare at cops in the rearview mirror or from the windows. Why attract attention? Besides, you look ridiculous rubbernecking and twisting your head around.

>> **TOSS THAT ROACH FROM YOUR WORKDAY COACH.** If you have to carpool to work with other guys, search the vehicle and get rid of dope, roaches, bongs, and residue. (See car search info in chap-

tcr 29). If other passengers insist on smoking dope or drinking, get another ride at any cost. If you work construction, have one of the guys wear a hard hat so cops will know you're workers, not crooks.

>> **CLEAR GLASS WILL SAVE YOUR ASS!** Avoid vehicles with darkly tinted glass or the dreadful, aftermarket tinting film that bubbles in the heat. If cops can't see into your vehicle, they may stop it just to check. Often they will want to use a handheld meter to measure the degree of the tint. This is done from *inside* your vehicle. Once you have agreed to this, guess what else you've agreed to—a search!

>> **LACK A LIGHT? DON'T DRIVE AT NIGHT!** Modern vehicles can have a dozen or more bulbs in the front and rear lights. Many of these are in sealed units that can be expensive. In the meantime, if any one of these lights is out, you can be stopped and ticketed. If you drive only during the day until you can get the lights fixed, cops are unlikely to notice you've got a light out. Get a clue here.

>> **DON'T BE A BOOB. TURN OFF THE TUBE.** Many new cars and vans now come equipped with flat-screen monitors. Some are connected to sophisticated, real-time traffic reporting and mapping systems that guide you through traffic jams. Others connect to DVD players and television tuners. Here's the problem. If you actually *look* at the things while at the wheel, you're guilty of unsafe driving. If you get pulled over and cops see a Hollywood feature flickering on your dashboard, expect tickets to rain upon you like delicate flakes of snow. A thorough search may be in order as well.

>> **YOU CAN'T SKATE WHEN THE PAPERWORK'S LATE.** Until recently, police had to radio in to run a license plate and wait on the air while a dispatcher checked the computer and read back the information. This meant that police ran plates sparingly so as not to overload dispatchers and tie up police radio frequencies

with low-priority traffic work. The installation in police cruisers of dashboard computers with high-speed wireless connections now makes running license plates a snap. Expect police to slide in behind you more frequently as they randomly check license plate numbers.

>> **CROOK WHEELS ARE BAD DEALS.** Cops know far more than the average person about cars. It's their work, and frequently their passion. They know all the makes and models, and what equipment comes standard and what's extra. They know about after-market equipment, custom paint jobs, custom upholstery, tires, etc. They know what things cost, and what types of people drive what sorts of cars. Most important, they know which cars are in fashion with bad guys. If the Mafia dons have switched from Cadillacs to Lincolns, the cops know. They know the wheels the drug dealers, gang leaders, and pimps are rolling in. This can be a problem if you're a car-crazed guy. You have to do some careful thinking if your current passion is for the same type of rides the crooks like, since this will get you stopped. A recent crook craze in my city was for Doves, extremely expensive ($4,000 per set) wheel rims. These snazzy add-ons have to be paid for up front and in cash, since no bank will finance them. Hot chicks love Doves, but so do cops. When cops see you riding around with these rims, they get curious about where you got the money. They may think you're into drugs or illegal street racing. So they check you out.

>> **500 WATTS CALL THE COPS.** Loud stereos or mufflers ought to be known as police-summoning devices. If you've got the subwoofers pumping out 500 watts per channel and rattling the windows, expect to spend time chatting with police. If you've poured concrete onto the floorboards to increase the bass to glass-*shattering* levels (this happens), expect your car to do time in the impound lot. Did I mention that police are not fond of rap lyrics about beating women and killing cops? As for lowriders, keep them in L.A. In any other city they're cop bait. (Curiously,

loud mufflers on Harley-Davidson motorcycles don't attract police, who love the sound of an expensive moto.)

>> **DO SOME THINKING ABOUT YOUR DRINKING.** Driving under the influence (DUI) is a criminal rather than a civil offense. Arrest and jail time are mandatory in most states, so once stopped you're on the plantations even if you have the $10,000 or so to beat the rap in court. Here's the most important point. Even if you're not legally intoxicated, the smell of alcohol will lead police to give you and your vehicle a thorough once-over, *which no rational person wants.* Basically this means that if you're driving, confine your drinking to one drink or less, especially if you weigh less than 150 pounds. Stop drinking an hour before you leave, so alcohol will be metabolized and not on your breath. If you have any question about your ability to drive, call a cab. Alcohol is a drug. When you purchase beer, wine, and liquor for home consumption, put the stuff in your trunk or backseat, *unopened*, with tax seals intact. Keep all your drugs, whether produced legally by liquor distilleries, breweries, and pharmaceutical manufacturers or illegally by Colombian, Bolivian, and Afghan peasants, at home.

>> **LOVE'S A FREAK IN THE BACKSEAT.** Having sex in the backseat worked in the 1960s, when cars were huge and seats were soft and squishy. Only pint-size contortionists can enjoy today's compact mobile units. So avoid doing it in the car. Use the no-tell motel instead. A double bed is much more fun than a backseat.

>> **JAIL'S YOUR CONDO WHEN YOU OVERUSE BONDO.** Most garages and toolsheds in America have a can of the famous gray goop used to fill dents. Shade-tree mechanics slap on the Bondo but never seem to get around to finishing the paint job. Cops figure that any car globbed with unpainted Bondo probably has *mucho* equipment violations and is therefore worthy of a stop. Dope dealers often buy Bondo-covered jalopies, rip out the backseats, and stuff the car with square grouper—the favorite seafood snack of your friendly local police/sharks.

Whether you get pulled, and whether the police interrogate you and search your car during the stop, depends on whether you fit the cops' unofficial crook profile for your city. The car arrestability quotient, or Car-Q, indicates how likely you are to get stopped and arrested. It's similar to the street arrestability quotient, or Arrest-Q.

CAR ARRESTABILITY QUOTIENT (CAR-Q)		
ARRESTABILITY METER		
SPEED	Excessive	Within limit, or just above
TOO SLOW, TOO CAREFUL	Yes	No
DRIVER IMPAIRMENT	Obvious	None
TAG	Expired	Current
LIGHTS	Not working	Working
LICENSE	Expired, none, revoked	Valid
REGISTRATION	Driver is not owner	Driver is the owner
INSURANCE	None	Yes
PASSENGERS	Four males	Couples, children
DENTS	Yes	No
PAINT	Rust	Good
BONDO	Everywhere-O	None-O
TIRES	Bald, mismatched	Good tread, matched

CONTINUED NEXT PAGE ☞

CAR ARRESTABILITY QUOTIENT (CAR-Q) CONTINUED

ARRESTABILITY METER	Low Medium High	Low Medium High
SMELL	Dope, liquor, BO, rot	Low
PASSENGER APPEARANCE	Thug	Citizen
VEHICLE INTERIOR	Nasty	Neat
STEREO	Loud	Off
DOPE	Yes	No
PRESCRIPTION DRUGS	Yes, no prescription	No, or yes w/prescription
WEAPONS	Unlicensed, stolen	No, or yes w/proper paperwork
DRIVER'S HANDS	Hidden	Visible
POSTURE	Slouched	Straight
SEAT BELTS	Unbuckled	Buckled
PASSENGERS	Quarreling	Quiet
SEX ACTS	"Cop-tus Interruptus"	Unthinkable
ALCOHOL	Open container	None or closed container
WINDOW TINTING	Dark or bubbled	None
GLASS	Cracked	Intact
EXHAUST/MUFFLER	Smoking/Loud	Invisible/Soundless

CONTINUED NEXT PAGE ☞

CAR ARRESTABILITY QUOTIENT (CAR-Q) CONTINUED		
ARRESTABILITY METER	Low Medium High	Low Medium High
CIGARETTES	In mouths	In ashtray
GUM	A-chewing	Gone
HATE/TERRORIST LITERATURE	Yes	Unthinkable
WEALTH APPROPRIATE	No	Yes
FLIPPING A BIRD	Yes	No
WEDDING BAND	No	Yes
LOUD JEWELRY	Yes	No
CONFEDERATE FLAG	Yes	No
BLACK POWER/ GANG STUFF	Yes	No
REACHING	Yes	No

AREN'T YOU TELLING ME TO ACT AND DRIVE LIKE WHITE-BREAD AMERICA?

Yep. This isn't fair, but this book is not about what's fair; it's about what *is*. In a better America, you should be able to drive any car you want without undue police scrutiny as long as it's street legal. Unfortunately, if you want to avoid encounters with police, a gray Honda carrying two passengers dressed preppy and listening to National Public Radio is the way to go.

This flies in the face of human nature, since many people need to be different. Guys need to stand out to attract women. Sexy ladies know that a cute convertible keeps the phone ringing with lovesick suitors. Cheerful eccentrics sometimes feel the need to attach cattle horns to the bumper or glue sea shells to the roof. An *Ah-OO-gah* Klaxon is also nice. Alas, to paraphrase a famous Japanese proverb, the car that stands out gets hammered down.

25 | STAYING FREE DURING A TRAFFIC STOP MEANS THE GUY WHO LOSES IS THE COP

T raffic tickets are mostly civil penalties. How you behave during the stop determines whether matters progress to criminal acts that justify arrest. Once you're pulled over and the blue lights are spinning in your rearview mirror, the situation is similar to a street stop. You want to *lose* the psychological contest and let cops prove they're the bosses. You want to *win* the custody contest and stay free. For cops, traffic tickets are small potatoes. When they don't make an arrest, they lose. Not that cops will cry into their coffee and doughnuts if they only give out a ticket. There are thousands of mobile Easter eggs rolling down the roads, and the supply of bad guys has been remarkably constant during 6,000 years of recorded history. Cops know there will always be someone to arrest. They're optimists by nature.

THE ROUTINE TRAFFIC STOP

There are two sorts of traffic stops: the routine stop and the felony stop. They are quite different and require different responses. Police make routine stops when they spot a traffic violation. They will flash the lights and give some whoops on the siren. Here's what happens and how you should respond.

1. Pull over quickly, from the right-hand lane, no matter where you are. Do not keep driving looking for a place to pull over. Police regard this as evasion. If police want you to drive further, they will instruct you through the loudspeaker.

   For ladies at night, the rules are different. Many women are terrified, with reason, of being stopped by rapists and stalkers impersonating police officers. At night, women should turn on their flashers and drive slowly to a safe, well-lighted place.

2. Once you're stopped, the cruiser will pull in behind you. If there's room, the officers will "porpoise" the cruiser in at an angle to protect themselves from being hit by oncoming traffic.

3. The officers will approach at an angle and shield themselves at the A-post, the frame that separates the front and rear windows. If the driver or passengers draw weapons, the A-post forces them to make an awkward, three-quarter turn and spoils their aim.

4. Turn off the motor, roll down the window, and await instructions. Do *not* duck down to look for the registration under a seat or in the glove compartment. This looks like you're reaching for a weapon. Do not reach for anything unless instructed to do so. Above all, do *not* make any sudden moves.

5. Place hands in view on the steering wheel.

6. Follow precisely instructions about presenting your license, registration, etc.

7. Do not argue. Police think that people who argue are trying to hide something. If you feel the ticket was not merited, contest the matter in court. You do not need a lawyer for minor matters in traffic court. Most traffic judges are blessedly lenient. If you have a reasonable case, you generally win. However, hiring a lawyer is always in your best interest. Lawyers know the system.

8. Sign the ticket.

SIGN THAT TICKET OR YOU'LL REGRET IT

Most people don't realize that what they're signing is merely a receipt that acknowledges that they have received the traffic citation. It is *not* an admission of guilt. It does *not* affect your right to appear in court to contest the ticket. In many states cops are supposed to tell you this, but they often forget or mumble. Not signing the ticket, however, is a *criminal* offense in many states. It can get you arrested at once.

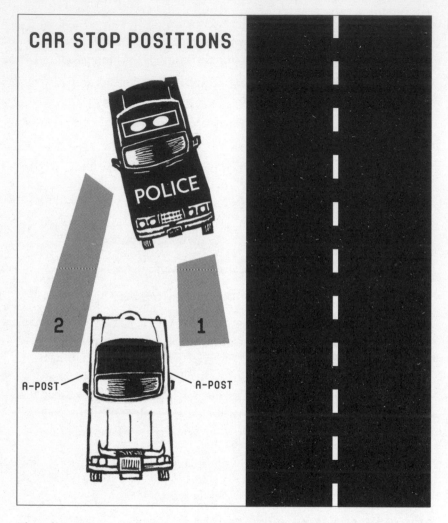

CAR STOP POSITIONS

POLICE

2   1

A-POST —   — A-POST

The police cruiser is parked at an angle to deflect a rear collision away from officer.

In position 1, the officer approaches the driver's side within the shaded zone of safety. The driver would have to twist 270 degrees to aim a weapon at the officer, who is protected by the car's A-post.

From position 2, the officer is likewise protected from passengers by the opposite A-post. In a two-man unit during a felony stop, the second officer would move to this position and jack a round into the Nine-Ball Machine, a shotgun whose shells are loaded with nine .32 caliber miniballs.

Schools, parents, and, especially, driving instructors are incredibly remiss when they do not explain this matter. An astounding number of people are arrested each year for failing to sign tickets. Every criminal attorney has several such cases. The resulting expenses and the lifetime arrest record are as absurd as they are avoidable. Sign the freaking thing!

THE FELONY STOP

A felony stop occurs when police think the driver or passengers have committed a serious crime. Felony stops are completely different from routine stops. If you've been in one, you'll never forget it. Felony stops can happen to anyone. Many upstanding citizens are felony stopped because their vehicles *resemble* those used in a crime. During felony stops, drivers and passengers are at serious risk of injury and can even be killed for making a wrong move. This is serious stuff, so listen up. Here's what happens.

1. Once the cruiser pulls you over, officers may draw weapons. They will immediately begin issuing commands, usually through the loudspeaker before they get out of the cruiser. The commands will get you and any passengers out of the vehicle and onto the ground, where you cannot threaten the officers with a weapon or use the vehicle to escape. They will go like this: "Driver, with your left hand, take the keys out of the ignition and throw them out the window. Put both hands out of the window. Open the door from the outside. Get on your knees. Face away from me. Place both hands on top of your head."

2. If the cruiser is a two-man unit, the second officer will go to the passenger-side A-post. You may hear the distinctive sound of a shotgun round being jacked into the chamber by the second officer. This will be the notorious Nine-Ball Machine.

3. In this situation, you must obey instructions *precisely*. Do *not* try to anticipate what officers want you to do and start rummaging for licenses and paperwork. Officers may consider this an attempt to reach for a weapon. Instead, react just like

a robot. If they say, "Place your hands on wheel," do it. If they say, "Put your hands outside the window," do it.

4. Do *not* argue with police officers aiming high-powered pistols and shotguns at you. Answer questions briefly and truthfully. Do not talk with passengers. *Shut up* unless officers ask you a question.

5. If you and your vehicle are not the ones police are seeking, they will let you go, unless police have discovered a violation of law. If you think police have infringed on your rights, hurt you, or damaged your vehicle, hire a lawyer and argue later in court. Do *not* argue with the officers on the scene and give them an incentive to arrest you. If they try hard enough, they'll think of *something*.

This is ammo for the Nine-Ball Machine, a magnum cartridge firing nine hardened steel miniballs. When an officer fires, the balls shred the vehicle and penetrate it until they bounce off the engine. With three rounds from the Nine-Ball Machine, police can kill everyone in a vehicle within seconds.

6. If you and your vehicle were involved in a serious crime, you're going to be searched and arrested. Important: During a felony stop, police already have probable cause to make a search. They do not have to ask permission. If this is the case, your only tactic is to minimize the charges brought against you. Therefore, do not resist. Do not flail your arms, as this is technically considered resisting in many states. When officers read your Miranda rights, they will ask if you understand. Say one word, "Yes." Then wait, saying nothing. If police ask for more than identifying information, registration, or insurance, say only the following words:

> **"I want a lawyer. I will not say anything unless my lawyer is with me."**

If you do not speak English well, just say three words, "I want lawyer," then be quiet. If you speak in your language, the officers may *translate* what they *think* you said into English in their reports. You are at a disadvantage. Yes, you do want lawyer.

If you're involved in a crime, shut up completely. Nothing you say will help. Anything you say will hurt. Talking is only an opportunity to lie, act out, resist, and rack up more charges. Many questions will be trick questions. For example, if officers ask if you've been arrested before or if you're on probation, they may already know the answer by having run your tag or license through their computers. Say the wrong thing and you've just committed another crime, lying to a police officer. *The officers will do everything possible to get you talking.* Silence is the only response that minimizes damage. Remember, you have a *constitutional right* to remain silent and to avoid incriminating yourself. Important: Don't *talk* about your rights, just *exercise* them. I will repeat Uncle Dale's Golden Rule #3, in language that is universally understood in police cruisers, in jails, and in the courts of this great nation:

> ≫ **GIVE COPS YOUR NAME AND BASIC INFO, THEN SHUT THE HECK UP!**

26 | "NO, YOU CAN'T SEARCH MY CAR"

Great news! Cops can no longer routinely search your vehicle during traffic stops—so says the Supreme Court of the United States of America. Here's the background. Prior to 2009, police routinely searched vehicles involved in traffic stops and filled the nation's jails with people found in possession of drugs, illegal firearms, and stolen merchandise. In many jurisdictions, arrests incident to traffic stops were the police's *primary* arrest tactic.

In Tucson, Arizona, Rodney Gant was driving his car with a suspended driver's license. Police stopped and then arrested him for the traffic violation. Afterward, they searched his car, found cocaine, and charged him with possession of narcotics with intent to sell and possession of drug paraphernalia. Note that the officers did not have a search warrant and that the search had nothing to do with the suspended license. Gant moved to suppress the evidence on the grounds that police had violated his rights against unreasonable search and seizure, as enumerated in the Fourth Amendment.

Over the next decade, the case made its way through the court system, all the way to the Supreme Court. In 2009, the high court sided with Gant, noting in its decision, "Countless individuals guilty of nothing more serious than a traffic violation have had their constitutional right to the security of their private effects violated." This opinion makes clear that your right to privacy and freedom from warrantless searches is more important than society's need for efficiency in policing. The Supreme Court was unequivocal: "Warrantless searches are *per se* unreasonable."

So is it time to stock your ride with whores, guns, booze, and bongs and roll down the highway in perpetual party mode? As cops roll alongside in this bright new century, should you wiggle your fingers in your ears, flip the bird, or wedge your pimpled and tattooed fanny against the window?

Not hardly. This vehicle search immunity has exceptions, and they're important.

>> **CONSENT.** When they stop you for a traffic violation, cops can always search your car if you agree to let them. Police will induce you to consent by asking the famous Cop Trick Questions. You *will* hear these words on your next traffic stop. They go like this:

> COP: "By the way, you don't happen to have any guns or narcotics in the car, do you?"
>
> YOU: "Who, me? Uh, hmm, uh . . . No!"
>
> COP: "Then you don't mind if I make a search, do you?"
>
> YOU: "Uh, well, er, hmmm, uh . . . Of course I don't mind!"

When you answer this way, you consent to a search and effectively waive your constitutional rights. Don't even try to answer these questions. Simply repeat the magic words: "No, you can't search my car."

>> **PROBATION AND PAROLE WAIVERS.** Check that balled up wad of papers you were handed at sentencing. In most jurisdictions, as a condition of probation or parole, you have to waive your rights against warrantless search and seizure. During any traffic stop, police will run your license and tag. If you're on probation and parole, they'll know, and they'll search. For details, see *Arrested*, by my coauthor Wes Denham, which explains why probation and parole are "outdoor jail," and why violations as trivial as not sending a change-of-address postcard can get you hard time in prison.

>> **WARRANTS.** If the check of your license and tag reveals an outstanding warrant, clearly you will be arrested. If you are

arrested for an activity for which your vehicle could have been used, it will be searched.

>> **EVIDENCE IN PLAIN SIGHT.** When police stop you for a traffic violation and see dope in plain sight, they can retrieve the dope and arrest you.

>> **OFFICER SAFETY.** Officers can make a cursory search of the interior of your vehicle if you are inside of or alongside the vehicle and they suspect it may contain weapons you might use to attack them. They can't, however, open the trunk or truck box, rummage around under the seats, pop panels, or grope around under the hood. The lesson here: don't give the police cause for alarm. Follow the advice in the earlier chapters about how to behave around police.

>> **POOCH POPS.** Police can always whistle up a K-9 unit to sniff your car for dope, explosives, and dead-body decomp. If the dog alerts, that's probable cause for search, seizure, and arrest, typically without a judge's warrant. However, it would not be unusual for a detective to be called to the scene and a search warrant obtained from the court.

>> **VEHICLE INVENTORY.** Cops can no longer routinely tow and inventory your car when they arrest you or declare your vehicle unsafe to drive. They have to ask you what you want to do with the vehicle. Always arrange for a friend or relative to pick up the vehicle. If you consent to have your car towed by police, you have also consented to an *inventory*, which is a search. Amazingly, tow yard employees sometimes forget to report large quantities of dope, cash, and guns they find.

>> **FELONY STOPS.** As explained in the previous chapter, when police make a felony stop, they're looking for you specifically or are searching for a vehicle whose description matches yours. If they arrest you, they can search your vehicle if it's reasonable to assume that it may contain evidence specific to the crime for which you are being charged. For example, using

your gun you rob a deli and escape with a bag of cash and a pastrami on rye. You flee in a red 1974 Pinto then run out of gas a mile from the scene and are stopped by the police. With these facts, the police will search your car to find the criminal proceeds, all of which will be admissible at your trial. Here's another example. If police arrest you for sale and possession of drugs, they can search your car, because vehicles are often used to carry dope. If, however, they arrest you for driving with a suspended license, they can't conduct a search. Why? Because there can be no reason to believe your car contains evidence relevant to the suspension.

You have, no doubt, noticed that this is a long list of exceptions. Unless you happen to be a criminal defense attorney of unusual mental and verbal adroitness, it is unlikely you will be reviewing these nuances while cops are barking at you through the window. Because this book is a practical guide to staying free, I simply recommend that you refuse vehicle searches. It's your right. Americans have fought and died for two centuries to preserve this right for you. Value it; savor it; exercise it.

In America, the people grant rights to government, not the other way around. Our Constitution is an effort from start to finish to limit, not extend, the rights and powers of government. Why should you *ever* allow agents of government to search you, your house, your vehicle, your papers, and your possessions to turn up violations? When you were a kid, remember how violated you felt when your parents tossed your room and found your cigarettes, your dope, your porn, your rubbers, and maybe even some gender-bender suspender undies?

You do not have to allow a search just because you think you have nothing to hide. Why should you have to prove this? As a practical matter, keep in mind that dope, guns, and contraband are considered to be jointly possessed by everyone in the vehicle at the time of the search, regardless of who actually owns the stuff or put it there. So maybe you didn't stash that contraband, but how about your knucklehead friends, relatives, and children? Gives you shivers just to think about it.

That said, when refusing a search, be smart:

>> Follow Golden Rule #2: Keep your dope at home. Keep liquor, wine, and beer *unopened* and in the back seat or the trunk.

>> Make sure that your personal firearms are licensed, that they're carried according to state laws, and that you have your permits with you, not at home.

>> When police ask for license and registration, hand them over. If you roll up the window and refuse, they can smash the glass then arrest you for interfering with police officers in performance of their duties. When they do this, they can top up the charges with those old favorites: resisting arrest, assault and battery on a law enforcement officer, fleeing and eluding, and lying to police.

>> Ask for permission before you reach for paperwork and wallets. If you lunge forward, bend down, reach for the glove box, or grope under a seat, officers may assume you're going for a gun. This can be unfortunate.

>> If officers ask you to get out, *step away from the vehicle*. This removes the justification for a search because of officer safety concerns.

So, with the above provisos, here is Uncle Dale's Golden Rule #4:

>> **WHEN POLICE ASK TO SEARCH YOUR VEHICLE, JUST SAY NO— POLITELY!**

It is standard procedure for police to talk fast or start yelling to rattle your cage and get you to agree to a search. They will try different approaches to get you to cooperate. Maybe they'll offer you some gum, or pal it up with an arm around your shoulder. They do this for one reason only. They want to *search your car and arrest you!* As I explained earlier, during a traffic stop the only safe thing to do is to tell a brief version of the truth and then say nothing more. If questioned further, refer inquiries to your attorney.

You have one advantage on the side of the road that is lacking for suspects downtown in the trick box—time. Unlike detectives, uniformed officers are required to patrol. If you refuse a search and they cannot quickly get a warrant or a dog, they will have to let you go lest their sergeant roll by and bite their heads off for "failure to respond to a higher priority call or to maintain adequate patrol activity." In general, police can detain you by the side of the road no longer than 20 minutes, the time it takes to write a citation. If they keep you beyond 20 minutes and only later conduct a search, anything they find may be ruled inadmissible. So refuse the search and wait them out. This works.

All of us now have new protections against vehicle searches granted by the Supreme Court. For this we can thank Rodney Joseph Gant, who for one shining moment, and with excellent legal advice, rose above the daily grind of the drug trade to strike a blow for individual freedom and the limitation of government power. For the better part of a decade, inmate 156398 was a guest of the State of Arizona. By day he labored in prison workshops; by night he slept amid the shouts, screams, and grunts that are the tragic chorus of American justice.

Now he's free. May he, and you, stay that way.

27 | TIPS THAT NEVER FAIL
TO KEEP YOU OUT OF JAIL

L ending your car is a disaster that lasts forever after. Never lend your car to anyone who is not listed on insurance and in other, written authorization in the vehicle—not to family members, not to neighbors, not to friends. Should the vehicle be involved in an accident, used in the commission of a crime, or stopped by police, the complications can be unending. You have civil liability, often uninsured by your carrier, for damages to other people and their property, and criminal liability if the car is used in a crime or stopped and found to contain drugs, guns, or stolen property.

Depending on the state, the vehicle can be impounded or seized. Most important, people to whom you loan your vehicle all too often leave dope in the ashtray or under a seat, kiddie narcotics between the cushions of the backseat, or a surprise or two in the trunk.

Lending cars is an enormous problem for the clueless. Their lives are usually in an uproar in which vehicles, or the lack thereof, are at the center of the drama. In the housing projects, barrios, and trailer parks of America, cars are always being stolen, vandalized, or repossessed. Drivers constantly have their licenses suspended or revoked for failing to keep the paperwork straight or pay fees or appear in traffic court. Habitual drunks who are banned for life from driving often get the urge to get behind the wheel again. Given this continuous state of vehicle emergency, clueless people often insist that friends lend them vehicles as a test of their friendship.

When your friends ask to borrow your car, it's a heavy burden. But don't do as the clueless do. Be smart about this. I suggest the following responses when your friends or family ask to borrow your car. These responses will keep you and your vehicle out of trouble.

1. Ask why they can't drive their own car. If their licenses are suspended or revoked, it's illegal for them to drive your car. You can go to jail for lending to your car to them.

2. Offer to drive your friends wherever they need to go.

3. Say your insurance agent (or a cop!) just gave you a stern warning not to lend your car to anyone. Agonize over this dilemma. Some drama, even tears, might be appropriate. "You're such a good friend! I just hate to say no!"

3. Offer to run errands for them.

4. As an emergency technique (if their friendship is worth it) offer them $50 as part of the cost of a rental car.

Whatever you do, *do not lend your car to anyone who is not a named insured on your insurance policy and who is not authorized in writing by you to drive the vehicle.*

FORGET THE RADAR DETECTOR. YOUR CAR'S THE REFLECTOR!

Forget radar detectors, gang. They don't work well and are illegal in some states. Increasingly, traffic patrols use lasers, which, unlike radar, give an instantaneous reading. By the time your detector warns of a laser hit, you're already hammered. First, some truthful disclosure here. I do use a radar detector, but for heaven's sake, do as I *advise*, not as I actually *do*. Remember, I have advantages.

>> I'm a golden-tongued lawyer with years of experience in interrogation. I can say almost anything convincingly. You can't.

>> I drive a Ford Crown Victoria that looks (on purpose) like an undercover law enforcement vehicle. This generally gets me a pass with the cops.

>> I'm a former cop and FBI agent. You aren't. Of course, after the publication of this book I expect to be arrested at least weekly.

Cops know all about radar detectors and how to defeat them. They generally aim radar at an angle so that the signal will not register until it's too late. They also set up on the low side of a hill so that the radar emissions are blocked until the last second. This means that your radar detector merely detects the fact that you're about to get hammered. Whoopee.

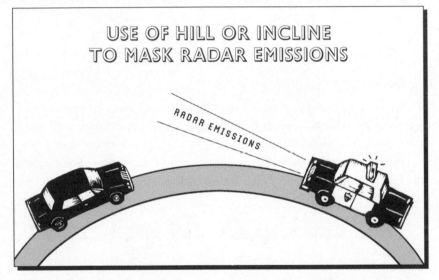

Cops use hills to block radar emissions from oncoming vehicles' radar detectors. Once you're over the top and your box starts to squawk, you're already toast. Cops also are adept at aiming radar at acute angles from roadside hiding places to accomplish the same thing.

BIKES, YIKES!

One of the "advancements" in law enforcement that truly disgusts me is the extension of vehicle laws to bicycles and the use of proactive policing techniques to pile felony charges onto children. Every criminal attorney in my city has cases of children *arrested* and *jailed* for such crimes as riding a bicycle at night without a light, riding without a helmet, and riding with their buddies on the handlebars. This enforcement is highly selective and never, *ever* occurs in wealthy neighborhoods. Poor kids, primarily poor black kids, are just Hoovered up into the system in industrial-sized quantities.

Poor kids often buy bikes at flea markets or pawnshops or from street vendors. Kids and their parents can be unaware that these bikes are often stolen, and that police have records on their computers of the vehicle identification numbers (VINs) of stolen bikes, especially the expensive ones. When a cop stops a kid on a bike and runs the VIN and finds the bike was stolen, the child is immediately charged with possession of stolen property.

Middle-class and wealthy people ride bicycles for fun and exercise. Poor people ride them out of necessity. Many poor people ride bikes to work and to stores because they have neither cars nor valid driver's licenses. Poor children ride bikes because they're their only means of transport. Their mothers often cannot drive or are at work or at home taking care of other children. There are no soccer moms hauling kids around in shiny vans in the ghettos, barrios, and trailer parks. Children have to ride bikes or walk to get anywhere.

Poor kids are more likely than middle-class kids to be afraid of police. They have been told scary stories by adults. Like their parents, they often do not have good manners and have no idea how to speak and behave around police. They are more likely to flee police or to flail their arms while being taken into custody. This will get them charged with battery on a law enforcement officer on top of the usual charges of fleeing, resisting, and lying. Thus, one moment a kid is riding down the street; the next, he's in the slammer facing a long list of felony charges, a stretch on the criminal justice and social services plantations, and a lifetime on the electronic plantation. This outrage can only be removed by legislation at the state or city level. In the meantime, you've got to protect your kids or your younger brothers and sisters.

>> Buy only new bicycles from stores.

>> Make sure that the bikes have lights and that the children use them.

>> Instruct the children to wear helmets where required and not to carry people on the handlebars.

Naturally, this takes much of the fun out of riding bikes, which for most kids is their first taste of freedom from their parents and an important stage in growing up. These bicycle laws were passed by city commissions and state legislatures to protect children's safety. Unfortunately, the welfare state has an unfortunate tendency to morph into the police state. For police, bicycle safety laws have become another means of making more arrests and racking up more points. Children need to stay free and out of jail long enough to grow up, straighten up, and become citizens. Help them out.

Help yourself out as well. Don't tool around on a stolen bike, and don't forget to use the light at night. To get arrested and dumped on the plantations due to a bicycle infraction is beyond tragic.

28 | CAR CREDS ARE THE KEY TO KEEP YOU FREE

C ar creds are lengthier than street creds for the simple reason that your car can carry more stuff that can get you arrested than your pockets or your purse. In addition, your vehicle can carry things secreted or misplaced by others that can get you arrested. Car creds are used like street creds. You hand them, all together in a business-size envelope, to the police officers who pull you over for a traffic stop. They establish that

1. you are not clueless arrest fodder

2. you have an attorney and social backup

3. you are who you claim to be

Creds stop the interrogation as police read them. When cops ask you questions about your creds, use the street-creds answers in Chapter 19.

IMPORTANT: You will note that car creds call for photocopies of driver's licenses of the car owner and anyone else authorized to drive the car. *These copies in no way replace actual driver's licenses or release you from your legal obligation to carry a license.* An emergency backup, the copies are for those times you may leave home without your license. The only purpose of the copies is to help keep you out of jail.

Note also that car creds have spaces for you to grant written permission to relatives who are authorized to drive your vehicle. Any authorized driver should also be a named insured on your insurance policy. This permission will explain to cops why someone other than the registered owner is driving the vehicle.

Last, there are spaces for you to make copies of prescriptions for medicines you or passengers may be carrying in containers other than the orange plastic containers that have legal prescription labels on them. You must make these copies *before* you hand in the prescription to the pharmacist. If you carpool, make sure to get photocopies of prescriptions from passengers or insist that they carry medicines in legally labeled containers. Anyone taking prescription meds for long periods for chronic conditions is likely to ditch the orange bottle and put pills in handier, shatter-resistant containers that do not have legal labels. This is a problem.

Remember, some prescriptions should not be taken when operating machinery like a car. If you take such a medicine, do *not* include it in your car creds.

Moms, be ultracareful about kiddie narcotics. Kids who have been prescribed stimulants and tranquilizers frequently carry the pills loose in their pockets, where they fall between cushions in the backseats. Kids also sell these drugs and give them to friends who want to get high, often unseen by you in your very own car! You, not the child, will get hammered during a police search. Syringes used for injections of insulin, which is legal, or performance-enhancing steroids, which are not, also fall out of book bags and show up in cars.

CAR CREDS / YOUTH VERSION

PLACE IN ENVELOPE ON WINDSHIELD VISOR

CUT ON DOTTED LINES. FOLD ON SOLID LINES.

FOR POLICE USE ONLY

Name _____

Address _____

City _____ State _____ Zip _____

Parent/Guardian _____

Telephone _____

Cell Phone _____

Attorney _____

Telephone _____

Cell Phone _____

Friend in Police Dept. _____

Telephone _____

Cell Phone _____

Church/Mosque/Temple _____

_____

Pastor/Priest/Imam/Rabbi _____

_____

Telephone _____

Cell Phone _____

School _____

Homeroom Teacher _____

Principal _____

School Counselor _____

Telephone _____

Cell Phone _____

FOR POLICE USE ONLY

OFFICER, I'D LIKE TO ANSWER YOUR QUESTIONS, BUT MY MOTHER TOLD ME THAT, IN A SITUATION LIKE THIS, I SHOULD NOT SAY ANYTHING UNLESS SHE AND OUR ATTORNEY ARE PRESENT.

GLUE OR STAPLE ATTORNEY'S BUSINESS CARD HERE.

GLUE OR STAPLE POLICE OFFICER'S BUSINESS CARD HERE.

CAR CREDS / YOUTH VERSION
PLACE IN ENVELOPE ON WINDSHIELD VISOR

REVERSE SIDE

Name _____

Address _____

City _____ State _____ Zip _____

Spouse _____

Telephone _____

Cell Phone _____

Attorney _____

Telephone _____

Cell Phone _____

Friend in Police Dept. _____

Telephone _____

Cell Phone _____

Church/Mosque/Temple _____

_____

Pastor/Priest/Imam/Rabbi _____

_____

Telephone _____

Cell Phone _____

Employer _____

Supervisor _____

Telephone _____

Cell Phone _____

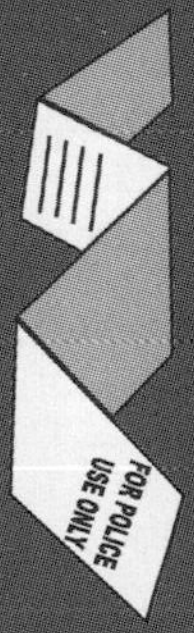

FOR POLICE
USE ONLY

OFFICER, I'D LIKE TO ANSWER YOUR QUESTIONS, BUT MY ATTORNEYS TOLD ME THAT, IN A SITUATION LIKE THIS, I SHOULD NOT SAY ANYTHING UNLESS THEY ARE PRESENT.

GLUE OR STAPLE ATTORNEY'S
BUSINESS CARD HERE.

GLUE OR STAPLE POLICE OFFICER'S
BUSINESS CARD HERE.

CAR CREDS / ADULT VERSION
PLACE IN ENVELOPE ON WINDSHIELD VISOR

REVERSE
SIDE

CAR CREDS 2
LICENSE, REGISTRATION, INSURANCE
PLACE IN ENVELOPE ON WINDSHEILD VISOR

PHOTOCOPY OF OWNER'S DRIVER'S LICENSE

PHOTOCOPY OF INSURANCE CARD

PHOTOCOPY OF VEHICLE REGISTRATION

CAR CREDS 3
PERMISSIONS AND PRESCRIPTIONS
PLACE IN ENVELOPE ON WINDSHEILD VISOR.

PERMISSION TO OPERATE VEHICLE

I affirm that I,

_____,

am the owner of this vehicle.

I affirm that

_____

has my permission to drive this vehicle.

_____

Signature of vehicle owner

PHOTOCOPY OF <u>AUTHORIZED</u> DRIVER'S LICENSE

PHOTOCOPY OF PRESCRIPTION

PHOTOCOPY OF PRESCRIPTION

29 | DON'T GET IN A LURCH. DO A SEARCH!

Having cops search your car is a real nail-biter. Will they find something? Am I toast? You can avoid substantial aggravation by searching your own car. The time to search is now, in the quiet of your home, where you can discreetly dispose of anything found, and *not* in the confused moments before a traffic stop when the blue and red lights are in the rearview mirror. I advise everyone to search their vehicles in the following circumstances.

>> Your children drive your car.

>> Friends or relatives drive your car.

>> You drive passengers who enjoy the magic herb or other controlled substances.

>> You drive children who take kiddie narcotics such as Ritalin or Valium.

>> You leave your vehicle unlocked at work so people can get tools.

>> You actually *lent* your car to someone, despite sage advice to the contrary.

>> Your car was stolen and returned to you by police.

Car searches are simple. The situation we're confronting is not sophisticated concealment by professional smugglers, who secrete contraband behind upholstery and door panels, in the gas tank in fuel-proof containers, and in specially welded compartments under wheel wells and inside bodywork. What we're concerned with here is the hastily hidden stuff that gets most people busted for possession of drugs, guns, or stolen property.

In most states, cops can seize vehicles in which drugs, guns, or stolen property are found. You will have to go to a forfeiture hearing to get your ride back. The attorney's fees often are more than what the vehicle is worth. Cops generally cannot seize a vehicle that was financed because the lender, not the driver, holds the title. Of course, if your car is seized, your lender will not be pleased. Many will insist that the loan be paid *in full* before they will release the car to you. Unless you have a cash stash, this means your wheels are gonzo.

Drugs are, by far, the most likely items to be secreted in your car without your knowledge. Basically it goes down like this. Passengers or drivers carry some dope aboard. They see a police cruiser behind them, running the tag number or just putting on the pressure in hopes of flushing a rabbit. They panic and stuff dope under a seat. People also carry dope or guns in your car, then forget to take them out because they're stoned out of their gourds. As for the kids, they're forever scattering their chemical straitjackets on the backseat cushions.

The basic places to search are

>> the ashtray, console and door storage areas, and glove compartment

>> overhead storage in windshield visor pockets

>> under all seats

>> the trunk (don't forget to check around the spare wheel)

>> the tire tool area

>> behind all seats that fold down and, in pickup trucks, the area behind seats

>> in SUVs, the storage lockers in the back or on top of the vehicle

>> between seat cushions

>> inside the air filter holder in the engine

SEARCH IT, BABY!

Gloves will keep your fingerprints off contraband. There's nothing like genuine cowhide to protect you from needles, knives, razor blades, dope, used condoms, dead cats, and whatever else knuckleheads stash in your car.

Check the ashtray first, then wash that bad boy out or get rid of it. Now go for the glove compartment, the center console, and the door storage. Don't forget the windshield visor compartments, doo-dad caddies, and trash bags.

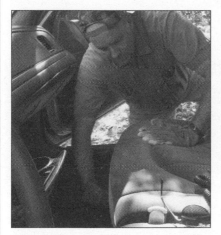

Mirror, mirror, under the wheel, Searching for dope is no big deal!

Poke way, way up underneath those seats and root around in the corners. Careful; this is where the junkies dump needles!

Use an old CD or compact mirror to peek up under the steering wheel enclosure, a favorite place to hide crystal and weed. Use your music so you don't have to face the music!

CONTINUED NEXT PAGE

CAR SEARCH (CONTINUED)

The trunk is where dummies hide the bad stuff like guns. Take some time here and probe in all the corners and in the back. Don't forget to look in the tire well and among the tire tools. It helps to toss out all the trunk junk first and give it all a good shaking.

Take a minute to peek into the air filter. Many clueless types think cops don't know to look there. Wrong.

YOU FOUND SOMETHING. NOW WHAT?

I said searching was easy. But what if you find something? What follows is extremely important. Do it right and you stay free. Do it wrong and the stuff can hit the fan. Obviously you want to search your car somewhere you're not visible to police or nosy neighbors who would love to dial 911 when they see you taking something illegal out of your vehicle. Even though you're the innocent victim here, you can get hammered for possession.

ALWAYS WEAR GLOVES WHEN SEARCHING YOUR CAR. Leather gloves will not only prevent your leaving fingerprints and DNA on anything you find, but will also protect you from needle pricks from syringes. If you discover drugs or guns, throw away your gloves after the search. You do not want to possess gloves that contain traces of illegal drugs or gunpowder residue.

IF YOU FIND DRUGS OF ANY KIND (weed, powder, crystals, blotters, spliffs, roaches, pills), here's what you do.

1. Put them into an opaque plastic bag so nosy neighbors can't see what you're up to.

2. Take them indoors into your own house (where police cannot search without a warrant). Grind up everything in the disposal if you have one. Otherwise, flush the stuff. If there is any quantity, dispose of it *a bit at a time* so as not to stop up the pipes. Plugging up plumbing with dope comes under the heading of hitting the fan.

3. Wash out any bags with soap and water, then toss them.

After you find dope in your car, ban any passenger who left it from ever entering your home or car again. If children are the culprits, you need to have a serious chat. Use the masculine approach. Don't ask them why they carry dope, what they're feeling, why they need it, and what they're thinking. Just tell them the stuff is illegal. Keep it simple. Dope does not enter your car now or ever, under any circumstances, period. Take immediate disciplinary action. Do not let this go uncorrected.

IF YOU FIND PARAPHERNALIA of any kind, here's what you do.

1. Place glass or ceramic bongs between cardboard pieces and smash them with a hammer.

2. Place metal pipes and bongs on a hard surface and smack them with a hammer.

3. If you find a syringe, *carefully pick it up so as to avoid a needle-stick*, which can kill you if the needle is infected with AIDS, hepatitis, cytomegalovirus, or other horrors. Pull out the plunger and soak everything in undiluted liquid bleach. Squirt some bleach through the needle. Now place the nasty thing between cardboard and give it a smack with the hammer.

4. Place paraphernalia in an opaque bag so nosy neighbors can't see anything.

5. Don't put it in your own garbage or your neighbors'. Use a municipal dumpster only. Many dumpsters are filmed by video

cameras, so you want to be seen or photographed tossing a bag, not the paraphernalia itself. Wear a hat. Most security cameras take low-resolution images, and you cannot be easily identified while hatted.

The reason you destroy paraphernalia is that you may have to carry it in your car for disposal. You do not want to have usable paraphernalia in your car where you're subject to being stopped and searched. If cops do stop you and find the stuff, explain what you're doing.

IF YOU FIND STOLEN MERCHANDISE, call your attorney. Willful destruction of evidence is a crime. Ask first, dispose second. Don't keep the stuff, even if you want it.

IF YOU FIND A GUN, this is a dangerous situation. Pay attention. Clueless and criminal types leave loaded and cocked guns in other people's cars because they're wasted or because they used the weapon in a crime and need to dump it. When cocked or chambered, both revolvers and automatic pistols will fire easily if jostled. Make absolutely sure no one, including yourself, is facing the business end of a gun.

You *do* want to turn in this weapon to police, because to dispose of it on your own may cause you to commit the crime of withholding evidence. If you turn in the weapon in person, however, you risk being

>> arrested as an accessory to a crime

>> arrested as a material witness

>> interrogated by police

>> named in police reports and in police databases and questioned about similar crimes

>> subpoenaed to testify in court

Remember, you don't want to get into disputes, get arrested, and then be subjected to the usual pile-on charges. Here's what you do.

1. If you're familiar with weapons, uncock and unload the weapon. Be honest with yourself. If you've never handled guns, do not attempt this.

2. Do *not* talk to anyone about the weapon—not now, not ever. If the weapon was used in a crime, anyone you talk to can be compelled to testify against you and connect you to a weapon used in a crime.

3. Call a criminal defense attorney. Hire him or her to arrange to have the weapon removed and turned in to police. The attorney may send a private investigator to handle this, which is OK. Here's why you do this. When your attorney or your attorney's employee turns in the gun to police, neither can be forced to reveal who found it, where it was found, or under what circumstances it was found. Your attorney and your attorney's staff have ironclad legal protection against police interrogation. This is called attorney-client privilege. The cops will have the gun, but they won't know who found it.

   By hiring an attorney to turn in the gun, you've done your legally required civic duty. You also have an attorney to protect you, extremely credible witnesses to back up your story, and an expert mouthpiece to do the talking in case the gun is ever linked to you and there's blowback from cops and prosecutors. Paying the attorney's bill will annoy you, but go ahead and fork it up. Until you've been grilled by homicide detectives about a murder weapon, you don't know what real annoyance is.

4. Don't even *think* about keeping a weapon you found, no matter how valuable it is and how much you need the money.

5. Gloves, gang. Wear gloves!

6. Talk only to your attorney. When you find a gun, shut the heck up! Never talk about it except with your attorney or pursuant to a court order.

30 | YOU CAN TELL COPS "TOODLE-OO" WHEN YOU SQUIRT THE YELLOW GOO

This chapter is about an emergency procedure for arrest-proofing a vehicle. The procedure consists of filling every void in the interior of the car with nasty, yellow, gap-filling foam. You also should rip out the backseat, then permanently lock the trunk so the car cannot be used to secrete dope, guns, or stolen property. Use this procedure when your vehicle is driven by

>> friends or relatives who may carry drugs, guns, or stolen property

>> people whose *passengers* may carry drugs, guns, or stolen property

>> a young guy who carries three of his buddies in the car, creating a four-male-passenger crew cab that is a high-value target for police

ABOUT CARS FOR TEENAGERS

It is insanity to buy a new car for a kid. The car is not a status symbol. It is a rolling load of civil and criminal liability, mostly unfunded and mostly uninsurable, that will not be lifted from your shoulders and removed from your nightmares until the kids are 18 to 21 and no longer living in your home. If teens need a vehicle, get them a good used car or pickup truck.

NOTE TO PARENTS: This procedure is tough on the car, but not nearly so tough, or expensive, as an arrest that keeps kids from working in decent jobs for the rest of their lives. Remember, if anyone leaves dope or guns in your car, you, too, could get arrested. If your kid gets busted for a felony, the attorney's fees alone will be more than the value of most used cars. If you've got a problem driver, just get out the foam (*nonflammable* foam only!) and start squirting. If the kid yells and throws a fit, tell the little darling to take the bus. Donate the arrest-proofed jalopy to charity, take a tax deduction, and feel better fast.

Here's how this arrest-proofing procedure goes down. Check the photos for details.

1. Remove the backseat from the vehicle. This makes it impossible to stash drugs under the seat and allows only two people to use the vehicle. Thus it is impossible for four young men to ride in the car in a crew-cab formation that attracts police.

2. Fill every space where drugs and guns can be hastily secreted with gap filler. This is a yellow foam that dries hard and is normally used to fill gaps where conduit and pipes enter houses. The stuff is available at home-improvement stores. Make sure to adjust the seats to the position that the driver will use before you start squirting. Once gap filler is under the seats, the seats will be immobilized.

3. Remove the tire and tire tools from the trunk, place them in the back where you removed the seat, firmly secure them so they don't become projectiles during driving, then weld or superglue the trunk lock so the trunk cannot be opened.

6. Fill out the additional page of car creds (see page 274) and place them in the vehicle.

Of course the vehicle is pretty well trashed, but it's still street legal. It can only be used for transportation. With the ashtray foamed up, it will be difficult to smoke dope, tobacco, or anything else, but what's so bad about that?

If police stop the vehicle, they will want to know why the car is filled with weird yellow foam. Instruct your driver to hand car creds to the cops. Kids can never explain this stuff adequately when cops are staring at them from behind a high-powered flashlight. For that matter, neither can you.

YOU CAN TELL COPS "TOODLE-OO" WHEN YOU SQUIRT THE YELLOW GOO!

Gap filler looks gross (its primary purpose is to fill holes in houses to keep out cockroaches), but it's easy to use. The foam swells as it cures. Once dry, it can easily be shaped with a knife. Gap filler makes it tough for your children or their druggy-thuggy friends to hide dope, guns, or stolen property. When your children develop common sense and prudence, you can remove the stuff. It will occur to your kids to get rid of it, so check periodically. For your children, having no storage is a certain amount of aggravation, but so what? Until they get arrested, they don't know aggravation. If they whine, let 'em. It's your car, your money, your insurance policy, and your children's future.

Start by squirting the gap filler into the door storage areas. The stuff swells as it dries, but once it's dry you can cut it easily with a knife if it's gotten out of control.

Fill up the ashtray if you can't get rid of it. It's the first thing cops reach for when searching a car.

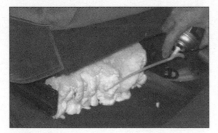

Yes, gang, you do want to foam under the seats, where so many nasty things can hide. Be sure to adjust the seat first, because when the foam hardens, the seat ain't moving, nowhere, nohow.

Say good-bye to the glove box. The kids will have to carry everything in plain sight, which is the point of the exercise.

ONLY ELEPHANTS SHOULD HAVE TRUNKS

Remove the backseat so that the vehicle cannot carry four young men in the "crew cab" formation that sends cops vibes that say, "Arrest me!"

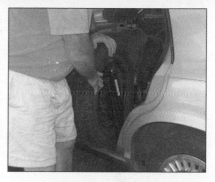

Take the tire AND THE TIRE TOOLS out of the trunk and place them in the now seatless rear of the car.

Disconnect the trunk opening switch if you have one, either by cutting the wire or pulling out the fuse.

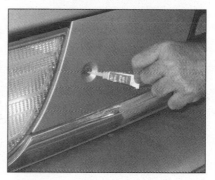

Weld or superglue the trunk lock shut. If you, the parent, sometimes need the use of the trunk, get the lock rekeyed instead. You keep the key, not Junior.

CAR CREDS 4
ARREST PROOFING
PLACE IN ENVELOPE ON WINDSHEILD VISOR

PHOTOCOPY OF <u>OWNER'S</u> DRIVER'S LICENSE

POLICE OFFICERS:
ARREST-PROOFING PROCEDURE EXPLAINED

I affirm that I, _____,
am the owner of this vehicle. I do not want anyone to be able to conceal illegal substances or items in this vehicle. In order to make concealment more difficult, I have done the following:

❑ I have filled voids throughout the interior with gap-filling foam.

❑ I have removed the rear seat.

❑ I have glued or welded shut the trunk.

You have my permission to search this vehicle, to cut out all the foam to assure yourself that nothing is concealed within, and to open the trunk by force.

_____

Signature of vehicle owner

PART IV

GUNS, KNIVES, AND SELF-DEFENSE

31 | GUNS, KNIVES, NUNCHAKU, AND NONSENSE

I 've carried a knife since I was a kid and a firearm for more than 40 years. I strongly recommend the legal carry of firearms for self-defense. As a former police officer and FBI sniper, I know plenty about weapons. As a criminal defense attorney, I defend people who don't understand their legal use. In chapter 32, I'll give you my personal recommendations, based on years of law enforcement and criminal defense experience, for the best firearms for self-defense and home defense and will discuss a special type of ammunition. But first, this chapter will discuss the ignorant, sometimes crazy behaviors involving weapons that will get you injured, killed, or incarcerated. I'll also review the legality and practicality—and lack thereof—of other weapons, gadgets, and gizmos that are more likely to end your freedom than to save your life.

Police are weapons experts. Throughout their careers, they study weapons, legal and illegal, and the state laws, federal laws, and court decisions that govern their use. They have an uncanny ability to find hidden firearms and to discover incorrectly registered, unlicensed, or illegal firearms, all of which will earn you distressingly long prison sentences. Most important, police officers react differently to various *legal* firearms and knives you may have when they encounter you. In this chapter, I'll also inform you how laws make knives and guns legal in one circumstance and illegal in another, regardless of whether the weapons were legally permitted. Lawyers call this "inchoate crime." This means a crime that's incomplete or unfinished. In standard English, this means getting busted for carrying a weapon in the wrong place at the wrong time.

GUNS ARE FUN

Owning and using firearms is intimately related to men's desires to be strong, dangerous, and capable of defending what's theirs. To confirm this, just visit your city's best gun shop, as I did when I took photographs for this chapter at Shooters of Jacksonville, one of the largest gun stores in the South.

Even at closing time, the place was jammed. Guys were going nuts over hundreds of automatics, revolvers, hunting rifles, and assault rifles, and some intriguing little derringers. Between the guns and ammo were bowie knives, bush knives, throwing knives, stilettos, bayonets, and extra-large diamond hones that put a razor edge on this hardware.

To say a gun store is a man's paradise is an understatement. There everybody talks the fine points of polygonal versus machined lands, right- versus left-hand spins, barrel length, trigger pulls, laser sights, German versus Japanese glass in scopes—and bullets, bullets, bullets. Need to stop a grizzly from interrupting your nap? Try the .50 caliber Desert Eagle. . . . With the exception of Apple stores on iPhone launch day, no other retail

Ruger .22 Mark III with integrated suppressor. This is a Title II firearm, which requires a permit from the Bureau of Alcohol, Tobacco, Firearms and Explosives. Photo courtesy of Shooters of Jacksonville

establishments in America have customers so excited about the merchandise and so eager to shove cash and credit cards across the counter.

My coauthor nearly got a chubby handling "The Judge," by Taurus International, a revolver chambered for .410 shotgun shells as well as .45 cartridges. The rifled barrel spreads the shot so that accurate aiming and no aiming at all have similar results. I, who should know better, nearly succumbed to the urge to buy a Ruger .22 Mark III with an integrated suppressor so slick that the discharge is quieter than a gnat's fart.

The first thing you notice at the best gun shops is walls lined floor to ceiling with assault rifles, all by famous manufacturers, based on the designs of their military counterparts. They've all got big clips, flash suppressors, lasers, scopes, even infrared emitters for night-vision gear. Chambered for rounds from .223 caliber to 7.62 × 45 mm, they look, and are, bad to the bone. As soon as sales are completed, everybody can't wait to head to the range or the woods and fire some rounds through those perfectly machined barrels.

Now and then I get together with my old law enforcement buddies, head out to the range, and blow up targets with machine guns and assault rifles and give my pistols a workout. It's interesting to put .308 rounds into four-inch groups a thousand yards downrange using rifles with floating barrels that are custom tuned by master armorers. What could be more relaxing? Guns, you see, are fun.

This assault rifle, by FN Herstal, can be chambered for rounds from .223 caliber to 7.62 × 45 mm. Photo courtesy of Wikimedia Commons

And that's the problem.

The powerful emotions we feel about owning and using firearms turn off rational mental functions. The ego inflation of gun ownership—you're no longer a nobody, you're a Man with a Gun—can tempt anyone into crazy, dangerous, and illegal behaviors. Gun law penalties are harsh. Many states have heavy minimum and add-on sentences, such as Florida's notorious 10-20-Life law, for crimes in which a firearm is used. These emotions also make you forget the obvious: guns are *dangerous*. Unlike on TV, where good guys who get shot suffer only flesh wounds that heal before the next commercial, in real life, bullet wounds have horrible consequences. Some take months to heal; some never do. Quite a few kill, and there's no going back after that.

To protect yourself from both legal and physical injury, beware the following firearms situations that will get you hammered, hurt, or both:

ACCIDENTAL DISCHARGE. Thousands of times a year, people accidentally fire weapons and cause injury or death. When you harm someone in this way, expect the police to arrest you, then file charges that will land you in jail, then prison, where you can reflect at leisure on your folly. The civil lawsuits that pile up while you're behind bars will make you think that "Defendant" is your new first name.

Sometimes accidental discharge is the result of ignorance, such as attempting to clean an automatic pistol that has a round in the chamber. More often, it occurs when you play around with handguns. The key factor in most cases is not being present mentally. You get distracted and start thinking of other things while you're handling a firearm. For example, while loading your gun you start thinking about the car, beer, lawn mowing, etc. These thoughts require your *conscious* attention, so that only your *subconscious* remains focused on loading the gun. This lack of conscious control can make you fire the weapon if you're startled or hear a noise.

The moral? Pay attention when handling a firearm. Put the thing down if your mind starts to wander.

SHOWING OFF. While planning this chapter, I handed a revolver, unloaded of course and with the cylinder opened, to my coauthor. What did he do?

He started *waving it around!* I practically dove over the armchair seeking cover. Waving guns around, of course, is what everybody does who is not knowledgeable about firearms. Worse, people pull the trigger to hear the click. Sometimes, unfortunately, they hear a *bang*. (I will not even discuss Russian roulette or other suicidal craziness.)

Women are not immune to gun foolishness. They will huddle with girlfriends, show off some "chick gun," then start waving the thing around and pulling the trigger. Sometimes they shove guns into their bras, where an accidental discharge can enter the torso and be fatal.

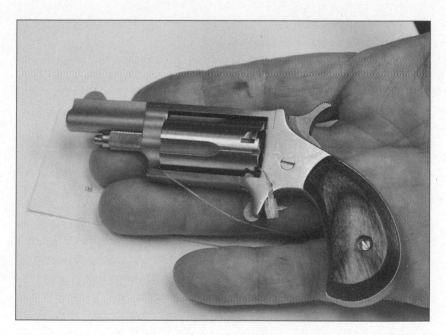

This North American Arms .22 derringer is the ultimate chick gun. It fires five Magnum rounds. It's as cute as lace pants. Photo courtesy of Shooters of Jacksonville

The takeaway? The most important "safety" on every firearm is the direction in which the barrel is pointed. Train yourself to point your weapon only where a bullet could safely go—even when the gun is unloaded. This will become a lifesaving habit.

IMPRESSING CHICKS. The urge is almost irresistible. You buy a firearm, and you want to show your girlfriend how tough you are and how you can protect her against bad guys with your big, bad gun. Naturally you think she should reward you with vigorous practice with your *other* gun.

As mentioned above, you need to stay focused and avoid distraction when you're holding a weapon. Another important reason not to flash your gun is that as far as firearms are concerned, you have no friends, only "frenemies." Today's friends, lovers, and business partners are tomorrow's complainants and plaintiffs.* If you're boning your lover's best friend, it may occur to your soon-to-be-ex–sweetie pie to call police and swear that you threatened her with your handgun, which she will then describe in excruciating and incriminating detail.

Never display or talk about your guns to casual acquaintances or even friends. Sensible women will be impressed that you are knowledgeable about firearms and careful about their use. If your significant other is interested in firearms, she can get a permit and you can train together. Couples that shoot together stay together.

CELL PHONES, CAMERAS, FACEBOOK. Nearly every person in this country carries a cell phone with a microphone, still camera, and video recorder. So when you show off your gun, you're likely to get photographed, recorded, and filmed. Being digital, these recordings will soon appear on Facebook, YouTube, and elsewhere on the Web. This can be unfortunate when a potential employer sees you playing with a firearm. It can be disastrous if you're on probation or parole or are subject to restraining orders that prohibit you from possessing a firearm. Think your probation/parole officer doesn't look you up on the Internet? And that furious ex-spouse/lover?

Think again.

BRANDISHING. Displaying a firearm in public, whether showing off or threatening someone, is called brandishing. This is a serious offense. In chapter 33, which explains self-defense and Stand Your Ground laws, I'll

---

* Just ask my former wives, a.k.a. Plaintiffs #1, #2, #3, and #4.

discuss the problems that occur when firearms laws conflict. In too many states, it's *legal* to protect yourself from attack with a firearm, but *illegal* to brandish the weapon before you are in fear of death or great bodily harm. These statutory niceties usually get sorted out while you're in jail.

GOOGLED INTO CUSTODY. Google sends video trucks through every public street in America to update their famous Google Street View service, which displays a picture of every building that has an address. With disheartening regularity, their photo trucks capture images of guys brandishing firearms on front porches and on the streets. The photos conveniently give cops the exact address for an arrest.

GUNS AND KIDS. Nothing is more tragic than children being shot while playing with firearms. After the funeral, Mom and Dad often get locked up for their failure to observe firearm safety laws. Most states have requirements for securing firearms and ammunition at home. This usually involves trigger guards, weapons lockers, or gun safes. Each state is different. The personnel at the best gun shops are extremely knowledgeable about these requirements, and they sell all the equipment your state requires to secure firearms at home.

Don't forget to secure the ammo as well. Boys have an almost irresistible urge to see what happens when they whack a cartridge with a hammer or toss ammo into ovens and fires.

TOY GUNS. Toy guns are a lousy idea. In low light, they look real. This may make the bad guys fire first. If you draw a toy gun on a cop, expect to get blasted. You should also expect, whether you survive or not, that the shooting will be ruled righteous. Even plastic squirt guns cause problems. Many "chick" guns are powder-coated in bright pinks, yellows, and blues, and these small-caliber automatics look just like—you guessed it—squirt guns.

What about air guns and CO_2 guns that fire BBs and pellets? They're great for blasting varmints, sending cockroaches to their just reward, and making precision holes in coffee cans. Although capable of wounding people, they don't have the stopping power of a handgun. Unfortunately, they look amazingly like real automatics and will make bad guys and cops shoot first and ask questions later. Ditto paint guns.

Many people are doing long stretches in prison because they robbed people, stores, and banks with toy guns. Here's a news flash: a robbery with a toy gun is still an armed robbery. The law is based on what the victim believes, not what the robber knows. A toy gun gets you the same tough sentences as the real thing.

SHOOTING BLANKS. Blank ammunition is used for firearms training, movie and TV stunt work, powering nail guns, and starting athletes at sports competitions. Although blanks don't have slugs, they are fully charged with primer and powder. The cartridge is sealed with a paper wad or a plastic cap, or by crimping at the end of the shell. Some movie and TV blanks are charged with specialized powder that produces photogenic fireballs and a big *boom* for the cameras and microphones.

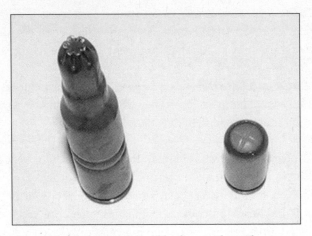

Crimped and plastic-capped blank cartridges. Photo courtesy of Wikimedia Commons

Quite a few dead, blind, and deaf people have discovered that blanks are not harmless. Even without a slug, the blast of a blank is spun by the lands and grooves and compressed into a focused explosion of intense energy. In 1984, actor Jon-Erik Hexum, purportedly to relieve the tedium of shooting the TV series *Cover Up*, put a blank cartridge into a .44 Magnum, spun the cylinder à la Russian roulette, put the barrel to his head, and pulled the trigger.

Bang! He dead.

Here are some of the other pants-on-head stupid ideas that occur to people monkeying with blank ammo:

» Load the blank then stuff the barrel with dirt, sticks, and BBs, muzzle-loader style. Sometimes this junk fires out and kills people and pets. Sometimes it jams the action and causes the weapon to explode. Shrapnel can be hard on your eyes.

» Make homemade blanks by snatching the slug off a cartridge with pliers.

» Fire blanks at other people. The paper wad, plastic cap, or shattered bits of crimping at the end of the shell will penetrate and kill when fired at close range.

Movie and TV guns are specialized weapons that fire blanks only and are serviced and managed by professional armorers. Actors are trained to offset their aim, i.e., aim slightly away from the bad guy, before firing. This avoids injury from debris and unburned powder grains. Careful angling of the cameras artfully disguises this prudent practice.

Dangerous as they are, blanks are lousy for self-protection. They also tempt people to carry unlicensed firearms in public, because they mistakenly believe that blank ammo makes obtaining permits unnecessary. This has the usual criminal justice consequences: jail time for Bozo.

WANNABE COPS WANNA BE ARRESTED. Want to be a cop? Be a real one. Study, get your degree, apply to the academy, work hard, sweat harder, and train even harder. When you graduate, take the oath, get the badge and the weapon, then hit the streets to serve and protect. Avoid like poison joining the netherworld of guys who obsess about cops but don't do the work that earns the uniform. Particularly scary are those who join neighborhood watch organizations then get that urge to be a cop on the cheap. As a neighborhood watchman, you're supposed to watch—period. See anything? Dial the number and wait for the constabulary.

You are not—repeat *not*—authorized to patrol, to snoop, to get into peoples' faces, or to make arrests. You are especially not authorized to pack a pistol and wave your piece to make the neighbors say "How high?" when you say "Jump."

GUNS AND LEGAL DOPE. Marijuana for recreational use is now legal in several states. Before you holster your gun and rush out to your friendly neighborhood dope store, put that bong down for a minute and pay attention. In many states, driving while under the influence of any drug, legal or illegal, cancels your firearms permit, and can subject you to arrest on firearms charges.

When it comes to firearms laws, what matters is whether your mental functions, coordination, and reflexes are impaired. Whether the drug that impairs them is legal or illegal doesn't matter. The only way you should carry a gun is stone-cold sober.

Need I mention that when dope slows you down, it makes it easier for bad guys to shoot you first? It causes you to be careless, which increases the risk of accidental discharges. It makes you shoot wild, which can bring death or injury to family and bystanders. After a shooting, when the cops are asking a thousand rapid-fire questions, dope will make you babble like an idiot *then forget what you said*, which is dangerous to your freedom.

Regardless of what state you live in, keep your dope at home, behind closed doors, away from cops, away from bad guys, and with your firearm secured in the manner prescribed by the legislators and judges of your state.

When you strap it on, be wary, be sober, and be cold as ice.

FIREARMS PERMITS

Whenever you carry a firearm, your gun permit has to be to on your person. It doesn't matter that the permit is back home in a drawer. If you don't have it with you when a cop asks for it, as far as the law is concerned, *you do not have a permit.*

Police find a gun permit reassuring. First, if you have a valid permit, you are by definition *not a felon*. Second, people with legal firearms and up-to-date permits are significantly less likely than the general public to commit crimes.

All states issue firearms permits, although the District of Columbia does not. Each state's laws are different. An excellent source for permitting and training requirements is your local top-tier gun shop—*not* a pawnshop and definitely not the Internet, which is full of out-of-date and incorrect information. Your gun dealer can also explain federal laws governing the purchase of firearms over the Internet, from out of state, or at gun shows, and how to get these legally delivered to a federally licensed firearms dealer for pickup. Another source for up-to-date information on permitting is www.atf.gov, the Web page of the Bureau of Alcohol, Tobacco, Firearms and Explosives. The bureau even has an app for your smartphone. The best source of information, always, is a local criminal defense attorney. Carry his or her business card along with your permit.

Gun permits from your state may be valid in other states or they may not. States that honor your state's gun permit are said to have *permit reciprocity*. You need to check reciprocity before you travel. This is not easy, since gun laws change constantly. For current information, go only to the most trustworthy source, the National Rifle Association (www.nra.org) and its Institute for Legislative Action (www.nraila.org). If you have a firearm, I strongly recommend that you join the NRA. Their information on legal and responsible gun ownership is second to none.

The federal Firearms Owners Protection Act (FOPA) makes it legal to transport firearms from one state to another. It *does not* make it legal to carry, have access to, or use the firearm while you are transporting it from one place lawful to possess to another place lawful to possess. Typically this relates to hunters. The NRA's Institute for Legislative Action has published these guidelines on how to transport weapons:

> *Under FOPA, notwithstanding any state or local law, a person is entitled to transport a firearm from any place where he or she may lawfully possess and carry such firearm to any other place where he or she may lawfully possess and carry it, **if the firearm is unloaded***

and locked out of reach. In vehicles without a trunk, the unloaded firearm must be in a locked container other than the glove compartment or console. Ammunition that is either locked out of reach in the trunk or in a locked container other than the glove compartment or console is also covered.

Travelers should be aware that some state and local governments treat this federal provision as an "affirmative defense" that may only be raised after an arrest. The U.S. Court of Appeals for the Third Circuit has also recently held that FOPA's protections only apply while the firearm is not readily accessible to the traveler, and that a firearm is readily accessible during a hotel stay.

Get this wrong and you can get seriously busted. Perhaps you remember the case of Plaxico Burress, the National Football League wide receiver. In 2008, he accidentally discharged an improperly holstered Glock in a Manhattan club. The bullet entered his thigh. Cops discovered he had only an *expired* Florida handgun permit. He was convicted on several felony counts and served two years hard time at New York State's Oneida Correctional Facility. When you've been making millions and living large, inhabiting a concrete cage, sleeping on a steel shelf, and eating beanie-weenies is tough.

Gun permits are unusual in that they are subject to instant cancellation when your circumstances change. It doesn't matter that you still have the permit itself, or that the permit is shown as valid on government computers. Under federal law, you are a "prohibited person"—i.e., your firearms privileges are cancelled—when you are

>> convicted of a felony or adjudicated delinquent while a juvenile (the delinquency prohibition remains in effect until you are 24 years of age)

>> adjudged an addict or a user of illegal drugs

>> an alien, unless you are admitted as a permanent resident

>> subject to domestic restraining orders

>> convicted of domestic assault, including misdemeanor convictions

>> a fugitive from justice

>> dishonorably discharged from the military

>> classified as mentally ill

>> a minor under the age of 18 for long guns and 21 for handguns; if you are under 18, you can't have a handgun

>> a person who has renounced U.S. citizenship

>> caught carrying a firearm in a school zone

Most state gun laws include these federal disqualifiers. Some states add additional disqualifiers. It pays to check.

The minute you are subject to a restraining order or are convicted on felony or domestic assault charges, gather up your firearms and give them to a trusted friend or relative. Do not put pistols in your safe deposit box. In the bank, the guns are still legally in your possession. Most of all, *do not wait*. You must be able to say truthfully to a police officer and under oath to a judge, "No, I do not have any firearms."

If police later arrest you and discover guns you are prohibited from possessing, you can be charged with firearms violations with severe penalties and mandatory minimum sentences in many states. If police merely seize your weapons, you might be able to have them returned once the dispute or divorce is decided or after the protection order is lifted, but don't get your hopes up. Vehicles and real estate require judicial hearings before seizure by the government. Not so with guns. Cops grab them and they're gone. The attorney fees necessary to have them returned are, in most cases, far more than the cost of any ordinary firearm.

An astonishing number of people have outstanding warrants and restraining orders that they thought were handled. Warrants and orders do not have a "handled" status. They're either there or not there. When your former neighbor/lover/spouse/friend/business partner tells you that a restraining order will get handled, say thank you, wait two weeks, then rush to the courthouse to verify. Get a copy of the paperwork from the clerk and keep it in your car. Don't be a sap and think that people who hate you won't let those orders stand and get you busted downrange. Verify also when an attorney tells you a warrant is quashed. Get it in writing and carry a copy in your vehicle. Otherwise you may be the one getting quashed.

When used in a crime, even permitted guns become illegal. If you are arrested for committing a crime, particularly a felony, possession will enhance the penalties in many states—big time.

When you encounter police officers, they will often inquire whether you're carrying a firearm. If you are, just say so. Cops encounter people carrying firearms legally all the time, and they have procedures for verifying ownership and permits. I recommend, however, that you do *not* volunteer this information unless you're asked. You are not required to do so, nor is it advisable to let them know you have a permit or guns. First, you're opening yourself to police interrogation. Second, once you volunteer this information, police might boot up the cruiser laptop and check government databases to see whether any of the disqualifiers listed earlier in the section apply. If they find one, you're busted.

If the police ask to see your weapon, just follow their directions. *Ask permission* before you reach for your firearm. Say something like this: "My pistol is in the glove compartment. What would you like me to do, officer?" Do the same when an officer asks for your permit. Do not hurry. Move slowly, calmly, and with your hands visible to the officer. Obviously, you never *point* a pistol at a law enforcement officer, since this is usually fatal.

TITLE II FIREARMS

There is a class of firearms that require permits from federal, not state, government. The issuing agency is the Bureau of Alcohol, Tobacco, Firearms and Explosives. These weapons are called Title II firearms, because of the section of the Federal Firearms Act that describes them. (They are frequently but incorrectly called Class III firearms, because the gun dealer

Clockwise from top left: the Daewoo Precision Industries USAS-12, a full-auto shotgun; a cell phone gun; an automatic pistol mounted on a shoulder stock, and the Serbu Super-Shorty, a smoothbore handgun that fires shotgun shells. Photos courtesy of Wikimedia Commons

must have a Class III permit to sell them.) They have stiff permit fees, require a background check, and often necessitate an attorney to process the paperwork.

Title II firearms include machine guns and machine pistols, short-barreled or sawed-off shotguns, short-barreled rifles (usually meaning pistols mounted to a rifle stock), firearms with noise suppressors (silencers), and those with bores greater than .50 caliber (½ inch), such as cannons. Title II also includes a catchall category, "Any Other Weapon," for regulating disguised firearms, trick guns, and weapons that are just plain weird.

GUNS THAT MAKE COPS SNOOP AND PRY

Cops know which firearms are commonly used for hunting and self-defense and where they're likely to be carried. Certain firearms, even when legally permitted, are frequently used for the commission of crime. Why are you carrying these things? Inquiring cops want to know. Here are some examples.

Huge .50 caliber automatics are used to blast through bullet-resistant glass and kill store clerks during robberies. If cops ask why you've got a .50 caliber Desert Eagle stuffed into your gym shorts, don't tell them you're hunting elephant in downtown Chicago.

Cops don't like assault weapons at all. Reason? They are, of course, derived from military weapons designed primarily to kill soldiers. In the 'hood and in the boondocks, hoodlums use them for drive-by shootings and, with illegal armor-piercing rounds, for firing through cars and houses.

Charming.

Any of the Title II weapons discussed in the previous section will make cops' antennas tingle. This includes noise suppressors, because they are primarily mounted on assassination weapons. If you're packing a machine gun or a full-auto shotgun like the Super-Shorty, or the 12-round "Street Sweeper" shotgun, you'd better be a member of a riot control squad. Permits for civilian use of these weapons are next to impossible to obtain.

While on the FBI SWAT team, I often carried an MP5 SDA3. This is a fully suppressed, select-auto, subsonic 9 mm Heckler & Koch with a collapsible stock. On the civilian market, this weapon sells for $15,000. The four-tube night-vision gear that goes with it costs $150,000. None of this equipment is for the faint of heart or the light of wallet.

The people who do legally own these weapons are primarily firearms enthusiasts and weapons experts. They have the time, the paperwork skills, and the money for expensive weapons, expensive Title II permits, and expensive attorneys to obtain them. When cops encounter these guys, they're usually going to or coming from the shooting range. Their firearms are cleaned, oiled, and generally nestled in expensive hard cases locked in the trunk.

Gun enthusiasts are immediately recognizable. They wear clean, pressed hunting and shooting outfits and tend to chatter, extremely articulately, about the finer points of this or that weapon. Why don't the police adopt the Sig Sauer P226, which Navy SEALs use, instead of those stupid Glocks? Cops, of course, find such talk boring. They're interested in bad guys and illegal guns. They don't mind a bit if hoodlums are incoherent and smell like long-dead mullet.

OPEN CARRY

Ten states in the South and West allow you to carry a handgun in plain view *without any permit*. Other states allow permitted open carry. In these states you can wake up, brush your teeth, and strap on a heater just like Wyatt Earp. Everybody knows you're packing. Perhaps the bad guys will give you some respect.

Perhaps not.

I recommend against open carry, because its disadvantages are considerable. Like the legendary Wild West marshal, when you strap pistols to your hips, you may be heading for a shoot-out in your own O.K. Corral. Worse, it can make you cocky and tempt you to confront hoodlums, or argue with people who annoy you and who may be carrying their own firearms. In a street fight, open carry gives your opponent a weapon to grab.

Most important, people *know* you have a gun. So if your enemies make a false complaint against you and state that you pointed a gun at them, they are at least 50 percent correct, because you do indeed have a gun that everyone can see and accurately describe for the police report.

Last, but not least, most states have conflicting firearms laws. They may allow open carry but harshly punish you for brandishing a weapon, firing a warning shot, or otherwise using a gun to defend yourself. After an attack, you could be arrested and sentenced to years in a state penitentiary while your attacker laughs on the courthouse steps as you are led away in chains. In chapter 33, I'll discuss these problems in detail.

ILLEGAL BULLETS, SUSPICIOUS BULLETS, TRICK BULLETS

Incendiary and armor-piercing bullets are absolutely illegal for civilian use. Unfortunately, they are smuggled into the country and sold to criminals on the street. If you encounter such ammo, do *not* touch it and leave your fingerprints or your DNA residue (now called TR, "touch residue"). Don't lecture the hoodlums selling this stuff about the law. They couldn't care less, and they might decide you're a snitch. The best response is to pull down your baseball cap, in case there are cops and cameras about, and fade away.

Certain ammunition is legal but makes cops suspicious. For example, if you're carrying a .50 caliber handgun, with its huge, half-inch cartridges, anywhere other than the shooting range, cops will inquire. Ditto if they find sabot rounds. Sabot is French for "shoe" and refers to an adapter that allows you to mount a small bullet, such as a .22, atop a much larger shell, such as a .30 caliber.

The large powder charge imparts tremendous speed to the bullet. Some sabots increase bullet velocity more than 400 percent. This causes a pistol bullet to go supersonic. In addition, rifling does not mark slugs encased in sabots. Thus, such slugs cannot be matched to a specific firearm. This is a huge concern for police. (Sabots themselves carry rifling marks, but often they cannot be located.)

Sabot rounds, .50 caliber ammo, hardened steel flechettes (arrows) fitted into shotgun shells, and other tricky cartridges have unusual ballistics that interest enthusiasts and professional armorers. Most ammo of this sort has to be loaded by hand. This is dangerous for unskilled people.

On the street, these types of rounds have no use other than shooting through bullet-resistant glass to kill store clerks and penetrating body armor to kill police. Naturally, a cop who finds this stuff on you will want to turn you over, in chains, to a detective for extensive questioning.

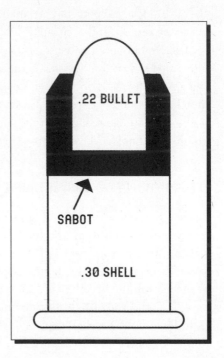

Diagram showing how a plastic sabot allows a small bullet to be seated into a larger shell.

KNIVES LEGAL AND ILLEGAL

Knives are handy gadgets. I don't leave home without one. Mine are legal; yours may not be.

ONE-HAND OPENERS. One-handed folding knives that extend the blade with a thumb push are generally legal. My coauthor, who currently is saving humanity by not owning a gun, carries the Kershaw Blur. The blade is managed by a torsion bar and opens in a fraction of a second.

The Kershaw Blur opens quickly with a push on the thumb stud, then locks.

Note, however, that this is a functional knife that does not *look* threatening. It will slice and dice vegetables and carve your sweetie's initials into a tree. In an emergency, it might also save your life.

TWO-HANDED OPENERS. I myself prefer a boring electrician's knife, which requires two hands to unfold the blade. It can be used for self-defense as a last resort but is ordinary enough not to excite cops should they encounter it. Of course, except in court, I'm always packing real heat should any of my clients charged with violent felonies become too frisky.

Electrician's knife, useful but boring to cops.

SHEATH KNIVES. Everyone has a sheath knife. They're great to wear on your belt when you're hunting and fishing. They're not great to carry in plain view on the streets, because they attract cops who want to know why you're carrying one. Open-carry knives are not good for self-defense. They frighten some people and challenge others. When real crooks see your knife, you'll see their guns.

I also recommend against carrying boot knives. The time it takes to bend down and unsheathe the knife is the time when you *should be running*. In addition, boot knives can stab your ankles at inconvenient times.

Never carry bowie knives in public. Bowies were designed specifically for fighting and were popularized by Colonel James Bowie after he thrust one through an assailant's chest and cut off another's arm in the famous Sandbar Fight in 1827 on the Mississippi River outside Natchez. Because of their size and weight, these knives are useless for hunting or fishing. Keep them where they belong, in display cases on the mantel or in the showroom area of your man cave. Ditto for swords, katanas, scimitars, battle-axes, and other blades designed for lopping off arms, legs, and heads.

KNIVES REQUIRING PERMITS. Some knives make cops want to stick it to you, even though they're legal with a permit. These are knives designed specifically for fighting and would be your last choice to whittle a stick or slice a burger. They include push daggers, spring-actuated switchblades (side-opening), and stilettos (the blade shoots out from the handle). Ring knives, spiked wristbands, and belt buckle knives also require permits in many states.

Fighting knives require special permits in most states. From left to right are a push dagger, a side-opening switchblade, and a stiletto whose blade shoots straight out of the handle. Photo courtesy of Shooters of Jacksonville

Balisongs, or butterfly knives, almost always require permits. They look cool when Asian movie villains whirl them around in Hong Kong chop-socky spectaculars. Try this yourself and you're likely to slice off your jeans, your jewels, and the organ of reproduction. Balisongs also excite police interest because of their association with hoodlums.

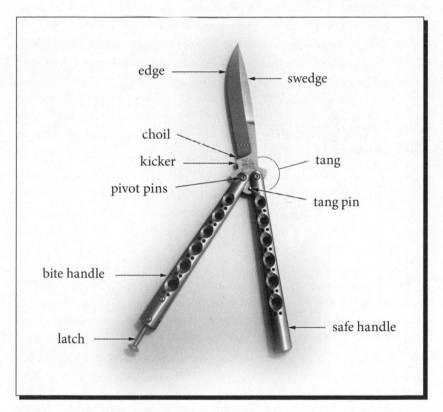

Balisongs, or butterfly knives, are risky to open in an emergency and conspicuous to cops. In the Philippines, where they originate, they are simple farm tools. Photo courtesy of Wikimedia Commons

People generally remember to carry permits with firearms but forget to do so with knives. When cops find a regulated blade without regulatory paperwork, it creates a pointy little problem.

PROHIBITED KNIVES. Utterly illegal are "ballistic knives" with detachable blades that are fired as projectiles by powerful springs or CO_2 cartridges in the handle. These nasties were developed by the Soviet Red Army, which noticed that many recruits were hopeless at throwing knives. With these contraptions, there's no need to throw, just aim at the center of mass and mash the button. Federal law bans transportation and sale of ballistic knives across state lines. Nonetheless, these things come into the United States illegally from Europe and the East. If you see one, don't pause to admire. For heaven's sake, don't handle the thing and leave fingerprints or touch residue. Just do a 180 and start running.

WHEN TO HOLD THEM; WHEN TO FOLD THEM; WHEN TO LEAVE THEM AT HOME

Knife laws are a hodgepodge. Some states limit the length of a knife blade, some don't. To check laws in your state, go to www.akti.org, the Web site of the American Knife & Tool Institute, to get links to the statutes. Knife laws are also highly situational. A knife may be illegal when carried during the commission of a crime but legal when you're walking down the street lost in your iPhone.

Most important is what you say about your knife when questioned by police. Imagine the following all-too-common scenario: You're outside your girlfriend's trailer, with a knife in your pocket. You are detailing, perhaps unwisely, her shortcomings as a lover and as a human being. Your girlfriend, naturally, cancels your booty call and, for emphasis, tosses your clothes out the window and stomps your $700 quad-core smartphone. You exchange fuck-yous at high volume.

Suddenly her brother runs out of his trailer with a billy club, someone looses the pit bull, and now the scrum is on. As you're on the ground working hard to prevent the pit bull and the girlfriend from biting through major arteries and the brother from beating out your brains, the police arrive to save the day.

Once the cops get you dusted off and mop up the blood, they'll ask if you have a knife. When police ask this, *answer truthfully*. Never lie. If you do, and police find your knife, they will charge you with lying to a police officer, obstructing justice, and anything else the booking sergeant can think of—even if you're the victim.

Remember this also. Most lowlifes are "frequent flyers" and have been through the criminal justice system many times. They know how to push cops' buttons. They know that cops have an inherent mental weakness. In the police worldview, people are either perps or victims. Cops favor victims, naturally.

Scumballs know this. They will shout, "I'm the victim," when cops appear. They will lie, but no surprise there. Thus, in the scenario above, the guys beating the crap out of you might tell police that they were defending themselves because you, they declare, have a knife. Even if the bad guys don't know whether you have a knife, they'll say so, because it's a good guess and it will definitely muddy up matters with the cops. It might even get them off the hook for aggravated assault, battery in all its flavors and colors, or attempted murder.

Be aware of no-knife zones. Knives of any kind, like firearms, are absolutely prohibited in schools. Ditto courthouses and airports. As to ceramic knives, often seen slicing tomatoes on late-night infomercials? Leave them in the kitchen. Manufacturers now add steel dust to the ceramic, so these blades *will* set off metal detectors. Naturally, they're uncool in school.

BATS, BILLIES, BATONS, BLACKJACKS, AND SAPS (HUMAN AND OTHERWISE)

Bats, batons, and billy clubs are illegal in most states when carried for offensive purposes. So if you're carrying a baseball bat in plain view of police, don't forget the hat, the ball, and the glove. "Tire thumpers," a type of billy club, are used by truckers to check tire pressure. They excite police attention when carried by non-truckers.

Leather-covered lead tubes and bars, known as coshes or saps, and blackjacks, which are rods with a leather-covered lead ball on a chain, also elicit police suspicion, since they're used as knockout weapons in robberies and fights. Sappings were a staple of police shows in my childhood.

The hero got knocked on the head, then moments later jumped up and caught the villains. In real life these weapons cause horrible brain injuries, and they're rarely seen now on television. They are nearly useless for self-defense, since they require you to get up close and personal with opponents who generally have guns. The proper place for them is in police and weapons museums. If you carry one, you're the sap.

TASERS AND PEPPER SPRAY

People who are leery of owning a handgun but who worry about self-protection are often interested in electroshock weapons and pepper spray.

Electroshock weapons—Taser is the best-known brand—are legal in most states, usually with a permit. Some Tasers fire steel darts attached to wires. On impact, the unit delivers a debilitating shock. These weapons are classified as "nonlethal" and work great—until they don't.

First, the darts bounce off thick winter clothing. Even when you do get a direct hit, the bad guy may keep coming, especially if he's hyped on angel dust and surging adrenaline. Heck, there have been guys who survived the *electric chair*—2,000 volts, five amps, straight into the coconut. For a seriously crazed tough guy, a Taser is a buzz, not a bother. Sometimes Tasers work too well and kill someone.

The second type of electroshock weapon requires you to push the unit's two electrodes into the attacker's skin and pull a trigger. To use these, you have to get nose to nose with your attacker. Sound scary? It is.

Pepper spray? It's nasty stuff. When directed into the face—mouth, nose, and eyes—the spray causes tearing, choking, and agonizing pain. The active ingredient in the stuff is oleoresin capsicum, which, translated into English, means resins derived from ground-up hot chili peppers. Some of the peppers used, like India's bhut jolokia, are so hot that farmers smear them on fence posts to deter rampaging elephants.

As a civilian, you can't buy large cans of pepper spray. Most states allow only two ounces or so of spray in a tiny canister. That's enough to stop an enraged kitten, but it won't floor a hoodlum unless you get a direct hit on the eyes or into the open mouth. One or two squirts are all you've got. If you miss or your attacker keeps coming, then what?

I do not recommend these weapons for personal use. First, they are subject to conflicting state laws and municipal codes. Many jurisdictions require permitting. Second, they are not as effective as a firearm. If your life and the lives of your family are at stake, put your trust in Messrs. Winchester, Smith, Wesson, Colt, and Ruger, and those jolly brothers Sig and Sauer. Save the hot peppers for the stew pot.

NINJA TOYS

Nunchaku (nunchuks) are fun to watch in Asian action flicks, where the fighters spin them around, somersault backward, and fly through the air while giving villains whacks to the noggin. Developed in Okinawa and China, they are used in certain forms of karate. Nunchaku are currently illegal in California, Arizona, New York, and Massachusetts. Interestingly, they are also illegal in Hong Kong, where Bruce Lee made them famous in his knock-'em-sock-'em thriller *Enter the Dragon*.

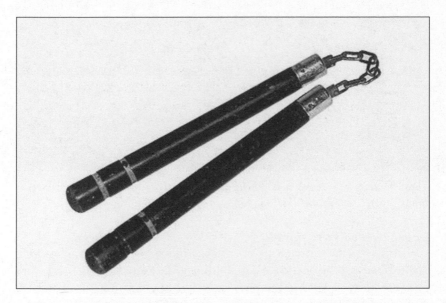

As for nunchuks and other ninja toys, you're a numb nuts if you play with these things in view of the police. Photo courtesy of Wikimedia Commons

Nunchaku are useless for self-defense in a world where the bad guys are packing automatic pistols and illegal machine guns. 'Chuks also tend to swing around and smack uncoordinated users on the knees or in the head. When you swing these things in public, you're more likely to look like one of the Three Stooges than Bruce Lee.

Shuriken, or throwing stars, are a staple of every teenaged boy's bedroom, and that's where they should stay. In the movies, ninjas saw off peoples' heads with these doohickeys. In real life, all you're likely to do in an emergency is nick the bluing on a bad guy's automatic before he blows your head off.

Throwing stars might come in handy if you're attacked by senior citizens on oxygen. Photo courtesy of Wikimedia Commons

ARRESTABLE CLOTHING

In the photo on the next page, I'm holding a "tac," or tactical, vest. I wore one when I was a sniper. Tac vests carry lots of guns and ammo and are the garment of choice for mass murderers. Cops know this, and if they see you wearing one of these on the street or at a shopping mall or movie theater, here's what will happen: The cops will hit the "panic button" on their radios. Within seconds, dozens of cruisers will light up and roar to your GPS location. Back at the station, while the police helicopter spins up from the pad, the SWAT Suburban will burn rubber out of the garage. Next, the police command vehicle will deploy, then the armored personnel carrier will rumble forth as the crew feed combo belts of .50 caliber tracer, incendiary, and armor-piercing rounds into the machine gun receivers and load 105 mm shells into the cannon.

Is this disco enough for you?

Wearing tac vests on the streets is like sending up a flare that signals "Arrest me!"

Tac vests are legal, but their effect on police is situational. So if you're wearing one in the woods during hunting season, no problem. Back in the city, enjoy styling them in the mirror and impressing your women. Otherwise, leave them at home. If cops are called out because you're wearing one on the streets, expect some quick kicks to the butt biscuits—if you're lucky.

The main takeaway from this chapter is *don't carry a weapon that makes you look like a badass.* You may think such a weapon is cool; police, prosecutors, and juries will not. If you keep a firearm for self-defense or home defense, keep it simple and keep it functional. As for a pocketknife, choose one that looks functional and nonthreatening. Carry sheath knives only while hunting and fishing. Enjoy ninja toys on TV and at the movie theater.

32 | WANT A REAL GUN? GET A WHEEL GUN

"There's threats everywhere, and the world is draped in camouflage."
—*Unnamed Navy SEAL in* Act of Valor

You're never safe. Anywhere, anytime, bad things can happen. It's easy to get lulled. You think, "I've been doing so-and-so for years. Nothing's happened yet, so it probably never will." Psychologists call this the "normalcy bias." I call it being stupid. Here are actual examples:

>> A club owner in Miami opens his cash box and counts his take at the same time, year after year, then gets shot one day when an employee leads in a crew of robbers.

>> In Jacksonville, a wealthy couple trust their tool safe* and high-tech alarm system to protect millions in gems. Expert thieves bribe the maid for the contractor/cleaner alarm code. After she scoots back to Nicaragua, the bad guys remove the safe, load it onto a boat, and motor down the St. Johns River to crack it at leisure in a workshop.

>> Just a few weeks ago my coauthor nearly had his snazzy road bicycle hijacked while riding in Jacksonville's notorious

---

* Safes are rated in the United States by Underwriters Laboratories. "Tool safe" is tech slang for a safe that has been rated to withstand, for a specified period, cracking attempts by experts using the best electrical and mechanical tools. A Class TXTL-60 safe, for example, can withstand 60 minutes of attack by tools and oxyacetylene torches and a blast from eight ounces of nitroglycerin.

Police Zone I, where, alas, he lives. Fortunately, he is as wary as a ferret and was able to spin a 180 on the bike and vanish into side streets before the bad guys could turn their SUV around. Now he rides on stated-owned "rail trails" with solid citizens who wear helmets and spandex and listen to National Public Radio while their iPod Nanos monitor their pulse, their miles, their ergs, and their happiness.

I've carried firearms nearly every day for 40 years, and I endorse responsible gun ownership for sport and self-protection. In this chapter, I'm going to recommend two weapons that, I believe, provide the most reliable self-protection for most people. Some military and law enforcement personnel, hunters, and firearms experts will find my recommendations laughable; ordinary people will find them lifesaving. You pros can skip this chapter and proceed to the next, where I explain how Stand Your Ground laws and the Castle Doctrine can get you tossed into prison and all your fancy guns seized if you don't understand the nuances.

FIRST THINGS FIRST

Get a permit. Carrying any firearm, particularly concealed, without a permit is a serious felony. Once you have the permit, keep it in your wallet. Keep copies in your house and in your car. Without it, you're toast.

GUN ONE

For your first firearm, I recommend the .38 Special, manufactured for over 60 years by Smith & Wesson, or similar .38s made by all the famous firearms companies. These are "wheel guns," police slang for revolvers with rotating cylinders that hold the cartridges and retain the spent shells after firing.

Already I can hear your objections: "Dale, are you nuts? Those antiques only hold five cartridges. The bad guys are packing Glocks and Sigs with 15-round mags and rip-off Chinese AKs that fire 30 to 100 slugs full-auto.*

---

* Until their pot-metal barrels melt.

This is the classic .38 revolver, which I recommend as your first weapon for self-protection.

When the excrement hits the fan, I want all the bullets I can get and extra magazines in every pocket."

Cool your jets and I will explain. Nearly all retired FBI agents carry revolvers, not automatics, for personal protection. These guys are weapons experts, and they carry revolvers for the same reasons you should:

>> Revolvers are defensive weapons precisely because they have limited ammunition. They are less likely than automatics* to tempt you to go into neighborhoods where you don't belong and to confront dangerous people whom you should leave alone (and consign to the expert attention of police officers).

---

* Technically, the available alternatives are *semiautomatic* pistols, since they require a trigger pull for each discharge. I use the more common nomenclature. Full-auto pistols are Title II weapons designed for use by police and military personnel— who, by the way, do not have to pay for ammo.

>> If you're in a confrontation with lots of pistol-packing bad guys, you need to be running, not shooting. You need to be jinking left and right, leaping fences, and turning every corner you can. If you're lucky, the bad guys will be drunk, wasted, or both, and won't be able to focus their eyes, much less aim. Pistols are notoriously inaccurate in inexpert hands. If you bolt, you have a reasonable chance to survive.

>> Revolvers are highly reliable, because their mechanisms are extremely simple. When you pull the trigger, they will fire, year after year, even when not properly maintained.

>> Ammo for .38s is universally available.

>> A .38 makes a big bang. In self-defense, noise is as important, perhaps more important, than accuracy. Watch any YouTube video of surveillance footage of armed robberies. As soon as the storeowner starts firing, the hoodlums skedaddle, even if they're not hit. Bad guys are not necessarily tough guys. They're willing to risk your life, but not theirs, to grab your wallet, your car, your cash, and your goodies.

>> A .38 has serious stopping power, yet is small enough to carry unnoticed in one of the holsters I'll recommend shortly.

>> Revolvers are not susceptible to the notorious "limp-wristed effect" that causes automatics to jam. Most automatic pistols malfunction not because of a fault in the mechanism but due to the physics of recoil when fired by beginners who are scared of weapons and do not hold the gun firmly. Limp-wristing occurs when a weak grip allows the automatic to jump backward. When the jump offsets the momentum necessary to cycle the slide and load the next round, the weapon will jam. This can be annoying or fatal, depending on the circumstances.

Your revolver should not have scopes, lasers (except grip-installed), suppressors, or other toys attached. These make the gun heavy and likely

This is the famous Glock 9 mm semiautomatic. You need meat on your wrists to fire this thing.

to snag in clothes and holsters. If attacked you won't need even the iron sights, since you'll be firing from less than 10 feet away. If you shoot an attacker who is *more than 10 feet away*, it causes the legal complications I'll discuss in the next chapter.

Your revolver should be matte black, not silver, not some crazy color, and *absolutely not* gold-plated. Avoid fancy engraving, too. Matte black is stealthy. It does not glint with reflections of light, and it is difficult to see or to describe accurately, especially at night. If you draw a black revolver in self-defense, then decide that the draw is unnecessary, you can stealthily *re-conceal the revolver* and possibly avoid a complaint and an arrest for brandishing a weapon.

Carry one pistol only. When you own multiple handguns, it can be difficult to remember how to fire each one unless you train constantly. A moment of confusion as to whether your handgun is *single action* (you have to cock the hammer first before firing) or *double action* (you can fire without cocking) can be fatal. In an emergency you may not be able to fire soon enough if you are confused about which handgun you're holding. If you have ammo of different calibers all over the place, you could insert the wrong cartridge and blow yourself up.

BULLETS, BULLETS ON THE WALL, WHICH OF YOU ARE THE BEST OF ALL?

The varieties of ammunition are endless, so let's start with basic ammo info. The slug at the end is called the *bullet*. The *casing* or *shell* holds the powder. Below is the *rim*, which is grasped for ejection in the case of an automatic, or in the case of a revolver simply holds the round in the chamber. When the hammer hits, the primer ignites and sets off the powder in the casing, then—*boom*—the bullet fires. Bullet, casing, and rim together are called the *cartridge*.

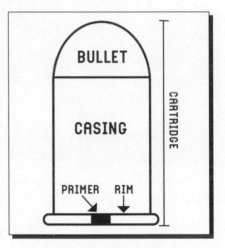

A cartridge consists of the bullet or slug, the casing or shell, and the rim.

MILITARY AMMO. Military rounds have a full metal jacket of copper or alloy surrounding a lead, steel, or composite core. The jacket lessens lead buildup in the barrel and complies with the Geneva Conventions regarding humane-kill ammunition. These rounds are unsuitable for self-defense, because they penetrate the attacker then ricochet and sometimes shatter, which can kill innocent bystanders, including you. Military incendiaries and armor-piercing rounds are illegal for civilians.

WADCUTTERS. These are square bullets designed to shoot at paper targets, not people.

Full jacketed 5.56 × 45 mm rounds that load into automatic rifles such as the M4 carbine used by U.S. military forces.

SELF-LOADS AND HOMEMADE BULLETS. Self-loading, which entails loading primer and powder into empty casings and crimping the slug to make a finished cartridge, is for experts only. Avoid trick bullets, like hardened paper and wood, plastic bullets, and that hoary movie and TV favorite, the mercury-filled bullet. These last are bullets, supposedly tipped with mercury fulminate, $Hg(CNO)_2$, that explode upon impact. Mercury fulminate, be advised, is the explosive used in blasting caps. Homemade mercury bullets usually explode in the bullet maker's face, or, if he's unlucky, blow up inside the action and convert the handgun into shrapnel.

When you file Xs, crosses, or your own secret symbol into the noses of bullets, or drill holes into slugs, you, not your ammunition, become the dumdum. See above remarks about explosions and shrapnel. Stick to store ammo. It works great.

HOLLOW POINTS. My *second* choice for self-defense is that universal favorite, hollow point ammunition. These bullets have a void or dimple in the center, or a polymer Pow'RBall molded into the lead. When they impact an attacker, they expand, tumble, and make huge holes. They tend to shatter upon impact and are less likely than solid slugs to overpenetrate, kill bystanders, and ricochet all over the place. Because they expand and "mushroom" after firing, they deliver more of the bullet's kinetic energy to the target, and thus have more stopping power. Hollow points are available everywhere.

At left, a partially jacketed hollow point. At right a dimpled hollow point. Photo courtesy of Wikimedia Commons

A .38 Special bullet showing the distinctive mushroom effect of a hollow point round. Photo courtesy of Wikimedia Commons

UNCLE DALE'S SAVE-YOUR-LIFE AMMO LOAD

My *first choice* for self-defense, based on years of experience on the firing range, on the crime scene, and in the courtroom, is a bullet you may not be familiar with: the frangible round. *Frangible* means breakable, and that's what these bullets do. Some are rounds with machined grooves on the side of the slug. My preferred round, however, is the Glaser Safety Slug. It's manufactured in Sturgis, South Dakota, home of the famous motorcycle rally that draws tens of thousands of bikers to the desolate hardpan of the Great Plains and where more than a few Glaser cartridges are concealed, more or less lawfully, in Harley leather jackets.

To quote the company Web site, "The Safety Slug uses a copper jacket and it is filled with a compressed load of either #12 or #6 lead shot. It is then capped with a round polymer ball that enhances feeding and reloading." The Glaser is, practically speaking, a miniature shotgun shell.*

---

* Rat shot, which is similar, is less precisely machined and less accurate. Rat shot is OK for blasting vermin in your basement—with safety glasses—but not recommended for bad-guy removal.

The Glaser Safety Slug is has a copper jacket, polymer tip, and birdshot load.

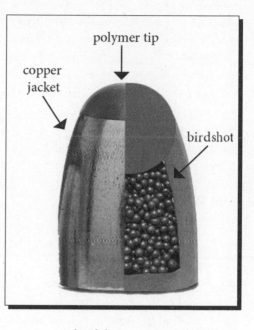

copper jacket

polymer tip

birdshot

Ballistically, Glasers are interesting. Being lighter than lead, the plastic-capped rounds exit the barrel at higher speed than metal rounds. They shatter immediately upon entry and deliver 100 percent of their kinetic energy to the target. (Rounds that by virtue of their hardened construction travel completely through their target, by contrast, carry much of their energy with them.) Glaser shot will bounce off walls and not kill bystanders, but the wounds they cause attackers are devastating.* Glasers are precision manufactured and nearly as accurate as match-grade ammo.** For all these reasons, I recommend Glasers as the perfect self-protection for ordinary people.

However, I have one refinement. In your revolver, I recommend that you load the first cylinder to fire with a .38 *solid* round (*not* hollow point). Load chambers two through five with Glasers. To determine which chamber is first, note whether your cylinder rotates clockwise or counterclockwise while loading. If clockwise, put the solid round in the chamber immediately to the left of the hammer; if counterclockwise, put it in the

---

* Air marshals use Glasers because they kill hijackers without penetrating the fuselage and depressurizing the aircraft.

** Match-grade ammo is manufactured to high tolerances. Identical amounts of propellant are loaded into the casings so all cartridges have precisely the same muzzle velocity and spin when fired. This allows snipers and competition shooters to precisely zero their weapons for each distance and to correct windage and bullet drop accurately.

chamber immediately to the hammer's right. That way the solid will be the first round to revolve under the hammer and fire.

Why should you do this? A solid round will not expand. It is less likely to kill your family or you in case of accidental discharge or when fired wildly amid the fear and confusion of a home invasion at night. The solid gives you time to recover and, with rounds two through five, shoot attackers. This combination of a solid slug with Glasers is my save-your-life load, and the one I use personally in the revolver I carry every day and everywhere.*

HOW TO HOLD 'EM

Everybody has seen crime shows where the detective strides wearily into his grimy office, grabs a cup of bad coffee topped with a cigarette butt or a cockroach, then removes his jacket to reveal a super-cool shoulder holster holding a monstrous pistol, such as the .44 Magnum made famous by Clint "Make my day!" Eastwood in the Dirty Harry film series.** Before you race off to the gun shop to get your shoulder unit, consider this. How often do you wear a weapon with a jacket or a suit?

Not often.

That's why I recommend a holster that's more practical and stealthier, and that will give you an edge. The photo on the next page shows a pocket holster. It fits inside your pocket, holds your .38 securely, and can be reached faster than a holster behind your back or on your shoulder. You can wear it in your jeans or even in white tie and tails (in case you're attacked by the hostess of a charity ball.)

It is not unusual to stand with your hands in your pockets; consequently, you can put your hand on your gun and nobody will be the wiser. Because no one can see the weapon, no one will be able to describe it accu-

---

* Note to Jacksonville bad boys: Don't get frisky thinking you can chance a Glaser. I have other guns, and even with my cataract lens replacements, can shoot the fanny off a flea.

** Dirty Harry movies are all-time favorites among cops. Of course, in real life, any police officer who blasted everyone who annoyed him would be fired and indicted, and his city would be successfully sued for millions.

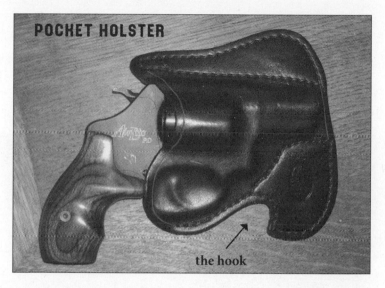

This is a pocket holster. In your pocket it looks like a wallet. The holster has a hook that will catch your pocket hem and allow your pistol to slide out cleanly. The revolver is the Smith & Wesson AirLite PD with a stealthy matte-black finish. It's dark as night, light as a feather, and deadly as a snake.

rately to police in order to swear out a false complaint that you threatened him or her or brandished a firearm. If an armed robber sticks you up, what's he going to ask you to do? Hand over your wallet, which is, of course, in your pocket.

Establish a firm routine for carrying your revolver. First, take the holster out of your pocket. Next, place the gun into the holster. Finally, pocket the entire assembly, holster plus gun. Never jam a pistol into a holster that's already in your pocket. This can cause an accidental discharge.

Never carry a pistol in your pocket without a holster. If you do, gravity will cause the pistol to rotate in your pocket, with the heavy butt down and the barrel pointing up. An accidental discharge from this position will put the bullet into your liver or stomach or into the brachial artery in your upper arm.

Practice drawing, then replacing, your handgun—gently, no jamming, with your finger *off* the trigger—into the holster while it is in your pocket. The gun should be unloaded for this practice.

Ladies, you may have to wear your piece differently. The one place you don't want to have your weapon is in your purse. Reason? That's the first thing bad guys grab, since they figure they can get your goodies and your gat at the same time. If you wear trousers *all the time*, then a pocket holster is best. If not, I recommend a waist holster, popularly known as a bellyband.

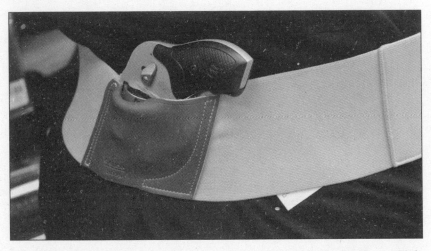

This bellyband, made by Galco, has two holsters and works for both right- and left-handed shooters.

Bellybands wrap around your midsection. They are ambidextrous, meaning that they have two holsters, one on each side, so both left- and right-handed shooters can use the same band. You wear these under your breasts with a blouse or dress that gives easy access

Unless you are an expert shooter, I recommend that you stick to one type of holster. You don't want to wonder "Where's my gun?" when bad guys attack. And nix those ankle holsters. You'll shoot off your little piggies as likely as not.

THE BIGGER BANG

Some of you will be tormented by the thought that a .38 is just not gun enough. Maybe you're paranoid; maybe you're prudent; maybe you're stuck on Mean Street until you save enough money to escape or until your U.S. Marine Corps enlistment papers come through. For you guys, there's only one choice: The Judge,* by Taurus International. It's chambered for both .45 pistol cartridges *and* .410 shotgun shells. The shotgun shells will have qualities similar to those of the Glaser. The shot will devastate attackers, avoid through-and-throughs and ricochets, and bounce off walls.

So the supersized version of the Dale Carson save-your-life load is this: Load a .45 *solid* round in the first chamber to fire. Load chambers two through five with .410 shotgun shells packed with birdshot (not larger buckshot). (See page 313 if you need help determining which chamber will fire first.)

Blammo!

Here come da Judge! This revolver is chambered for both .45 standard ammunition and .410 shotgun shells.

---

* The Judge got its name because actual jurists carry it under their robes. Many states encourage judges to pack a pistol in court. This is another reason to be polite, even humble, before his or her honor.

THE VIRTUES OF ORDINARINESS

Observe that both these revolvers appear *ordinary*. This is important, because if you shoot someone in self-defense, you are likely to be prosecuted. As the saying goes, it's better to be judged by 12 (jury members) rather than carried by 6 (pall bearers). It is, but only just.

A 6-pack or a 12-pack (lawyer jargon for 6- or 12-member juries) is unlikely to have weapons experts on the panel. If your weapon is tricked out with lasers and extended magazines, or engraved ghetto fabulous–style with skulls, tombstones, and naked bosoms, the jury may ignore any evidence your attorney presents in your defense and convict you just because you had a scary gun. So before you buy a fancy gun, think of the reaction it would cause when passed around in an evidence bag to a jury composed, as most of them are, of retirees, church ladies, and government employees.

GUN TWO

For your second gun, to be kept in the house and used to shoot home invaders, I recommend a 12-gauge shotgun. The reasons are obvious. A 12-gauge releases a huge blast of shot with a deafening *bang*. Any attackers left alive will be dazed, confused, and partially blinded. They may decide to beat feet out of there. Again the proper load is birdshot, not buckshot or solid slugs.

I recommend a pump-action shotgun. These are simple to operate and fire up to seven rounds. The iconic sound of a shell being racked into the chamber may be enough to save your life and protect your family. A

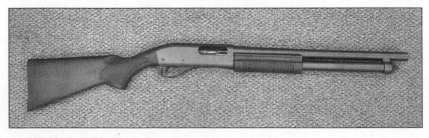

Mossberg 12-gauge pump-action shotgun.

12-gauge will take out sheetrock and do a number on the studs, but the pellets will have far less ricochet and cause less collateral damage than solid or hollow point bullets.

RIFLES? JUST SAY NO!

Rifles are good for one thing only: long-range shooting of targets, animals, and enemy soldiers. They are the wrong choice for self-defense. First, they're long and heavy. That makes them slow to aim and fire in an emergency. Second, they fire bullets at supersonic speed,* with tremendous kinetic energy. Fired indoors, rifle bullets will pass through entire buildings and kill innocents blocks away. They will penetrate body armor and may kill police officers coming to assist you. This is not optimal.

Save your rifle to shoot wild critters from long, long distances. Enjoy that Zeiss glass on your scope and use those mil dots to blast moose a mile away.

KEEPING YOUR GUN AT NIGHT

A gun won't do you any good if you forget where you put it. You should routinely keep your firearm in the same place at night. A handgun should be kept secured in a safe box in the nightstand. The box should be secured to the nightstand, the weapon inside and available with a finger combination. This will protect you from criminal and civil litigation should a child wander into your bedroom, extract a gun, and hurt him- or herself or someone else.

Your shotgun should be stored in a locked case on an inside inner wall of your bedroom. There are two schools of thought as to whether a shell should be kept in the chamber. Certainly, for long-term storage the preferred method is to untension the hammer spring by pulling the trigger on an empty chamber and retaining the rounds only in the magazine. This permits you to operate the charging mechanism and create the much-

---

* Supersonic bullets produce a loud crack when they break the sound barrier. Most pistol ammo is subsonic.

feared sound of a shotgun being racked. However, racking the gun might permit an intruder to determine your location. The stealthier choice is to keep a round in the chamber, safety on, ready for action.

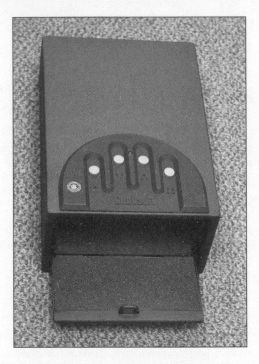

This is the Gun Vault tabletop handgun storage unit. Buttons on top must be pushed in a predetermined pattern to unlock the box. Unauthorized access is prevented, but with practice, you can grab your pistol in a jiffy when you need it.

WHAT HAPPENS WHEN YOU SHOOT SOMEBODY?

I laugh when I see TV shows in which the good guys shoot bad guys who, when hit, appear to get blown backward 5 to 10 yards. Sometimes you can see the wire cables attached to hidden body harnesses that the actors wear under their shirts. This may be the origin of the term "blown away."

Unfortunately, real life is not like this. As someone who has been on scene of many shootings, I can tell you this. When people are shot, one of two things can happen. They run away or they keep coming. The first outcome is desirable for self-defense. The second is every victim's, and every cop's, nightmare. I worked a case in which a bank robber was shot five times by a bank guard using a .357 Magnum. The perp was still jabbering to me as he was transported to the hospital! Police officers have shot assailants *through the heart*, then were shot and killed themselves when the perp kept going long enough to pull his own trigger.

How can a cop, or you, be killed by a bad guy who has been shot through the heart and is, in most respects, already dead? The answer is the adrenaline effect. When under attack, the human body pours adrenaline into the bloodstream. Superhuman strength and endurance are two of the effects. These effects are increased by orders of magnitude when an attacker is amped up on phencyclidine, a.k.a. PCP or angel dust. This is an illegal drug that produces mania, hallucinations, and, unfortunately, immunity to pain. On angel dust or similar drugs, bad guys don't feel bullet wounds and don't realize, or care, that they're going to be toast in 30 to 45 seconds. Even if you shoot out their left ventricle or put a round through their head, they will keep coming and will fire their weapon or stab you with a knife before they drop.

The most notorious incident of this kind occurred in 1986, when bank robbers William Russell Matix and Michael Lee Platt killed FBI special agents Jerry Dove and Benjamin Grogan. In a standoff with the perpetrators, Dove got out of his car, returned fire, and hit one of the perps directly in the heart with a 9 mm, semi-jacketed hollow point round. The perp continued to shoot for nearly five minutes before several .12 gauge shotgun rounds finally put him down.

I represented a woman who used a Ruger .357 loaded with hypervelocity rounds to shoot her boyfriend twice through the heart as he lay in bed. He got up, snatched the gun, and shot her twice. He died; she survived. Afterward, she was convicted of second-degree murder. As they say, love hurts—bad.

SELF-DEFENSE AFTER BRAIN SHUTDOWN

Adrenaline also has powerful effects on victims, i.e., you. The most important is brain shutdown. Adrenaline turns off the conscious, reasoning functions of the front part of the brain, known as the cerebral cortex.

Adrenaline is readying you for fight or flight. Conscious thought is slow, and in an emergency, there's no time to think, only to act.

Don't even imagine that if your car is jacked or your home invaded, you will be able to choose the proper weapon from your extensive collection, then reach among the numerous boxes of ammo and load the correct cartridges. In real life, you could be killed 10 times during the few seconds it took for you to read the preceding sentence.

Brain shutdown can be compensated for by practice. Repetition trains the superfast, superefficient unconscious mind to perform specific actions. We all do this. Nobody, for example, *thinks* about hitting a baseball or tossing a basketball through the hoop. You just do it. Even complex tasks can be performed flawlessly with no conscious thought. How often have you driven someplace "on autopilot?" You start, stop, make turns, change lanes, and can't remember doing any of it.

All this applies, in spades, to self-defense. To responsibly own and use firearms, you must practice two very different things. First, you must master the firearm and be able to load, aim, and fire, with reasonable accuracy, without using the gun sights.

Second, you must practice *making decisions* on whether to fire or not fire. This is the practice that too many people avoid. It's the most important, and the skill most stressed in military and law enforcement training. Standing calmly and making holes in paper targets just won't cut it. You need to practice this:

>> A figure pops through a door. Do you shoot or not shoot?

>> Is that a bad guy or citizen 50 yards downrange? Decide. Do it now!

>> A person lunges at you while babbling incoherently. Do you shoot or give him spare change?

Fortunately, many of the best gun stores have installed specialized equipment in their ranges to train unconscious decision making. These are "snaps," targets that pop up, and "movers," targets that move across your field of vision, each made to resemble either bad guys with guns or mommies with babies. Ranges can lower the lights, add smoke, and blast loud, annoying music or sounds to accustom you to real-world conditions. To make things hyper-real, before the targets start to pop, drop down for push-ups until your arms burn and you collapse to the floor. Then pick up your firearm with trembling hands and *try* not to hit grandma when she pops up. This is how they do it in the military.

THE NIKE/GOODYEAR DEFENSE AND THE RED ZONE

There is, of course, a defense better than handguns when you're out and about. It's the Don't Go There Defense. Stay away from trouble. Even if you are armed, you're more likely to protect yourself and your family by turning around and running from bad guys. The cardinal rule of protection is to put distance between yourself and potential attackers.

Most serious crime occurs between 9 P.M. and 3 A.M., what cops call "the red zone." During red-zone hours, you *don't* need to go out to a 24-hour store to get food, smokes, or booze. If you get late-night cravings, tough it out or take a pill. You should never be in the high arrestability quotient areas listed in chapter 12 (page 158)—clubs where guys fight over women and drugs, dope holes, and any place where guys consider leaning on walls and lampposts a full-time job. Do your partying *at home*, where walls, doors, and the Fourth Amendment protect you.

When confronted by strangers who ask about time and directions, say nothing. These are ploys used by robbers to lure you close. Don't speak; just go. Use the Nike/Goodyear Defense—burn shoe and tire rubber rather than gunpowder. If you think you need a gun where you're going, you're going to the wrong place. Be smart. A gun is always a last-ditch defense.

Practicing with a weapon makes you think carefully about personal safety and about the inadvisability of going into bad areas or confronting street people and crooks. The problem with firearms, even when used legally and in self-defense, is what happens *after* you shoot someone. That's the topic of the next chapter.

33 | STAND YOUR GROUND (AND DRESS THE HOG)

When you shoot someone in self-defense, it creates a legal, financial, and political mess of astonishing magnitude. To illustrate this, let me relate a parable, just as in the Bible. A parable is appropriate because this book you're reading is criminal justice scripture—the Good Book of Staying Out of Jail.

THE PARABLE OF THE HOG

It all started when a hog got my dog. My wife noticed that the Labrador was moping. We looked, and the guy had been slit from chest to chin by a wild hog. When I say hog, I don't mean your typical bacon-and-ribs porker rolling around behind the barn. I'm talking about wild boars, the sharp-tusked monsters that make hikers flee and Boy Scouts shinny up trees whenever they come crashing, like midget rhinoceroses, through the palmetto scrub.

I received a wifely command: "Kill it, Dale. Kill it!"

Magic words. Once again I would be the primeval hunter coming home to the village to protect and feed the tribe. In my imagination I saw bonfires roaring, women dancing, and elders nodding while the children clapped in glee. Yahoo! It was time to do some killing.

So I set out the bait, lurked in darkness with a red light that the beast could not see, and readied a .22 rifle. Yes, a .22, the smallest caliber. There would be one chance, and one tiny bullet, to even the odds against an animal that can kill you with a swipe of its head.

Near midnight I heard a grunt. He was at the bait! In the red hunting light, I could see he was huge. From 100 feet away, I took a stance and looked through the scope for the spot, one inch below the ear and one inch down, that is the spinal column. I took three slow breaths, let out half a breath, aimed, squeezed . . .

Pop!

He dropped. I had split his spinal column with a perfect central-nervous-system disconnect, the only shot that will drop rampaging beasts or men. My machismo was confirmed. My sniper chops were recertified. I stood over this 400-pound monster. He was covered with mud and fleas, and ticks danced on his hide. It was midnight; he was dead. Now what?

Here's what. At an age when I should be getting ready for Medicare and the rocking chair, I was out in the middle of the night with a dead hog. You shouldn't kill animals unless you eat them, so I dragged the carcass to the cabin's front porch and hoisted it, splayed, on a gambrel. I whipped out my skinning knife and started to "cape" the carcass. This means to strip off the hide and the fat in one piece. This takes hours. While cleaning hogs, you have to wear steel mesh gloves atop latex gloves to avoid cuts and infection from their parasites, worms, and bacteria. In steel and rubber gloves, I sawed, sliced, and disjointed. More hours.

When the sun rose, I had 200 pounds of meat. Half of it filled the freezer and the fridge. The other half I buried. I was whipped. Needless to say, when the meat came out of the frying pan later in the day, it was foul and disgusting.

The aftermath of a self-defense shooting—hit *or* miss—is so nasty it makes dressing a boar look as simple as washing dishes. The consequences will go on for years and will turn your life upside down. If you're religious and moral, they will turn your soul upside down. So let me walk you through what happens when you shoot someone and what you need to do. Brace yourselves. It's a bumpy ride.

FIRST, WHEN CAN YOU LAWFULLY SHOOT?

For you to be granted Stand Your Ground immunity or to argue self-defense successfully, a number of conditions have to be met. Some of these you can control; some you can't.

>> You must be lawfully present where the shooting occurs. You cannot trespass or be in someone else's house or car without

permission. Note: As soon as you get into an argument with someone on his or her property, you are *not* lawfully present. The law assumes your invitation expired as soon as the argument started.

》》 You cannot be engaged in *any* unlawful act. So if you're over the legal alcohol limit in public, or you toked a joint or took a hit from a bong, you may not lawfully fire in self-defense and employ Stand Your Ground in order to get immunity from prosecution.

》》 You must reasonably (and the key here is *reasonably*) be in fear of death or great bodily harm before pulling the trigger. If you are defending someone else, you must reasonably believe that person is in fear of death or great bodily harm. "Great bodily harm" is not easy to define in the courtroom.

Does great bodily harm include being threatened? Being hit? Being pushed? It all depends on the judge and the jurisdiction. In parts of the South and West, getting stomped on a barroom floor may not be considered "great bodily harm," merely a routine ass-whipping. If a video shows you smooching some guy's wife or copping a feel, all bets are off, especially in Texas.*

》》 You must not be the aggressor. This isn't simple either. Imagine a scenario in which an attacker is bashing your head on concrete. Suddenly you kick his balls and he falls back. You get on top, bounce *his* head on the concrete, pull your piece and put his brains on the ground. Would this be justifiable homicide? Courts could rule either way.

》》 You must not pursue your attacker or shoot him in the back if he flees. This is not simple either. Imagine that you're attacked. You break away, go to your car, grab your gun, then return

---

* In Texas, until 1973, if you caught some lowlife boning your wife, you could blast both of them and walk away free.

and cap the bastard. Were you "pursuing" your attacker? If the government proves you had an opportunity for reflection, you will be charged with first-degree murder, because you premeditated the shooting after you had effectively escaped.

>> You must not fire a warning shot. If you pull your piece before the threshold is reached at which you are reasonably in fear of death or great bodily harm, then by firing a warning shot you may be charged with attempted murder or aggravated assault. If you kill someone, you can be charged with murder.

>> In many states, you must not brandish a weapon or hold a potential attacker at gunpoint.

WHAT HAPPENS IF YOU'RE NOT IN DANGER OF GREAT BODILY HARM?

Whenever you use your weapon in circumstances that lead a court to conclude that you were not in fear of death or great bodily harm, the results can be dire:

>> If you *pull* your gun, you can be charged with brandishing or improper display.

>> If you *point* the gun at someone, you can be charged with felony aggravated assault.

>> If you *fire* a round, you have illegally discharged your weapon and are subject to felony charges with stiff minimum mandatory sentences.

>> If you *hit* someone, and they survive but suffer serious bodily injury, you're looking at charges up to attempted murder.

>> If you *kill* someone, it's murder or manslaughter. A dream-team defense, with private detectives, independent ballistics experts, and specialized secondary attorneys to argue rules of evidence and police procedure, will start at six figures and top a million in a hurry.

SELF-DEFENSE AND STAND YOUR GROUND LAWS

All states allow arguments of self-defense. Most recognize the so-called Castle Doctrine, which says that your home is your castle and you may defend it with deadly force with no duty to retreat if invaded.

A few states have expanded this zone of protection to include vehicles and any location where you are attacked. These expansions of the self-defense zone are called Stand Your Ground, Line in the Sand, or No Duty to Retreat laws.

The distance between you and the person you shoot is critical. If the perp is a mile away, he's not a threat to you. If he's holding a gun on you from three feet away, he is a threat. But what if he has a knife and is 15 feet away? If he's not an imminent threat, *you do not have the right to shoot him*. It is difficult to make a case for self-defense when you shoot from more than 10 feet.

Stand Your Ground laws in general do two different things. First, they expand the definition of self-defense to say that you have no duty to retreat when attacked. So you do not have to be trapped, with your back to the wall, before you can blast somebody and successfully argue self-defense.

Second, Stand Your Ground laws enable you to go before a judge at a preliminary hearing and ask the court to immunize you from prosecution and to dismiss pending charges. If you're granted immunity, it's great. You're free!

If not, you've got problems. First, judges rarely grant immunity even though the standard used, known as preponderance of evidence or 51 percent, is low. All of the conditions listed on pages 325–327 have to apply. There are, alas, some political considerations, especially for elected judges. If a judge grants immunity to an unpopular defendant, especially if there is media uproar, interest groups will begin raising money to defeat his or her honor in the next election. The simplest expedient is to refuse immunity and kick the whole hairball to a jury. Let *them* figure it out. In law as in life, shit rolls downhill.

Your second problem is that at the immunity hearing, you must testify under oath as to the facts and the events. If you fail to get immunity, you have revealed your entire defense strategy in advance! Your testimony will be picked apart by prosecutors and compared with any statement you were foolish enough to give police. Any discrepancies can sink you.

At your trial, *your attacker can become the victim!* Expect the family to show up and state how their darling's life was shattered or snatched away by that evil guy sitting over there in the defendant's chair, your honor sir or ma'am. Expect to see photos introduced into evidence to show the perp as a choirboy. You might see crayon pictures, with a happy house and yellow sun, that he made his momma while in nursery school. The perp's long rap sheet will be glossed over.

If you merely wounded the attacker, expect him to appear in court with bandages and crutches, with a little blood opportunely dripping. His formerly horrifying rooster, mullet, or Fu Manchu hair will be buzzed into an all-American crew cut, and all his jail tatts will be artfully concealed by a Wal-Mart "court suit."* A dab of makeup will hide the tattooed tears that indicate kills he made for his gang. Expect witnesses to lie, disappear, or be confused. Expect the police report not to say what you told them, or not exactly.

Even if you're acquitted, it's not over. The perp and/or his family and his *carnales* now know where you live. It may occur to them to drive by and exterminate you and your family, or merely get payback by torching your car and house.

If you dodge those bullets, there's more incoming artillery of the legal variety. In the back of the courtroom, in suits that definitely are not from Wal-Mart, members of the plaintiff's legal team will observe the proceedings in order to determine whether the family can sue you and grab your money and property. Civil proceedings have lower thresholds of evidence than criminal cases. It is entirely possible for a shooting to be ruled self-defense in a criminal trial and wrongful death in a civil proceeding.

Consider O. J. Simpson. He was acquitted of murder, then adjudged guilty of wrongful death in a civil trial. The victims' families seized his

---

* Wal-Mart sells two-piece men's suits, in gray or charcoal with pinstripes, for under a C-note. Defendants swear by them.

house and cars, his cash and investments, and even his Heisman Trophy! Afterward, O. J. prudently moved to Florida, where his home could not be seized for debt. Years later, he imprudently used a handgun to settle an argument in a Las Vegas hotel and is now a guest of the great state of Nevada for the next 5 to 33 years.

THE INCREDIBLE DISAPPEARING GUN

One of the greatest complications of self-defense claims is that the bad guys' guns and knives vanish. If police do not recover the perps' weapons, it will be hard to convince a judge and jury that you were in fear of your life. Bystanders grab guns on the ground to score a few C-notes fast and easy. When the bad guys you shoot remain undead, they will flee and toss their hardware. In my city there are dozens of bridges over the St. Johns River and its tributaries. I shudder to think how many guns have flown over the rails and into the drink over the years. Their magnetic signature could probably be detected from outer space.

SELF-DEFENSE IN THE CONFUSION

Real life attacks are seldom simple. If an unknown attacker breaks into your house, the situation is clear-cut. If the home invader has a key, or is someone you know, or employed, or had sex with, it isn't.

Carjackings are also not as simple as they seem. After the bad guys' weapons vanish, expect them to tell cops that you—yes, you—made an unprovoked attack. They merely approached you to ask directions to the nearest bus stop!

What if people menace you? Should you shoot them? A court will have to decide whether the people who menaced you were crazed street people off their meds or potential killers. If a schizophrenic comes at you and you defend yourself with a gun, the cops will listen to him chatter to his demons and realize immediately that this guy is a loony tune. Will they arrest him or you?

REAL PEOPLE, REAL MURK

To illustrate how confused things get in real life, consider a murder case currently pending in my city. The defendant is a woman accused of stabbing her lover to death. She had a passionate, fight-and-fuck relationship with the deceased. One day she goes over to the guy's house with a *former* boyfriend in tow. Drinks get drunk, words get exchanged, and the soon-to-be-dead guy drags her around the yard by her hair and administers some well-placed smacks and punches.

She dashes off and whistles up her brother and his homeboys. They arrive, and a general scrum begins. The girl's team starts administering a level-two Brooklyn stomping* to the victim. Then, she rushes back to the house and returns with a long, wicked knife and plunges it into the guy's chest, with predictable results.

The woman has been charged with second-degree murder. Her defense is that, during the melee, the victim got up and lunged at her. She was in fear for her life, and therefore the stabbing was justified. Her relatives and friends support this view.

The victim's friends, naturally, tell a different story. They say victim was on the ground receiving the mother of all beatings and the woman simply finished him off, up close and personal. Which version of the story the judge believes will determine whether the woman goes free or spends her life in prison.

Here's another actual case. A middle-aged man got into an argument with a car full of snotty teenagers in the parking lot of a convenience store. He and his girlfriend stated later that one of the kids lowered the window of his vehicle and pointed a shotgun. The man grabbed his nine-millimeter from the glove box and fired multiple times into the kids' car. He killed one of the boys.

Not having absorbed the wise counsel of this chapter, the man and his girlfriend did *not* report the incident to police. They fled and were

---

* New Yorkers set the standards for beat-downs. In a level-two stomping, you crack ribs, pop teeth, and work on the knees and the innards. In level one, you kill the guy.

arrested hundreds of miles away after a bystander captured their license plate number. The shooter is currently on ice with a murder charge and is asserting a Stand Your Ground defense. To be acquitted he will have to prove that there actually was a shotgun. Absent corroborating witnesses or a video, this will be tough. The shotgun, if it ever existed, is probably sleeping with the fishes.

The moral of these stories is that shootings are never simple. The facts will be in dispute, the witnesses' stories will conflict, and the physical evidence will be ambivalent or nonexistent. In every shooting, witnesses lie, shade the truth, or trim it back. In many cases, the witnesses have experience talking to cops or scamming insurance companies for phony injuries. They know how to coordinate their stories fast before the popo and the paramedics arrive.

WHEN LAW AND POLITICS COLLIDE

When the excrement hits the fan, you will be angry and confused. Aren't you the victim? Maybe you are in God's eyes, but maybe not in society's eyes after the media and criminal justice system finish with you—particularly if the shooting resulted in a death. The reason is simple. *A dead body cries out for justice.* The person you shot cannot testify in his or her defense. People are predisposed to think of the dead guy as the victim.

Your other problem is that laws often conflict. States that have strong Stand Your Ground laws, like Florida, also have draconian gun laws with severe, mandatory minimum punishments. Worse, laws often conflict with politics! Do you think elected judges are not affected by mobs protesting outside the courtroom? TV correspondents and reporters will swarm judges as they drive away from the courthouse. Talking heads who understand less about the law than a grasshopper will decry "gun violence" on the TV news at 5, 6, and 11 o'clock. When judges escape these media maniacs, they want to drive home and reach for the Pepto-Bismol and a fine adult beverage, preferably a double.

I don't blame them.

STAYING OFF THE HOOK

1. If you decide to shoot, you will necessarily have to shoot until the threat is eliminated. In the confusion, you won't know whether you've hit an attacker. If he turns and flees, *stop shooting*. Otherwise you are looking at a murder charge. Ditto if you shoot him in the back.

2. Once he's down, kick his gun away. Do *not* put your fingerprints on it. And don't kick it *too* far away, lest bystanders steal it. If this sounds complicated, it is.

3. Do *not* administer a coup de grâce shot to the head. This turns self-defense into murder.

4. Dial 911. When the dispatcher answers, say the following:

   "I was attacked. There's been a shooting at [your address or whereabouts]. Send an ambulance and a supervisor."

   Now hang up. Don't say another word. Do not allow the dispatcher to interview (i.e., brain search) you on a recorded phone call.

5. Take photographs of the victim, gun, witnesses, and the scene. Make sure your camera or tablet is password protected so it cannot be dumped without a warrant.

6. If the guy you shot is alive, you must render aid. Obviously you must first have secured his weapon, as indicated in #2.

7. If your attacker flees, you must report it to police. If you hit the guy and he goes to a hospital, medical staff will report the shooting. When they ask the perp what happened, he will lie and say that *you* attacked *him*! That's a guarantee. Nobody ever says, "I was robbing this guy, and he got the drop on me."

8. When cops arrive, they are looking for two types of people to be there, a victim and a perpetrator. Police are human and are likely to incorrectly tag the injured party, or in some cases the deceased, as the victim. If this happens, you will be arrested.

Once you're in handcuffs, you will have an overwhelming desire to plead with police that you were the victim! You will want, with every fiber of your being, to convince them that you fired in self-defense, that you were standing your ground.

Don't do this.

Say only this:

1. "I was attacked."

2. "I am the victim."

3. "I acted in self-defense."

4. "I will swear out a complaint against my attacker."

5. "I will be glad to talk to you *after* I have consulted my attorney."

Then remain calm. The cops have seen this all before. Let them figure it out. That's what they do for a living

Practice these statements in the mirror. Forget about looking silly. This practice can save you years in the penitentiary. Practice also will impress upon you how serious shootings are and how dire the consequences. It will make you think about using the Nike/Goodyear Defense—running like hell—*first*.

In chapter 19 (page 186), I recommended that you carry "street creds" containing your basic info and your attorney's name and phone number to cut short police interrogations. If you have a gun, I suggest that you also carry a self-defense card, like the one shown at the end of this chapter, listing the statements discussed above. Place it in your wallet alongside your street creds, license, and firearms permit. If you shoot in self-defense, simply hand the police these documents and remain silent. The self-defense card is your full and complete written statement.

Do not talk further to police or volunteer that you have taken photos of the scene or the victim or witnesses. Keep in mind that police themselves are allowed 24 hours to reflect and speak to an attorney before they are interviewed after discharging a firearm.

Once the body is bagged and tagged (or resuscitated and treated) and the sun rises, the fun begins. You will have to appear at an initial hearing to testify about what happened. Pray to God that you've talked with an attorney *before* you take the stand. You will not know the nuances of your state's law on self-defense. You will need expert help.

GETTING DEPRESSED YET?

Maybe you read the preceding chapter and rushed out to buy the .38 Special I recommended, or the supersized version, The Judge. You've invested beaucoup bucks in ammo and range time. Now you're wondering, how can I ever use this thing?

If you're inside your home or in a car, and the attackers have guns or knives that are later found, you are likely, but not guaranteed, to be exonerated if you shoot them. If you are attacked in the street or on property outside your home, the outcome is less certain.

Make shoes your first weapon of self-defense. Running like hell, with jinks, turns, and fence leaps, really works.

Remember, if you don't go a dangerous area in the first place, you won't need to use a gun to protect yourself. If you are forced to shoot, do so only when proper conditions are met. When you do shoot, be ready to dress the hog. It's nasty, risky, and can take years.

Always consider your first response to be flight rather than fight. Forget male pride! Spin that wheel, turn those sneakers, and get away from trouble. Leave the thugs, the rage-heads, and the whack jobs to the police. They're experts at handling them, and often well compensated for doing so.

DISCLAIMER

I'm not your lawyer and this is not legal advice. Each state has different laws, different community standards, and different court opinions on self-defense. Consult a local criminal defense attorney for legal advice applicable to your city and state. The foregoing is merely practical advice that *may* be helpful if you have to use deadly force to save your life or those of your loved ones.

SELF-DEFENSE CARD

PLACE IN WALLET OR PURSE

CUT ON DOTTED LINES. FOLD ON SOLID LINE.

FOR POLICE USE ONLY

FOR POLICE USE ONLY

STATEMENTS FOR SELF-DEFENSE SITUATION

1. I was attacked.
2. I am the victim.
3. I acted in self-defense.
4. I will swear out a complaint against my attacker.
5. I will talk to you after I have consulted my attorney.

PART V

AMERICA, LAND OF THE SURVEILLED

34 | BIG BROTHER'S DIGITAL EXAM

Back in the day, the only deep probe you got from the criminal justice system was the cavity search with a rubber glove and what the low bidder laughingly called lubricating jelly.* Nowadays, police prefer to probe your cell phone, your tablet, and your laptop, which hold more secrets than your fanny. They're looking, naturally, for reasons to arrest you.

Police routinely search your mind through questioning. Now they can search your digital *auxiliary* minds. They can also search digital devices you may not know about, such as the computers, sensors, cameras, and microphones built into your car. They can follow your digital tracks on the road and on the airwaves, from up high in space to deep down in cyber netherworlds you never knew existed. Like a satellite, you're emitting telemetry all the time. Increasingly cops, and their computers, are tracking, listening, looking, and sifting through your digital brains. Total surveillance through total telemetry is a reality. It's here, it's now, and it's scary.

THE ILLUSION OF EVANESCENCE

What gets you, and everyone, into trouble is the illusion that digital data is easy to dispose of. Finished with an e-mail or a document? Just toss it into the trash can, click the button, and—*poof*—it vanishes. Or so it

---

* Technology is replacing even this hallowed ritual. Nowadays, any up-to-date jail or prison will have a digital "butt scanner" that shoots X-rays through your hindquarters to discover any razors, shivs, dope, and flash drives you may have tucked up where the sun don't shine.

seems. In fact, digital data is more permanent than written records. First of all, it remains for quite a while in your computer. When you erase a file, all you're doing in a technical sense is removing the first letter of the file name, to indicate that the space the file is taking up is available to be overwritten. The icon disappears, but until something else actually overwrites the space, the original file is still there. Want to check this out? Erase something, then run unerase software. The file will reappear, instantly. In order to defeat unerase technology, you'll need a *secure erase* program, which immediately overwrites the file 7 to 30 times with 0s and 1s.

Getting rid of data on cell phones and tablets is even more difficult than on computers. Unlike laptops and desktops, tablets and smartphones run on flash memory, not hard drives. Their operating systems do not allow you to secure erase files you want to obliterate. More important, phones and tablets continuously send and receive information from the vast server farms that make up the wireless telephone system and the World Wide Web. Much of this information is stored indefinitely. Think you deleted those dodgy e-mails and those naughty photos of yourself with booze, dope, guns, hoodlums, and nonspousal sexmates?

Think again.

Using data extractors and subpoenas, cops can transform *your* phones and tablets into *their* Digital Prosecution Assistants. For example, if they see hot pics or sexts sent to a girl (or a boy, you cougar ladies), they might check state databases. If the kid is underage, you're busted.

Don't get fooled by ads for "cyberscrub" software that purports to hide your presence on the Internet. To law enforcement agencies, supplied with the latest cyber search software by the major computer companies and armed with code-cracking technologies developed by the CIA and Israel's intelligence services, defeating cyberscrub is about as difficult as stomping a bug.

Amazingly, people who should know better still get hammered over e-mails and texts. In 2012, the director of the CIA was shit-canned over e-mails to his mistress. That our top spy sent breathless love letters through a zero-security nongovernmental e-mail account makes you doubt the value of his Princeton Ph.D. It also shows which head does the thinking in these matters.

SKYNET AND THE RISE OF THE MACHINES

Who hasn't enjoyed a bushel of popcorn in the theater or on the couch while watching the Terminator movies? The story posits the existence of Skynet, a self-aware system of interconnected computers. Skynet deploys android assassins called Terminators to wipe out humans in order to remake Earth into a machine planet. Back in 1984, when Arnold Schwarzenegger starred in the original *Terminator*, Skynet was Hollywood hokum. Now it's real. Computers, tablets, cell phones, and other digital devices are all interconnected all the time. The data? External storage and retrieval of digital information is managed by groups of interconnected server computers known collectively as the Cloud.

You too are connected, whether you know it or not, because the telemetry you emit all day every day is also out there in the Cloud. Exactly who owns this data, the extent to which you can control it, and the ease with which police and government can use it to surveil you may determine whether you continue your happy life in freedom chattering away on your cell or rot in a cage with no phone, no Internet, and nothing to do except read out-of-date magazines.

We've discussed in earlier chapters that there is no right to privacy in the U.S. Constitution. Various courts have inferred (English translation: sort of decided) that there is such a right, but it exists at the ever-changing level of court decisions. As for your right to the privacy of digital data, court decisions change faster than a porn queen's Web site. Unfortunately, many courts have ruled that your information in the Cloud is owned by corporate America, not by you. When these corporations are served with subpoenas, they will disgorge your texts and e-mails faster than your dog can puke up a dead rat.

PADDLED BY YOUR PAD, FUCKED BY YOUR PHONE

To you, your tablet and smartphone are super-cool tools, toys, even fashion accessories. Who doesn't get a rush going into a hipster coffee shop and flipping open the newest fully loaded iPad while the other losers are pecking on laptops, which are so *yesterday!* Tablets and smartphones are just like laptops, however, in one essential: they are powerful hand-held computers. Their quad-core processors would have been considered supercomputers 15 years ago and prohibited from export as strategic military technology.

Tablets and phones collect amazing amounts of data—not only music, photos, video, and other files you create or download but also information the devices automatically assemble about where you've been, when you placed a call, and to whom. If your cell phone is equipped with a NFC (Near Field Communication) chip, which allows it to be used as a credit or debit card by touching it to a store checkout receiver, authorities can find out what you buy, where and when you buy it, and, naturally, your credit card and bank account numbers. Needless to say, government, police, and plaintiff attorneys are quite interested in these things.

THE DIGITAL BRAIN DRAIN

On TV, cops grab cell phones and within seconds find exactly the telephone number, photo, or e-mail they need to arrest the bad guy and clear the case.* In real life, it takes hours to dump a phone and decide whether the data recovered is evidence or trivia. That is about to change. In New York and Los Angeles, and in more cities each year, police employ digital data extractors. These gizmos, about the size of a dictionary, are super-fast flash-drive computers. They are equipped with cables that connect to every kind of phone, tablet, hard drive, flash drive, memory card, and computer made in the last 20 years. All the cops do is plug in the extractor, and the magic begins.

The capabilities of these devices are extraordinary. Let me quote from the brochure of Cellebrite, a leading manufacturer:

>> "Complete logical extraction of data from a wide range of devices such as: BlackBerry, iOS, Android, Nokia, Symbian,

---

* I hit the floor laughing when I see TV cops who hold their sidearms incorrectly or refer to prison as "jail." The most absurd shows depict fashionista CSI techs interrogating suspects, breaking down doors, shooting perps with sniper rifles, and roaring around in Hummers, for heaven's sake!

Windows Phone, Palm and phones manufactured with Chinese chipsets."

>> "SIM ID cloning which neutralizes the phone from any network activity during analysis and bypasses PIN-locked SIMs and missing SIM cards."

>> "Analysis, report generation and customization using UFED Logical Analyzer."

>> "Field-ready, easy-to-use—no PC required for extraction."

>> "Fully equipped mobile forensic kit with everything you need for your investigation."

Now I'll translate this tech talk into standard English.

"Complete logical extraction" means they probe your digital brains and drain the data to the last drop. They get everything, including root directories, hidden files, and—important for prosecution—invisible metafiles that show times, dates, and locations of photographs, videos, and recordings. They know *precisely* when and where you created or received info. Forget the gooey finger. This is a digital exam on steroids.

"Chinese chipsets?" This means they can drain even *fake* iPhones, not to mention those devilish devices people buy on the Internet to steal credit card numbers.

"SIM ID cloning." A Subscriber Identity Module (SIM) is the chip inside a tablet or phone that contains the unit's serial number and mobile subscriber identity and the authentication codes that identify your phone to cell networks. By cloning this information, cops can make an exact duplicate of your phone and record all your future calls, e-mails, videos, and pics, not to mention your movements. Once they return your phone and say "Drive safely and have a nice day!" they'll be listening in on a clone phone before you get into third gear.

"Bypass[ing] PIN-locked SIMS and missing SIM cards." PIN means Personal Identification Number, i.e., your password. So even if you protect your phone, tablet, and computer with a password, a data extractor will bypass it in a nanosecond. Think you're being cool by blocking your cell phone from showing your caller ID? Forget it. Cops blew though that stuff back when *72 actually worked, which is to say, when my college-aged son was in diapers.

"Analysis, report generation." Writing reports is an essential, and heretofore manual, police activity. These data extractors, however, write reports automatically. Data extraction reports are a prosecutor's road map to a conviction and your road map to prison (not jail).

"Field-ready, easy-to-use." This means that the brains are in the box and even the dumbest cop can extract data faster than the savviest geek.

"Mobile forensic kit." There's no need for police to go back to head-quarters or dial up some data wizard in a van. Now cops can plug and play on the street, while your hands tremble on the wheel and you sweat up your tee. At such times, as they say in text speak, "Sux 2 B U."

WHEN THE BLACK BOX PUTS YOU IN THE TRICK BOX

You may have a sophisticated computer inside your car you don't know about. This is an Event Data Recorder (EDR), the automotive equivalent of the "black boxes" on airplanes. In case of a crash, the EDR records all the events leading up to the impact, such as speed, direction, braking, acceleration, steering angle, seat belt status, etc. Airbags have similar units to record deployments. The federal government intends to make these data recorders mandatory in all new motor vehicles, having attempted to enact provisions to this effect in recent transportation bills. And you should know that all cars made by General Motors, Ford, and the large Asian manufacturers have been equipped with black boxes for years.

To extract data recorder information, cops just plug the unit into a PC, fire up the proprietary software, and copy it all. The problem for privacy is that these devices don't just record at the moment of a crash; they record *all the time*. They overwrite old data, but there is usually information for a half hour or more in the box at all times. Black box information has already been used in criminal prosecutions and in civil auto-crash litigation. In other words, your car can be a witness against you.

It gets worse. A program that analyzes the inertial data in the EDR can backtrack your whereabouts from the moment police dump your box. Digital backtracking can place you at the scene of a crime, or in a neigh-

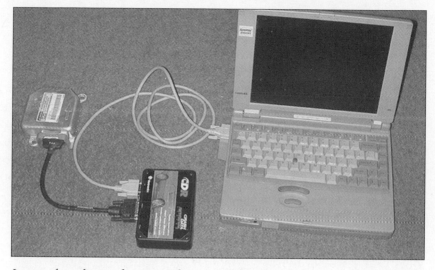

Laptop data dump of an event data recorder and an airbag data module. Photo courtesy of Wikimedia Commons

borhood from which you are banned by judicial order. If probation officers have a hard-on for you—and this happens—they can violate you back to prison.* Expect this software to be upgraded soon to generate traffic tickets.

Let's take a closer look at the criminal justice consequences. In chapter 33, I discussed Stand Your Ground laws, the use of firearms in self-defense, and the fact that a Stand Your Ground defense will collapse if you are engaged in unlawful activity, no matter how minor. How does this relate to data recorders? Imagine that some pistol-packing hoodlums try to jack your car. You reach for your .38 revolver (or the .45/.410 Taurus, for you yahoos who insist on a master blaster). You cock the hammer. . . .

Bang!

You smoke one of those hood rats. The noise makes the others vanish, along with their skeezer girlfriends. Now, as white wisps spiral from the

---

* Next to drugs, probation and parole violations are the greatest cause of felony incarceration. In the Sunshine State, one-third of the inmates of our fine prisons are there because they screwed up paperwork or annoyed the bureaucracy.

barrel, you see blue lights coming. You think, "He's dead. I'm alive. The cops are coming. Hallelujah!"

Wrong.

If you don't refuse search and interrogation, the cops may well search your vehicle and dump any digital devices, including the black box. If they discover erratic driving, excessive speed, or evidence that you stopped and waited for the bad guys (as in, you were doing business with these mopes) or that you pursued them in your vehicle before you fired, you're busted. You're looking at man one or murder two, and a long stretch. All you'll be doing around the clock is dancing to the jailhouse rock.

BIG BROTHER IS WATCHING YOU

In preceding sections we discussed how police can interrogate your computers, phones, and storage devices up close and personal. Now let's discuss how they can investigate you stealthily, from afar.

For years the FBI has been getting warrants to remotely operate General Motors OnStar systems. Once activated, the systems track vehicles' movements and transmit conversations via the interior microphones. The suits enjoy busting tech-stupid hoodlums who ride around to discuss their scores because they think the FBI has to use platoons of vehicles to follow them and has to sneak into their houses to plant listening devices. No chase vehicles are needed when vehicles track themselves. As to planting bugs, that is *so* last century.

Until quite recently, law enforcement's ability to monitor conversations, e-mails, and texts was constrained by manpower and costs. As an FBI agent, I was astounded at the effort required to man wiretaps, listen to days of conversations, transcribe the tapes into text, and then filter the verbal sludge for nuggets of incriminating conversation. It might be weeks, even months, before you knew whether the wiretaps had yielded evidence.

Computers and keyword search technology now make it possible to monitor conversations, spoken and written, in real time. A computer can monitor thousands of information streams simultaneously, flag interesting conversations and messages, and type them up *instantly*.

You may think, "Isn't that illegal if agencies don't have a warrant?" Unfortunately, the courts can't prohibit illegal monitoring if they don't know it's happening. Even if law enforcement agencies are prohibited from using warrantless intercepts as evidence in court, they can use them to begin investigating you. If you're up to anything, they'll get warrants soon enough. In any case, discovering that illegal wiretaps led to your arrest will take legal talent and money.

Here's an example. Let's say you're out of jail on supervised release and miss a probation meeting, anger management class, or monthly drug test. In the past you would get an ass-chewing from your probation officer and a letter warning about the violation. With the help of a crackerjack attorney like me, you could sort things out without getting rearrested and violated back to prison.

Now, in many states, probation officers can simply issue a warrant and have you arrested—no meeting, no phone call, no letter. Even if you're not wearing an ankle monitor, a probation officer can track you through the GPS chips in your phones and computers. He can query toll-road databases to see which tollbooths your car's transponder pinged recently. He can fire up your LoJack or, with a court-issued wiretap order, turn on your OnStar mike for a quick listen. Remember, on probation and parole, you waive your rights against warrantless search. Once your proby locates you, he will call a cop to hook you up.

Perhaps all you did was hang out in a restricted area near some hoodlum joints or drive by your ex's house after she took out a restraining order. You can still get busted. If you have a good lawyer, you'll be sprung. After all, the state can prove only that your phone, your computer, or your car were in restricted zones, not you. But what if, like 95 percent of defendants, you don't have a private attorney? The legal fees, court costs, restitution, jail costs, and probation fees detailed so terrifyingly in *Arrested*, my coauthor's companion volume to this book, may have tapped you out. Maybe you never had real money to start with. You'll be facing the music with a public defender who may have met you for the first time at the door and will try, possibly with success, to match your name to a file folder before the hammer comes down.

TRACKED BY THE TOWER, STUNG BY THE RAY

The ability of police and civil plaintiffs to track your movements via the modern version of Skynet is awesome. A smartphone, for example, bounces signals off cell towers, tracks your location moment by moment, and posts it to social networking map software. For many people, this isn't a problem. They want digitally connected friends to see where they are and dash over for chats, parties, and fun. Of course, geolocation also allows soon-to-be-former lovers, spouses, and business partners (and their private detectives) to dash over to get their own videos and photos. Police and probation officers will zero in for their own fun.

When tracking via GPS and cell tower triangulation doesn't work, police have their own mobile cell tower called the Stingray. This device measures the strength of your cell signal from one location, then takes another measurement from a second location. With two or more fixes, the Stingray's algorithms triangulate your position. The system can track you even if you use a cheap "burner" phone with no GPS and no brain. Ditto if you use those free "Obamaphones" that the government hands out.

If the government's tracking information is wrong, how can you challenge it in court? Who can testify as to the accuracy of tracking from outer space, in the case of GPS units, or tracking over the airwaves, in the case of cell phones? Only the government and its licensees and contractors know this stuff. Do you think an executive from a gigantic international electronics company selling trainloads of spy gear to government will take the stand and testify under oath that his gizmos don't work?

FOXED BY FACEBOOK

The real Skynet doesn't send Terminators through time portals. It has a happy face, a user ID, and a password. Facebook, Twitter, and similarly amazing services just want you to log in, check on your buds and your sweeties, and join the fun. They're hugely profitable and generally benign—except when commandeered by government and law enforcement through warrants, or by your enemies, exes, and other plaintiffs via a civil subpoena.

Skynet these days has a happy face.

The same thing that makes these services so useful and irresistible, their connectivity, causes the privacy problems. Post a message to a social networking site and—*bing-bong*—it's instantaneously on all the devices of all your friends, all over the world, all of the time. These services are insidious and habit forming, like crack. We all know people who "live on Facebook." They log their activities minute by minute and beam them through cyberspace to friends who, no doubt, are breathlessly waiting to learn which doughnut somebody selected with their half-decaf, nonfat, organic, Ethiopia-blend latte. On my computer, Facebook is forever chirping that it wants to connect to my address book, e-mail, Web browser, etc. In the future it will probably want to interface with my fridge and my toaster.

Once you upload your stuff, you can't take it back and you can't erase it, because it's in the Cloud. That's a problem when you're ensnared in the criminal justice system, subject to judicial orders, or involved with civil litigation.

Posts to Web sites and Facebook often contain more information than you know. Photos, for example, may contain date, time, and location metadata even though you can't see it. Don't think for a minute that "private" material you post to these sites is actually private. The cops can peel back those Web pages layer by layer, like a tasty Vidalia onion. So can insurance companies, government agencies, and individuals who buy specialized software.

What happens most commonly is that frenemies such as former friends, lovers, and spouses give law enforcement legal access to your data because *you* gave *them* your passwords in happier days. When this happens, no warrant is required, and your attorney will not be able to suppress the evidence.

Police aren't the only government agencies surveilling you. Intelligence agencies, even those in other countries, use software called Web crawlers that search social networking sites for prohibited speech and track suspicious persons both domestic *and* foreign. Let's say, for example, that you post some snarky comments about Fidel Castro on your page. Years later, if you travel to Cuba, you might get arrested and tossed into the notorious Combinado del Este prison, where you can spend your vacation chasing rats to supplement the protein ration. No *mojitos** either.

Professional criminals also love social networking sites. Here's how they exploit them:

STEP 1: Get addresses for target homes.

STEP 2: Look up owners' names on property tax Web sites.

STEP 3: Find social networking pages of owners and their children.

Jewel thieves and burglars search for posts like the following: "Going skiing for a week! My boring husband won't let me take my diamonds." Rapists and child molesters get excited by messages like this: "Mom and dad are gone for two whole days! RUH2?" (Are you horny, too?)

---

* Cuban cocktail of rum, mint, sugar, and lime made famous by Ernest Hemingway and beloved by barflies on both coasts.

All this suggests how guarded you should be about your posts to social networking sites. To protect yourself, observe this ancient Muslim proverb: "Never disclose thy tenets,* thy travels, or thy treasure."

Social networking services also display your "friends" and your recent communications with them. For law enforcement and prosecutors, social networking is a free Conspiracy Diagramming Service. What you call "friends" they call "criminal associates," "co-conspirators," and "accessories after the fact."

This is especially problematic if you're on probation or parole, because you're not supposed to be "consorting with known felons." If you're friending, texting, and swapping messages and pics with hoodlums, you done been consortin', as we say down South. You're going to be violated back to state prison for some hard time to ponder your digital ignorance.

The problem is aggravated by information and photographs *other people* post about you. Here's the classic example. Every day thousands of defendants and convicts are released on bail, on probation or parole, or via orders for diversion. What's the first thing they do?

Party hearty!

They rush out for booze, pizza, burgers, red-hots, and some fine Schedule I narcotics. They want to get wasted and get laid, and do it now. Inevitably at these celebrations, guests snap pics, record video and sound, and post everything to various Web sites. The next day there's a big *har har* as friends chortle over photos of the happy probationer slurping booze, sucking on a bong as big as a fire hose, and wrapping an arm around some underage jailbait who's grinning ear to ear. Flinty-eyed law enforcement types will be watching also, and things will get very "fugly," very fast.

THE SPYBOT IN YOUR POCKET

Law enforcement agencies soon will be able to extract the rest of your digital data remotely—no box, no cops, no hands. By inserting spyware into your computers, phones, and tablets, they can drain your data wirelessly and invisibly over the Internet. The U.S. Navy has even developed

---

* "Tenets" here means religious beliefs.

an ingenious program called PlaceRaider that, once introduced into your cell phone, switches on the camera, video, and microphone whenever the phone is used. The software then reconstructs, from fragmentary images and video, three-dimensional images of you, your car, your crib, your gun, your hangouts, and all your visitors, lovers, accomplices, dope buyers, etc.

POPO IN THE TV

In 2011, Verizon, the telephone, television, and Internet company, filed patent application 20120304206, contemplating a television set-top box with cameras, infrared motion sensors, and microphones that watch you while you're watching TV. The box, with appropriate computing power, will determine how many people are in the room, what they're doing, and what they're saying. Then it will send an activity-appropriate ad to the TV. I'm not making this up! Let me quote from this astonishing document:

> In certain examples, the targeted advertising may be based on one or more ambient actions performed by one or more users of an access device. . . . To illustrate, an exemplary ambient action may include the user eating, exercising, laughing, reading, sleeping, talking, singing, humming, cleaning, playing a musical instrument, performing any other suitable action, and/or engaging in any other physical activity during the presentation of the media content. In certain examples, the ambient action may include an interaction by the user with another user (e.g., another user physically located in the same room as the user). To illustrate, the ambient action may include the user talking to, cuddling with, fighting with, wrestling with, playing a game with, competing with, and/or otherwise interacting with the other user.

The gizmo will even know when you're playing a musical instrument. You won't be able to toot your sax without getting an ad for brass polish. If you've playing another instrument, the freaking box will send the TV ads for condoms, lube, and douche. If your woman says she has a headache, the TV will advertise aspirin!

Do you think law enforcement agencies aren't interested in whom you're meeting with, drinking with, drugging with, and knocking boots with? This patent describes with eerie accuracy the fictional "telescreen" used to surveil the drone society George Orwell imagined in his dystopian novel *Nineteen Eighty-Four*. This horrifying book was written in 1949, in an era when "computers" referred not to machines but to female arithmeticians who calculated the trajectories of artillery shells with paper and pencil. Should this set-top box become a reality, when you watch TV, government, with appropriate warrants, will be watching you.

DEOXYRIBONUCLEIC ACID TRIP

When you're arrested by federal law enforcement agents or by police in 25 states, the first thing correctional officers do after you're booked into jail is pop a swab in your mouth and mop DNA from your cheeks.* I think this is an outrageous violation of your Fourth Amendment rights against warrantless search and seizure. In these jurisdictions, you can refuse an interrogation or a search of your car, but once you are arrested you can't refuse your DNA.

Once processed, DNA is digitized and uploaded into the Combined DNA Index System (CODIS). In due course, your fair city and its police department will get a check from the federal government. These pay-by-swab bucks are important dollars, and they assure that pleas for privacy will fall on deaf ears.

DNA indexing has benefits. It clears old crimes, exonerates the wrongly convicted, and hammers serious criminals. It also causes serious problems. First, your DNA, like the contents of your vehicle, may not be relevant to the crime for which you are charged. Second, it may place you at crime scenes regardless of whether you were there at the time the crime was committed. Even when cops don't have your DNA, they can bust you using "familial searches" of your relatives' DNA.

I believe that, inevitably, non–law enforcement agencies and private corporations will gain access to the CODIS database, just as some of

---

* In states like Florida, correctional officers seize your DNA only after you plead guilty or are convicted.

them now have access to arrest records through NCIC. Many researchers believe that criminal behavior is partly genetic. I foresee a future in which you can be banned from higher education, gainful employment, and even public places because you have bad-boy DNA—even if you haven't done squat. When you're arrested these days, it's got'cha, baby, right down to your molecules.

POP A CHIP IN YO' ASS

Schools already look like prisons, with surveillance cameras, electric locks, entry and exit recorders, armed police, and escape-proof detention rooms. Several Texas school districts now mandate that students carry a magnetic card with an embedded Radio Frequency Identification (RFID) chip. These cards track students' locations, supposedly for safety reasons. Students, who can be punished for not carrying their cards, are freaking out. There are certain mildly naughty teenaged activities (smooching, sneaking a cigarette, masturbating) that need to be done in secret. They need to happen without children being busted, tossed into juvie jail, and given a permanent arrest record in the FBI's database. In Surveillance High, there's no place to run, no place to hide, and no place to grow up.*

Naturally, the kids stash these cards in their lockers or hide them in cracks and crannies when they need to vanish. Eventually and inevitably, it will occur to schools to strip the chips from plastic cards and implant them under students' skin, like you do for pets and livestock. Why stop there? Why not chip jail detainees, suspects, everybody?

Feel scared. Feel very, very scared.

A VISIT FROM THE BLACK SUBURBANS

Reviling our elected and appointed leaders is a great American tradition. Presidents, beginning with Thomas Jefferson, have been called whoremongers, Communists, lunatics, and worse. It's part of the game, and no

---

* These enormities were deplored in editorials in Russia Today, a 24-hour TV and news service. When former Communists lecture Americans about civil liberties, we have a problem.

one can earn the top spot without having emotional and intellectual rhino hide.

In this century, however, there's an electronic line you cannot cross. You cannot, even in jest, make an e-mail, text, telephone, or mail threat against the president, the leaders of the House and Senate, cabinet secretaries, and foreign officials, all of whom are under the protection of the U.S. Secret Service. The National Security Agency maintains acres of liquid-nitrogen-cooled supercomputers at their Ft. Meade headquarters. These scan phone calls, e-mails, and texts to match words and names.

Suppose you write an e-mail that contains the following:

Official's name + "I'm gonna get that motherfucker!"

Expect a visit from the black Suburbans with the weird antennas. Expect a grilling from the Man with No Eyes (a humorless Secret Service agent in retro sunglasses). Once you're on the Fruitcake List, you'll be interviewed whenever the target of your anger travels to your area. So will your friends, family, doctor, therapist, and probation officer.

THE EYE THAT NEVER SLEEPS

The devices most likely to put your freedom and your bank balance in jeopardy are Automatic License Plate Recognition (ALPR) systems. The new scanners are small, economical, and stealthy. They fit neatly under the light rack on a patrol car. Some can be mounted on poles. This is policing *without police!*

Some of these machines not only scan tags but also clock vehicle speeds. They scan traffic, identify everyone going over the limit, and issue citations automatically in industrial quantities. A computer in a remote document center will print a citation and pop it into the mail before your engine cools in the driveway.

Until recently, the number of license plates cops checked was limited by the need to call them in to dispatch via radio or to key them, one at a time, into cruiser laptops. Typically, an officer can manually scan 150 to 200 plates per shift. The new devices scan thousands of plates *per hour.* They use infrared spotlights to film tags in the dark. Automatically, they

WATCHING YOU!

Clockwise from top left are a pole-mounted scanner and camera array, a British prowler with quad license plate scanners, a stealthy under-the-rack plate scanner, a miniature IP (Internet Protocol) camera, a pole-mounted "intimidator" camera, and the Nano Hummingbird, which can fly through doors and windows to keep an eye on you. Photos courtesy of Wikimedia Commons

compare plate numbers to numbers associated with violations. When a match is detected, these gadgets beep, flash red, etc. so cops can pull the vehicle.

Plate scanners make possible thousands of easy arrests and generate gushers of revenue from traffic tickets, court fines, jail charges, and the unending fees of the probation and parole system. (See *Arrested* for the detailed list). The decrease in arrests initially caused by the Supreme Court's prohibition against traffic-stop searches has been more than offset by the increase in scanner-generated arrests. A plate scanner that costs thousands can pay for itself in a few shifts. Every arrest-hungry patrol officer, and every dollar-hungry tax collector, is lusting for one.

Police use the devices to scan for criminal offenses, arrest warrants, detainers (wanted for questioning by detectives or other agencies), BOLOs (Be On the Lookout for), stolen vehicles, traffic violations, and, increasingly, *administrative offenses* such as unpaid, expired, suspended, or revoked driver's licenses, unpaid traffic and parking tickets, unpaid child support, and probation and parole violations. Cops soon may be able to scan for professional and business license problems; zoning violations; unpaid property, sales, and income taxes; even unpaid driver's insurance and health insurance premiums. There are few legal barriers to using police as revenue agents and bureaucratic paperwork checkers. This mission creep is alarming. Citizens need more than a little wiggle room with government.

Another problem with traffic scanners is that they videotape *all the cars all the time*, in black and white and color, and keep all the data. Computers can track vehicles and people over extended periods. So if you're on probation or subject to restraining orders, they can reconstruct your movements retroactively. The scanners also will capture you on video if you're visible from the window or near your vehicle. Drive into a red zone and your proby can bust you back to the rock while he's snacking on a cracker at his computer.

Many states have formed networks to share license plate scanner data. So if you have a warrant and need to lie low while you scramble money for an attorney, crossing a county or state line will not get you off the grid. Law enforcement will be watching for thousands of miles in every direction.

The repo guys also use plate scanners. Now The Hook's got eyes and a brain. Repo scanners signal when a hot-listed vehicle is detected. If you're driving one of these and stop to take a leak, when you return, your car—like magic—will be gone.

As you pass under these cameras and scanners, you can sense the binary code flashing along fiber-optic cables, beaming up to satellites and bouncing among computers and servers from sea to shining sea. The machines are whispering to each other. They're thinking; they're planning. It's Skynet, coming alive. Soon there will be no place to run and no place to hide in America, the Land of the Surveilled.

STAYING FREE ON AND OFF THE GRID

If you want to live completely off the grid, there are any number of kook-fringe books and Web sites that offer advice. Much of it actually works—that is, it works if you're willing to eat cockroaches roasted on an open fire, live in a cave, and poop in a hole. I myself keep a small cabin deep in the piney woods of Georgia where I enjoy at least the illusion that I'm not being watched. During idyllic weekends, I forget that U.S., Chinese, Russian, and Iranian satellites in low Earth orbit can dial me up anytime day or night. Now and then a navy drone buzzes by, but they know I'm harmless, just an old guy running dogs and shooting hogs with an itty-bitty .22.

You cannot reasonably live off the grid in cities and towns. Nonetheless, with America crisscrossed with cameras, scanners, and digital trip wires, it's more important than ever to avoid traffic stops, autoticketing, and unwise release of information to the Internet. Here are some suggestions:

>> Obey traffic laws, obviously. Pay special attention to red lights. Some cities have shortened the yellow light interval, causing more tickets to be written by automated camera and computer systems. Courts have thrown out citations in these cases, but do you have the thousands of dollars for legal fees necessary to challenge a city legal department, no matter how outrageous the city's conduct?

>> Make sure the address on your driver's license is current. If you have moved recently, file a change of address with your state's department of motor vehicles. With more cities sending citations by mail, you may not receive the tickets timely if they're sent to an old address. You also will not receive notice of a license suspension. Suspensions are criminal offenses; cops can arrest you and tow your car. Sorting this out costs thousands. If you're moving around, have a friend or relative maintain a legal address for you.

>> Do not purchase fuel with a credit or debit card if you are on the run.

>> Check for warrants. It's prudent to call your police department's nonemergency number and ask if you have any warrants, detainers, or unpaid tickets or a suspended license. Many states will give you this information. If you're afraid to call, ask a friend or relative to call for you. They will need your full legal name and date of birth. Unfortunately, many states withhold warrant information. You may need to hire an attorney to assist. If you find a problem, get it handled. As the say on the TV show, "Whatcha gonna do when they come for you?"

>> Beware a common scam. If you have a citation or criminal charge, you may get e-mails saying something like "Remove your criminal record for just $400!" Get a clue. State and federal governments aren't removing anyone from their databases until Judgment Day, if then.

>> Fugitive squads can take years to run down warrant jumpers, but if a patrol officer gets a hit with a manual or automatic plate read, you're toast. If you're on the run with an outstanding warrant, detainer, or bail jump, don't drive your own car. Hole up with a friend or relative and raise money for a good criminal defense attorney who may be able to quash the warrant, reinstate the bond, or negotiate your appearance at a hearing without an arrest.

>> Always assume that everything you type onto a computer can be accessed by law enforcement. E-mails and texts are written evidence. Keep your mitts off the keyboard (and for heaven's sake, don't dictate) when you have nasty thoughts, words, and opinions about your employers, enemies, exes, judges, probation officers, anger management group leaders, etc. Prosecutors will construe these outbursts as threats and add on charges or violate your parole or probation.

>> Always secure your computer, smartphone, and tablet with a password *known only to you*. Even though this will not defeat a data extractor, it will prevent casual snooping by ex-spouses, enemies, and cops. Courts have ruled that when a device is protected by a password, police have to get a warrant to access its content. If the cops do nail you using evidence from your computers, a password will help your attorney get the evidence tossed. Without a password, when cops arrest you, they may state that you agreed to the computer search. They can read all your e-mails, texts, and addresses, then search your nav system to trace your movements. By the way, "1234" is not a good password.

>> On desktops and laptops, secure erase anything that might cause you legal, personal, and financial problems. You can use built-in software to do this on Macintosh computers. For Windows and Linux systems, use third-party apps like File Shredder. Periodically secure erase the "unused" space on your hard drive.

>> When troublesome stuff appears on your tablets and phones, plug the gizmos into your PC and do a software "restore." This will wipe the flash memory chips in the units and reinstall their operating systems. Now resynch the devices with your PC to retrieve apps, photos, and e-mails you want to keep.

>> If you must keep secret stuff on your phone and tablet, encrypt it. Note an important distinction: *Passwords* merely

block the document from view. *Encryption* scrambles the whole shebang. Encryption algorithms are extraordinarily powerful, easy to use, and blessedly cheap. They have funky names like Twofish, MacGuffin, and Triple DES. The best current encryption is called the Advanced Encryption Standard (AES). Once you encrypt your secret stuff, even with free golden oldies like Blowfish, the cops will get gobbledygook when they seize the file with an extractor.

>> Pay attention to which programs upload to the Cloud and which do not. Any program that is Web-based or that synchs info between devices is uploading your stuff to giant corporations that will keep it and will release it when a subpoena shows up.

>> Everybody has cameras and video recorders. If you get into arguments and fights, expect the cameras to pop out and everything to be uploaded to Facebook, shared with e-mail and text blasts, or even sent directly to the police.

>> Keep your kisser covered when other people get crazy around you. You don't want pictures of yourself with drunks, hoodlums, and drugs whirling around the Internet. When things go sideways, deploy *the most important anonymizing device in the world*—a baseball cap. When the cell phone cams start snapping, pull down the brim and ease toward the door. With the brim low you become, as far as law enforcement is concerned, that famous unsub,* the Man in the Hat.

Cameras clicking? Pull down your cap and fade, fade away.

---

* Cop talk for "unknown subject."

>> If you don't want law enforcement and enemies to track you via your cell phone, turning it off may not be enough. Yank the battery. Disable social networking features that pop your location to people on your "friends" list or e-mail address book. If you want your buddies to come over, call them. Voice communications enjoy greater statutory protection than text, photos, and video.

>> Whenever anyone e-mails or texts you about sensitive legal, business, or personal subjects, *do not reply. Do not write anything.* Talk these matters over in person, indoors, away from phones, cameras, and computers.

>> Beware of anyone, even so-called friends, asking you too many questions, especially if they have criminal records. They could be registered informants of the FBI or informal "pocket informants" of local police. Junkies and street people will rat you out for a burger and fries. For a fifth of real hooch, they'd testify against God Almighty.

>> In the wireless era, no one knows telephone numbers anymore. You, however, need to memorize those of your closest family and friends. Dial these numbers rather than using your contact list in order to plant them in your memory. If you get arrested, you will not have your cell phone. You can call family on the jail phone, but you have to know the number. Yes, there are phone books in jail, but the only listings are for wheezers who have landlines. In any case, most of the pages will be missing, since the guys use them to wipe jizz off their flip-flops and to start fires for jail tatts.*

---

* The ink for jail tattoos is made from burned paper soot and melted plastic razor handles. The needles are straightened staples pulled off the legal documents that litter jails. Paper from the Yellow Pages is also highly prized for another reason. When well chewed, mixed with toothpaste, and marked with a jail pencil, it can be formed into yellow dice, which are very hip in the slammer.

Here's another melancholy reality that should give you additional reason to guard your digital privacy. Do you think that elected local judges, with law degrees from Ho-Hum University, who make about the same money as a patrol cop without overtime, want to listen to geeky arguments about electronic privacy rights? Not in the five minutes you're before the bench. You're not facing justice as taught at Harvard Law. You're getting the rough-and-ready kind served up piping hot, all day every day, where you live—in Crime City.

PLAY iSPY; GET iBUSTED

You may be thinking, why should cops and the feds have all the fun? Surveillance equipment, once available only to law enforcement and intelligence agencies, has now been miniaturized, digitized, and made affordable for the ordinary Jack and Jane. Spy superstores are a nerd's playground. For less than a paycheck, you can get miniature still and video cameras with digital streaming. These gizmos are fitted into pens, neckties, clocks, eyeglasses, walls, ceilings, pinhole cameras—even teddy bears!

You can also purchase spyware for cell phones and computers. Once it's running, you can read e-mails, texts, and tweets. You can discover peoples' innermost thoughts as they write in "private" online diaries. With a matchbox-sized, magnetized GPS transmitter, you can follow cars.

Spying on other people gives you a weird sense of power and mastery. This can tempt you into trouble. Let's say you're in the neighborhood watch. The idea may pop into your head that instead of calling police when there's trouble, maybe you should get some evidence. Then the bad guys will get theirs, for sure.

Probably not.

Any digital evidence you gather most likely will be inadmissible against the bad guys. It might be admissible, however, to prosecute *you* for violating wiretap laws. When bad guys catch you spying or hear you testify against them at trial, they may not have warm feelings. When their posse find you, just hope they limit their weapons to knuckles, boots, and bats and leave the guns at home.

Spy gear and computers also collect information about the spy. Let's say you dictate to your computerized to-do list a note that says, "Buy GPS to track that lying, no-good motherfucker." Once you finish dictating, your computer uploads the audio file to the Cloud. In an instant, servers convert your words into text and add the item to your to-do list. But what goes on in the Cloud *stays* in the Cloud. Prosecutors can subpoena your note, with the exact date and time it was made, and your voice!

Sex, naturally, is the biggest driver of spy mania. Is my husband unfaithful? Is my wife untrue? Inquiring minds want to know. When you spy on spouses and lovers, you can be charged with wiretapping, stalking, computer hacking, threatening, sexual predation, and so forth. That you own the house where the person is living, or bought the computer that the person is using, is no defense.

If you are ever charged with stalking or illegal surveillance, *never* say to police the words "It's my house" or "It's my computer." These sentences are confessions. Remember, when interrogated by police, the only words you ever say are "My attorney will speak for me." In a pinch, "Gimme a lawyer!" and its Spanish translation, *"¡Un abogado, por Dios!"* also work.

Worse than the criminal jeopardy is the damage spying does to your character. When you sit up night after night reading other people's mail and reviewing clandestine videos, you become a creep. You're not living your life large and in charge. You're watching other people live theirs while you're being consumed by envy, jealousy, contempt, and rage.

Let me give you some fatherly, as well as lawyerly, advice. Next time your brain is in a testosterone- or estrogen-fueled uproar, pause before you burn tires to the spy shop. Do you really need to know which witch enthralled your husband? Is it necessary to geolocate the exact motel room, and record the precise date and time, that some poon-hound pounded your old lady?

You don't need to know because you already know. When the person you cherish removes that last iota of comfort and caring—what Ian Fleming famously called the quantum of solace—the relationship is irretrievably broken. What once was fire is now but dust. If you're smart, you'll sweep away the ashes and start a new life rather than a criminal sentence.

RECORDING COPS WITH YOUR PHONE, CAMERA, AND TABLET

Almost everyone has a cell phone camera. Nowadays even the cheesiest handset hanging on a hook at the gas station or neighborhood bodega records sound and video. You may immediately think, "Yippee! I'm going to record the next cop who interrogates me. Then, when he screws up, I'll get even!"

Think again. The laws and the court rulings on surreptitious recording are confused and conflicting. The only way you can safely record is if a police officer agrees to the recording. Nonetheless, as a practical matter, I do not recommend you record police interactions even if officers agree to it. They can always grab your camera, stomp it, drop it into a handy puddle, or just make it vanish. Antagonizing police is never prudent.

There is one form of "surveillance" that may actually work for you. If you're having a conversation on the phone with a third party when you encounter the cops, what the other person hears over the phone may later corroborate your version of the events. While you're on the phone, police typically behave themselves, because they understand that someone else is listening in.

"But," you protest, "what about all those cop interrogation videos on YouTube?" Did you notice that these videos are taken by *third parties*, not the person being questioned? The laws governing third-party recording of police in public places are different from those governing one-on-one recording. You rarely see surreptitious video taken by a driver that shows a cop's face in the window. In any case, police misconduct videos are usually uploaded to the Internet under names like "Bozo Anonymous." In a confused legal environment, it is safer, and easier, not to openly flout electronic surveillance laws.

Most important, do *not* push a phone into cops' faces. Never point *anything*, even fingers, at police. At night and during low visibility, they may mistake the camera for a gun, draw their sidearms, and shoot you dead. In states like Florida, land of warm sun and hot bullets, blasting you will, with few exceptions, be ruled a righteous kill. Your relatives can sue all the way to the Florida Supreme Court, and all they will get will be bubkes, which is Yiddish for zero, zip, nada.

WHAT IF YOU'RE A CRUSADER AGAINST POLICE MISCONDUCT?

You know who you are. You live to confront, not avoid, police. When questioned, you get tingly with excitement. You have a record of minor charges longer than the Dead Sea Scrolls from arrests during rallies, protests, and street riots. The American Civil Liberties Union (ACLU) phone number is on your speed dial. You dream of a day in court where stern judges, you imagine, will tongue-lash cowering cops whose misdeeds you revealed to the world via the Internet.

The balance between police power and individual liberty has to be renegotiated in every generation. Police misconduct crusaders do useful work. Nonetheless, it's risky. Pay a criminal defense attorney to advise you on your state's laws and court decisions before you dash after the blue lights. Practice using a camera as a third party. Practice responding to police questions. Drop some coin for apps that record video while leaving the screen blank. But remember, surreptitious recordings are generally felonies. You need some serious legal advice before you start doing this stuff.

Have you noticed that the most successful protesters against police misconduct have money? To get into the game, you'll need serious cash to pay bail bonds, court costs, and attorney fees. Don't delude yourself that the ACLU or Legal Aid will always give you a free defense. Even if they do, consider that the cute Yale Law School graduate they assign is not the one in jail. You are. When the moral high ground is a holding cell where drunks barf on your feet, it may give you cause to pause, and reflect.

NOW WE'RE DONE

Stay free, people. It's what America's all about. Get a clue from this book. Stay away from cops unless you need them, and never forget to *keep your dope at home!*

PART VI | AIDS TO LEARNING

THE GOLDEN RULES

Shout these out a few hundred times until they're burned into your memory. You *will* be glad you did.

>> **#1: IF COPS CAN'T SEE YOU, THEY CAN'T ARREST YOU.**

>> **#2: KEEP YOUR DOPE AT HOME.**

>> **#3: TELL COPS YOUR NAME AND BASIC INFO, THEN SHUT THE HECK UP!**

>> **#4: WHEN POLICE ASK TO SEARCH YOUR VEHICLE, JUST SAY NO— POLITELY!**

THE MAGIC WORDS

These are hymns of freedom. Sing them. Chant them. Use them. Next time you encounter a cop, go home instead of to jail.

When cops say, "Hey you, c'mere."
You respond, "Officer, have I done something wrong?"

When cops ask, "Why are you hiding?"
You respond, "Because I'm afraid of police."

RESPECTFUL WAYS TO REFUSE ANSWERING QUESTIONS

Youth Version: "Officer, I'd like to answer your questions, but my mother told me that, in a situation like this, I should not say anything unless she and our attorney are present."

Adult version: "Officer, I'd like to answer your questions, but my attorneys told me that, in a situation like this, I should not say anything unless they are present."

When cops ask, "Why are you giving me your credentials?"
You respond, "I wanted to write down my basic information so I wouldn't make a mistake when talking to police."

When cops ask, "Why do your credentials carry the text for refusing to answer questions?"
You respond, "I wanted to be able to read this phrase in case it becomes in my best interest to end this interrogation."

Last-ditch emergency technique to avoid arrest: "I've crapped my pants and peed on myself."

Words to use when seeking a young lover's driver's license: "Darling, our love is strong, and we've got to be strong. Showing me your license is the strongest proof that you love me, and that what we're doing is right, so very, very right. If you're too young, we can wait. Our love will only get better, sweeter, and closer over time."

What you say after hearing your Miranda rights: "I want a lawyer. I will not say anything unless my lawyer is with me."

How to refuse a vehicle search politely and ask to go free: "Officers, I apologize for the traffic violation. I have answered your questions and cooperated with you in every way. However, I am late and urgently have to be going. _____ (Fill in the blank with reason.) Are we finished? May I go now?"

INDEX